Accession no.
36165986

WITHDRAWN

Meaning in Interaction:
an Introduction to Pragmatics

D0318005

Learning About Language

General Editors:
Geoffrey Leech & Mick Short, Lancaster University

Already published:

Meaning in Interaction: an Introduction to Pragmatics

Jenny Thomas

LIS LIBRARY	
Date	Fund
8/11/12	1-che.
Order No	
2350245	
University of Chester	

An imprint of Pearson Education

Harlow, England · London · New York · Reading, Massachusetts · San Francisco
Toronto · Don Mills, Ontario · Sydney · Tokyo · Singapore · Hong Kong · Seoul
Taipei · Cape Town · Madrid · Mexico City · Amsterdam · Munich · Paris · Milan

Pearson Education Limited,
Edinburgh Gate, Harlow,
Essex CM20 2JE, England

and Associated Companies throughout the world

Visit us on the World Wide Web at:
www.pearsoned.co.uk

© Longman Group Limited 1995

All rights reserved; no part of this publication may be
reproduced, stored in a retrieval system, or transmitted
in any form or by any means, electronic, mechanical.
photocopying, recording, or otherwise without either the
prior written permission of the Publishers or a licence
permitting restricted copying in the United Kingdom issued
by the Copyright Licensing Agency Ltd.,
90 Tottenham Court Road, London W1T 4LP.

First published 1995

ISBN 978-0-582-29151-5

British Library Cataloguing-in-Publication Data

A catalogue record for this book is
available from the British Library

Library of Congress Cataloging-in-Publication Data

Thomas, Jenny, 1948–
    Meaning in interaction : an introduction to pragmatics / Jenny Thomas.
        p.   cm. — (Learning about language)
    Includes bibliographical references (p.) and index.
    ISBN 0-582-29151-8 (ppr)
    1. Pragmatics.   I. Title.   II. Series.
P99.4.P72T45   1995
302.2'24   dc20   95–16351
                                                      CIP

22   21   20   19
15   14   13   12

Printed in Malaysia, PPSB

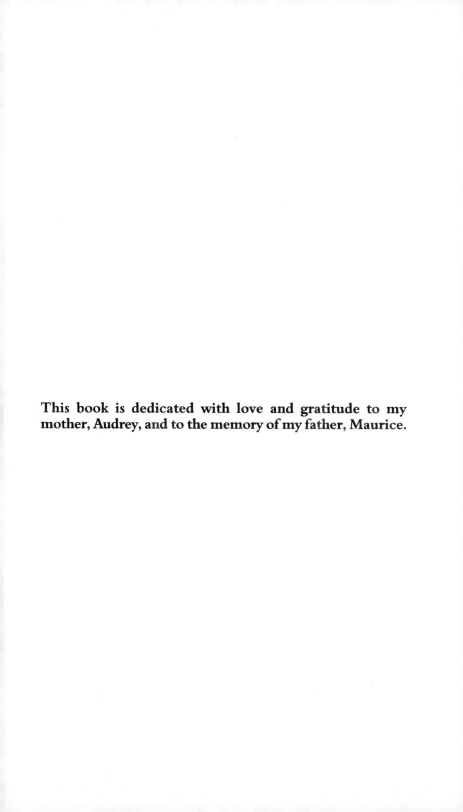

This book is dedicated with love and gratitude to my mother, Audrey, and to the memory of my father, Maurice.

Contents

Preface

Pragmatics is a relatively new area of linguistics and until recently there were no introductory texts available. Now, in response to the growing interest in the field in colleges and universities, a number of introductory books have appeared, each somewhat different in orientation. Marcelo Dascal (1983) offers a first class introduction to the field from the standpoint of the philosophy of language. Georgia Green (1989) provides a very accessible introduction, with particular emphasis on textual pragmatics and more formal aspects of pragmatics. Diane Blakemore (1992) takes a cognitive approach, firmly rooted within relevance theory, to which she offers an excellent introduction, while Jacob Mey (1993) approaches the subject from a social point of view.

So what makes this book distinctive? Firstly, it accords a central place to the roles of both speaker and hearer in the construction of meaning and takes account of both social and psychological factors in the generation and interpretation of utterances. Secondly, it covers basic concepts in considerable detail, drawing particular attention to problems in early work in pragmatics. Thirdly, it brings the reader right up to date with current issues in pragmatics. The theoretical points are illustrated with copious authentic examples taken from the media, fiction and real-life interactions.

Although I have presupposed that the reader well have no previous knowledge of pragmatics, I have presumed that he or she will be familiar with some basic linguistic terms and concepts.

Jenny Thomas
Lancaster,
February 1995.

Acknowledgements

First and foremost I would like to thank Geoffrey Leech, through whose work I first became interested in pragmatics. Without his unfailing encouragement and editorial support this (long overdue) book would never have been completed.

I owe a debt of gratitude to generations of Lancaster students, whose comments and criticisms have helped shape this work. Finally, to the many friends and relations, colleagues and strangers who, over the years, have provided me (often willingly, sometimes unwittingly) with the data on which this book is based — thank you!

CHAPTER 1

What is pragmatics?

1.1 Introduction

People do not always or even usually say what they mean. Speakers frequently mean much more than their words actually say. For example, I might say: *It's hot in here!*, but what I mean is: *Please open the window!* or *Is it all right if I open the window?* or *You're wasting electricity!* People can mean something quite different from what their words say, or even just the opposite. For instance, to someone who has borrowed my car for the weekend and returned it with no petrol in the tank, I might say: *It was nice of you to fill the car up!* or *What a shame you couldn't find the petrol tank!*

Several interesting questions arise from these observations: if speakers regularly mean something other than what they say, how is it that people manage (as on the whole they do) to understand one another? If a single group of words such as *It's hot in here!* could mean so many different things at different times, how do we work out what it actually does mean on one specific occasion? And why don't people just say what they mean? These, and many other issues, are addressed within the area of linguistics known as pragmatics.

In this introductory chapter I shall explain the way in which the term *pragmatics* will be used in this book and I shall outline the sort of work which is carried out under the heading of pragmatics.

1.2 Defining pragmatics

In the early 1980s, when it first became common to discuss pragmatics in general textbooks on linguistics, the most common definitions of pragmatics were: **meaning in use** or **meaning in**

context. Although these definitions are accurate enough and perfectly adequate as a starting point, they are too general for our purposes — for example, there are aspects of semantics, particularly semantics of the type developed since the late 1980s,[1] which could well come under the headings of meaning in use or meaning in context. More up-to-date textbooks tend to fall into one of two camps — those who equate pragmatics with **speaker meaning**[2] and those who equate it with **utterance interpretation**[3] (they do not necessarily use these terms explicitly). Certainly each of these definitions captures something of the work now undertaken under the heading of pragmatics, but neither of them is entirely satisfactory. Moreover, they each represent radically different approaches to the sub-discipline of pragmatics. The term *speaker meaning* tends to be favoured by writers who take a broadly **social**[4] view of the discipline; it puts the focus of attention firmly on the **producer** of the message, but at the same time obscures the fact that the process of interpreting what we hear involves moving between several levels of meaning. The final definition (*utterance interpretation*), which is favoured by those who take a broadly **cognitive** approach, avoids this fault, but at the cost of focusing too much on the **receiver** of the message, which in practice means largely ignoring the social constraints on utterance production. I am not going to undertake an exhaustive discussion of the relative advantages and disadvantages of the two competing approaches just now — this task will be done at appropriate points in later chapters. But we can begin to understand the differences between the two approaches if we examine what is meant by **levels of meaning**. The first level is that of **abstract meaning**; we move from abstract meaning to **contextual meaning** (also called **utterance meaning**) by assigning sense and/or reference to a word, phrase or sentence. The third level of meaning is reached when we consider the speaker's intention, known as the **force** of an utterance. We shall begin by looking at each of these levels in turn.

1.3 From abstract meaning to contextual meaning

Abstract meaning[5] is concerned with what a word, phrase, sentence, etc. *could* mean (for example, the dictionary meanings of words or phrases). The last four lines of the following excerpt[6] illustrate well the point I am trying to make:

Example 1

'What we want is the army to take over this country. See a bit of discipline then, we would ... The Forces, that's the thing. We knew what discipline was when I was in the Forces.' Pop always spoke of his time at Catterick Camp in the nineteen-forties as 'being in the Forces' as if he had been in the navy and air force and marines as well. 'Flog 'em, is what I say. Give 'em something to remember across their backsides.' He paused and swigged tea. 'What's wrong with the cat?' he said, so that anyone coming in at that moment, Alan thought, would have supposed him to be enquiring after the health of the family pet.

As Alan rightly observes, if you had not been party to the whole of the preceding discussion, you would probably have assumed that *cat* referred to a pet, rather than to the *cat-o'nine-tails*. In most dictionaries *cat* is shown as having two abstract meanings: *a small four-legged animal with soft fur and sharp claws, often kept as a pet* and *a whip made from nine knotted cords, formerly used for flogging people*.[7] But, quite clearly, the first meaning is by far the more common — the second meaning is restricted to a very limited **domain of discourse** — that of military life in earlier times.

More recently, *cat* has acquired an additional meaning — *catalytic converter* — which belongs to yet another domain of discourse, that of cars or air pollution. In the summer of 1990, one British television commercial for Volkswagen cars showed an elderly woman, cat-basket in hand, searching her new car for the cat, which, according to the advertisement, was supplied as standard. What this somewhat sexist advertisement rather tortuously illustrated is that if a hearer is in the 'wrong' domain of discourse, if, for example he or she thinks you are talking about pets when you are actually talking about cars or life on board ships in earlier times, the possibility of wrongly assigning sense is greater. Conversely, when you are in a known domain of discourse or when you know what social roles your interactant occupies, you will probably have little difficulty in assigning the correct sense to an ambiguous lexical item. So you will have no problem in knowing that a student who comes to ask you for *a handout* probably wants lecture notes, while the tramp who asks for *a handout* equally certainly does not.

The term *abstract meaning* does not apply only to single words. It can apply equally well to phrases or even to whole sentences. Supposing at a party you heard someone saying: *The*

Pearsons are on coke. Taken in the abstract (by consulting a dictionary of contemporary spoken English, for example) the word *coke* could (at least in theory) refer to *Coca-Cola, cocaine* or *a coal derivative.* And, accordingly, the whole expression *to be on coke* could have one of (at least) three abstract meanings: *to be drinking Coca-Cola, to use cocaine,* or *to have solid-fuel heating.* What the words actually meant on the occasion in question could only be determined in context.

In general, competent native speakers do not have to seek laboriously for the contextual meaning of a word, phrase or sentence in the way that the two previous examples may have implied. The contextual meaning is so obvious that it never even crosses our mind that there could be alternative interpretations. So, if a friend promises to send you a card from Rome, you do not agonize over whether it will be a picture postcard, a playing card or a business card. Unless your friends are particularly odd, the second two possibilities would never even enter your head. If we were not able to take such short cuts in interpretation, the process of understanding one another would be very inefficient. Nevertheless, there are occasions when we do quite genuinely experience difficulty in assigning contextual meaning and then we have to weigh up alternative interpretations. The likelihood of such problems occurring is increased still further when there are rapid changes of topic, as the following conversation illustrates:

Example 2
Speakers A and B had spent a long time discussing the relative merits of different computers, using terms such as 286, 386, RS/6000. A third person, C, had been in the room throughout this conversation, but had taken no part in it. Shortly afterwards B turned to C and said:

B: Do you know what fifteen fifteens are?
C: No, I don't know much about computer hardware.

In this case, a simple question about elementary arithmetic gets interpreted as a complicated question about sophisticated new computers, because speaker C thought he was in a different domain of discourse — thus *fifteen fifteens* is assigned the meaning of the name of a computer instead of the meaning *the number fifteen.*

The problems which confront people when they understand the abstract meaning (the range of linguistically possible meanings) without being able to determine the contextual meaning is, of course, the very stuff of which fiction is made — comedies, tragedies, romances and, above all, mysteries and detective stories. In Umberto Eco's *The name of the rose*, for example, the monks Adso and William only discover the secret of the *finis Africae* after many false trails (and 250 pages!). Although they were able from the outset to translate the words of the text containing the clue to the mystery, they were unable to understand what the original writer, Venantius, meant by those words.

Example 3
'Secretum finis Africae manus supra idolum age primum et septimum de quatuor.'
'Is that clear?' he asked.
'The hand over the idol works on the first and the seventh of the four ...' I repeated, shaking my head. 'It isn't clear at all!'
'I know. First of all we have to know what Venantius meant by "idolum". An image, a ghost, a figure? And then what can this "four" be that has a "first" and a "seventh"? And what is to be done with them? Move them, push them, pull them?'[8]

The monks in *The name of the rose* had to deal with two problems. The first was to assign **sense** to the word *idolum* (line 8) and the second to assign **reference** to the word *four* (line 9). We shall deal with these two problems separately.

1.3.1 Assigning sense in context

When people are engaged in conversations, they intuitively look for contextual sense (the sense in which the speaker/writer[9] is using a word) as the following example[10] illustrates:

Example 4
This exchange, which I overheard on a train, took place between two young Englishmen. Speaker A was reading a newspaper.

A: What's this lump they're always on about?
B: Read it out.
A: [*Reads aloud from paper*] Inland Revenue crack down on lump.
B: Oh, isn't it something to do with casual labour on building sites? The way they're paid — tax evasion and that?

Notice that speaker B did not list all the possible senses of *lump* (*a shapeless mound*; *a hard swelling*; *a heavy, dull person*; *to put up with*, etc.). To have done so would have been both irritating and unhelpful. Instead, he asked for sufficient context to enable him to tell his friend what, in his opinion, the writer of this particular article meant by the word lump.

As we have seen, part of the process of determining what speakers mean (as opposed to what their words mean) involves assigning sense to those words. In general, this process is very straightforward, but problems can occur and one of the most frequent causes of such problems occurs in the case of homonyms. We have already seen several instances of homonyms (words which have the same spelling and pronunciation but different meanings) causing misunderstandings — *cat*, *handout*, *coke* and *lump*. The following example, taken from a Scottish local newspaper, *The Dunoon Observer*, caused offence as well as misunderstanding:

Example 5

Correction

The 'old pouffe' which started the fire at 7, Douglas Cottages, as reported last week, referred to an item of furniture and not to the owner, Mr Donnie McArthur.

We also saw that in example 3 the Latin word *idolum* caused particular problems. There were several reasons for this. In the first place, *idolum* is polysemous[11] in Latin, that is, it had several closely related meanings — *image*, *ghost* and *figure*. It is very often the case that lexical items have different ranges of polysemous meanings in different languages. Thus in English you can speak of a person's *head* or *foot* and you can also refer to the *head*/*foot* of a staircase (the different senses of the words are in a very obvious way related); you can do exactly the same with the French words *tête* and *pied*. However, whereas in English the word *hand* can apply both to people and to clocks or watches, you cannot in French speak of **la main d'une montre* (although a French person would probably be able to work out what you meant). The problem was exacerbated for the monks, since they had no idea of the **context** in which the word was being used.

A potentially very serious example of the problems which can be caused by expressions having a different range of polysemous meanings in different languages was given to me by a colleague who was the chief interpreter (from Hebrew to

English) at the trial of John Demjanjuk.[12] This was an extremely sensitive, important and complex trial, one of the complications being that the trial was conducted in three languages — Hebrew, Ukrainian and English — and involved many interpreters. At one point in the trial a Hebrew-speaking lawyer presented an exhibit to the defendant and asked if he recognized this *tzilum* (צילום). In Hebrew the word *tzilum* is polysemous and has three (closely related) meanings — *x-ray*, *photograph* and *photocopy* (xerox). In English, of course, these are three quite distinct lexical items. Unfortunately, the interpreter was positioned towards the back of the court and she was unable to see the exhibit. In the circumstances, she could only guess at the correct interpretation of the word and, as it happened, guessed wrongly, to the considerable confusion of all those who could not speak Hebrew.[13]

Assigning the correct or intended sense to polysemous or homonymous lexical items can be especially problematic for non-native speakers of a language, because they may lack the cultural background knowledge on which native speakers draw. For example, I was once listening to two German university students trying to work out the meaning of the word *roundabout* in a newspaper article on international economics. They looked up the word *roundabout* in a dictionary and one read out: *Traffic island, merry-go-round, indirect*. So they had three possible meanings (i.e. abstract meanings) of the word and in normal circumstances it would have been reasonable to assume that they would have experienced little difficulty in selecting the appropriate one for their particular context. However, the text they were working on was in fact making a rather obscure reference to a children's television programme *The magic roundabout* — an allusion which would have been picked up instantly by anyone who had grown up in Britain, but which would probably be completely lost on anyone else.

While homonyms are one of the most frequent causes of problems in assigning sense correctly, **homographs** — words which have the same spelling but different pronunciation and meaning — can cause similar problems. The first line of the next example[14] was scrawled on a wall and the second line was added by way of comment by a different graffiti-writer. This is clearly an instance of wilful misinterpretation of the intended sense of *lead*:

Example 6
In People's China the workers take the lead!

[To which had been added]:
In capitalist England, the sods also take the iron, copper,
floorboards and fillings from your teeth.

A third cause of incorrect assignment of sense can be
homophones — words which have the same pronunciation, but
different spelling and meaning. The following example, which
appeared in the minutes of a management meeting at the BBC,[15]
was caused by the fact that the original newsreader spoke with a
Northern Irish accent.

Example 7
The solicitor reported that the BBC was being sued in
Ireland by a man who thought he had been described as
having herpes. The BBC's defence was that it had accused
him of having a hairpiece.

In each of the previous examples in this section, if the
hearer failed to assign sense correctly, he or she would probably
completely misunderstand what the speaker meant. In the
following example, caused by the homophones *chaste* and *chased,*
this is not entirely the case:

Example 8
'He's ever so funny, my dad. He gave her a lovely silver
bracelet, one of those chased ones.'

Alan couldn't imagine how one bracelet could be more
chaste than another, but he didn't ask.[16]

Even though Alan fails to assign sense correctly to the word
chased, he nevertheless manages to understand the general import
of what his girlfriend is telling him. We shall return to this
example in section 1.5.3.

1.3.2 Assigning reference in context

So far we have discussed abstract meaning only in terms of
assigning sense to words or phrases — i.e. working out what they
mean in context. But, in everyday life, you need only to call to
mind those tantalizing snippets of conversation overheard on

buses or in supermarkets to realize that it is perfectly possible to understand the sense of every word a speaker utters, yet still not understand what the speaker means. Years after having heard it, I still long to know what one woman was talking about when she said to her fellow bus passenger:

Example 9
And just think, if he hadn't fallen out of bed, I'd never have found out about it!

Why did I find it impossible to understand what this woman was talking about, when the sense of every word she uttered could have been understood by a three-year-old? The answer, of course, is that I did not know who *he* referred to, nor, more importantly, what was the *it* the speaker had found out about. In other words, I was unable to assign **reference** to her words.

In order to understand an utterance, we not only have to assign sense to words, but also to assign reference (i.e. to determine in context who or what is being referred to). Thus a notice which said: *Danger! Do not touch!* could be understood to some extent by all literate members of a community — they would know what the words meant and that the notice constituted a warning. But the notice could only fulfil its warning function properly if it was clear to the reader precisely what was being referred to — i.e. what must not be touched.

The practical joker who delights in stealing official signs and re-erecting them at appropriate (or inappropriate) new sites, exploits the fact that, whilst the notices may retain (more or less) the same sense when relocated, the reference can be changed to entertaining effect. Thus a sign saying *Reserved for the Vice-Chancellor* may vanish from the chair of honour in the Great Hall and reappear attached to a copy of *The Beano* in the Junior Common Room.[17]

Notice that the previous example simply said *Reserved for the Vice-Chancellor* and not *this (chair) is reserved*. Expressions such as *this* and *that* are called **deictic expressions**.[18] Deictic expressions are those which derive part of their meaning from their context of utterance. **Place deictics**, such as *here, there, this, that*, do not mean very much in isolation; it is only when you know where the speaker is standing or what the speaker is indicating that they become truly meaningful. In the same way, **time deictics**, such as *yesterday, tomorrow, now*, only become fully meaningful if you know when the words were uttered. Other categories of deictic expression operate in a similar way. These include **person deictics**, such as *I, he, you*; **discourse deictics**, such as *the former, the latter*; and social deictics,[19] such as *Madam, Your Grace*, which tell us something about the social relationship between the speaker and (in this case) the addressee.

Virtually all deictic expressions, by their very nature, cause problems of reference assignment when removed from their original context of utterance, as the following excerpt from a detective novel[20] illustrates. A man has just found a compromising letter in his wife's handbag, asking her to meet the writer this Monday lunchtime:

Example 10

Suddenly the thought struck him: how long had the letter been in her bag? There was no date on the letter — no way at all of telling which particular Monday was meant. Had it been *last* Monday? There was no way he could be certain about things; and yet he had the strong conviction that the letter, presumably addressed to her at work, had been received only a day or so previously.

Even without any remove of time or place, it can be difficult to assign reference correctly to any utterance containing a third person pronoun (he, she, it, they) since these have an almost infinite number of possible referents. This is well illustrated in the following excerpt form Tom Stoppard's play *Rosencrantz and Guildenstern are dead*,[21] which is at least three ways ambiguous.[22] Rosencrantz is talking to one of the actors:

Example 11

Act: The old man thinks he's in love with his
       daughter.
Ros: *(Appalled)* Good God! We're out of our depth here.
Act: No, no, no — *he* hasn't got a daughter — the old
       man thinks he's in love with *his* daughter.
Ros: The old man is?
Act: Hamlet, in love with the old man's daughter,
       the old man thinks.
Ros: Ha! It's beginning to make sense! Unre-
       quited passion!

Another example is to be found in Shakespeare's *Othello*,[23] when Othello, who has already begun to doubt his wife's fidelity, overhears a conversation between Iago, his adjutant, and Cassio, the man he suspects of being his wife's lover:

Example 12

… she is persuaded I will marry her, out of her own love and flattery, not out of my promise … she was here even now; she haunts me in every place. I was t'other day talking on the sea-bank … she falls me thus about my neck.

Othello, already consumed by jealousy, is convinced that Cassio is talking about Othello's wife, Desdemona, when in fact the *she* in question is Bianca, a prostitute. There are many such examples to be found in literature.

A more entertaining (albeit unwitting) real-life example of the problem of assigning reference was provided by a television commentator, the late Wynford Vaughn-Thomas, at the launching of the Cunard liner, *The Queen Elizabeth*. 'And there she is', he announced to the television audience. 'The whole vast bulk of her.' Unfortunately, at that very moment the cameras switched from the new liner to the Queen Mother, who was about to perform the launching ceremony.

As we have already seen with the word *Monday* in example 10, even what appear to be straightforward cases of definite reference can be problematic when the reader or listener is in a different part of the world from the writer/speaker. For example, it is intensely irritating for people in the southern hemisphere when international journals are dated by season instead of by month: what is Spring 1991 in Europe is not Spring 1991 in New Zealand. Likewise titles such as *The Queen* or *The Prime Minister* obviously refer to quite different people in, say, The Netherlands, Sweden and Canada, as the following incident, which took place in March 1976, clearly illustrates. The British Labour M.P. Roy Hattersley, then second-in-command at the Foreign Office, had flown to Bulgaria on an official visit:[24]

Example 13

'On the airport in the capital I was standing holding sheaves of flowers in both hands — they present a lot of flowers in Bulgaria. They'd played … the band of the Bulgarian Army had played *God Save the Queen*, they were playing the Bulgarian National Anthem, which is a rather long national anthem and the British Ambassador standing next to me holding a rather smaller bunch of flowers whis-

> pered from the corner of his mouth: "The Prime Minister
> has resigned." And I said to him, whispering behind my
> gladioli: "I didn't read that part of your briefing. Is the
> Prime Minister the *senior* figure here or is he just a figure-
> head, with the Party Secretary being the real boss?" To
> which Eddie Bolland — his name's engraved on my heart
> and mind — Eddie Bolland replied: "Not *their* Prime Min-
> ister, *our* Prime Minister!" To my eternal credit, I didn't
> drop a single gladioli, but it came as an enormous shock to
> me.'

You will have encountered similar problems when reading old books. For example, several books by Agatha Christie refer simply to *the war*; the reader is obliged to check when the book was written in order to establish which war the writer meant. And the further back in time you go, the harder it becomes to establish intended reference. Samuel Pepys,[25] for example' refers frequently to *The Duke of York* and *The Prince of Orange*. The identity of these people would have been perfectly clear to any contemporary of Pepys's, but modern readers may experience some difficulty in determining which of the many bearers of these titles were being referred to.

1.3.3 Structural ambiguity

In the two previous sections we have noted how we have to derive the sense and reference which a **speaker** intends from the range of possible senses and references which a **sentence** could have. A third cause of potential sentence-level ambiguity is structural. Consider the following example,[26] which relates to a report of a pilgrimage to the shrine of Our Lady of Walsingham:

Example 14
Afterwards, the Bishop walked among the pilgrims eating
their picnic lunches.

In this case the source of the ambiguity is syntactic. The hearer has to decide whether it was the Bishop or the pilgrims who ate the sandwiches.

1.3.4 Interaction of sense, reference and structure

In the three preceding sections I have given examples where

ambiguity is caused by single instances of ambiguities of sense, reference or structure. Very often, of course, these things will occur in combination.

In the corridor outside my room I once picked up a piece of card on which someone had printed OUT OF ORDER in large letters. Now, from my knowledge of the English language (that is, from my abstract linguistic knowledge), I know that the phrase *out of order* has a range of possible senses, including *not in the correct sequence* (e.g. of books on a library shelf), *not permissible* (e.g. of a question at a meeting) or *not working* (e.g. of a machine). My knowledge of the world (which here included knowledge of the sort of things people in my department usually put up notices about) told me that the last sense was by far the most likely and I surmised that the writer was warning someone that something was not (or had not been) working. Assigning reference — determining what was being referred to — was more difficult. I decided that the notice must refer to a machine in the corridor where I had found it, but there were several possible candidates, including a coffee machine, a laser printer and a photocopier. Moreover, since I had no idea when the message had been written and whether the notice had fallen off the machine or had been removed deliberately, I had no means of knowing whether or not the warning still applied.

I later found out that my initial guess had been wrong. A group of students had been trying to put several hundred M.A. dissertations back into chronological and alphabetical order. The notice I had found had fallen off a pile of manuscripts which had yet to be sorted. From this we can begin to see that the processes of assigning sense and reference are frequently mutually dependent: unless you know what something refers to, you may not be able to work out the sense, and conversely, if you do not know the sense of a word or phrase, it is more difficult to work out what is being referred to. The following examples show how structural ambiguity can lead to ambiguity of sense:

Example 15
Speaker B was a well-known cricket commentator, Brian Johnston, Speaker A was his wife.[27]

A: Have you seen the dog bowl?
B: No, but I've seen it play several good innings.

Brian Johnston is exploiting the potential structural ambiguity between *dog bowl* as a complex noun or a verb phrase.

Example 16

The late Brian Redhead, a well-known radio presenter, was discussing with Sir Geoffrey Howe (Foreign Secretary at the time), the reluctance of Britain's EEC partners to support the U.K.'s proposal to impose sanctions on Syria:

Was it because the EEC men were not all there?

Not all there is structurally ambiguous, as it could be analysed as either an adverbial or an adjectival complement. Analysing it as an adverbial would give you the meaning *absent (from the talks)*, while analysing it as an adjectival complement would give you the meaning *out of their minds* or *insane*.

1.3.5 Ambiguity and intentionality

Instances of surface-level ambiguities of sense, reference and structure are legion. Indeed, as Corder (1981: 39) has pointed out:

> Well-formed sentences produced by native speakers are mostly ambiguous when taken out of context.

Comparatively few ambiguous sentences are genuinely misleading when taken **in context**, although such instances do occur. The following example, which I read on a sign adjacent to Lancaster station, might not normally have caused any confusion, but it did in the historical context of the day on which I saw it (it was the day of the Duke of York's[28] wedding):

Example 17

> **Flags 2' x 2'.**
> **£11.50 per dozen**
> **Delivery free.**

I would probably never have realized that the word *flags* here referred to *flagstones* (paving stones) if I had not been puzzling over why anyone would need to have their flags delivered, even in fairly large numbers.

So ubiquitous are ambiguous sentences that speakers rarely notice that their utterances are ambiguous and cannot recognize the ambiguity even when it is pointed out. A particularly striking instance of this was provided by Mr Cyril Smith, at the time the

Liberal M.P. for Rochdale and a man readily recognized through-out the country because he was extraordinarily fat. During a radio programme[29] Smith was expressing the opinion that racist attitudes could not be altered by consciously changing the language people use, but he claimed to speak as someone who:

Example 18

'… does a very very great deal of work amongst the immi-grant population — I had sixteen of 'em for lunch at the House of Commons last Tuesday…'

The audience laughed so much that Mr Smith was unable to continue speaking for some moments, but he clearly failed to recognize the ambiguity of what he had said, and became extremely angry because the audience appeared to be doubting the sincerity of his regard for ethnic minority groups.

I have said that, in general, only one utterance meaning is intended by the speaker, but there are exceptions, the most obvious being in literary discourse (particularly poetry[30]) or in jokes.[31] But we can find examples outside these genres where it is not possible to understand the speaker's intention without understanding both meanings. Examples 19 and 20 are excerpts from a speech given by Glenda Jackson, M.P.[32]

Example 19

In this extract, Ms Jackson was making reference to the desire expressed by John Major on becoming Prime Minister to make Britain 'a classless society'.

'They call it a "classless society". And it is classless. There are no classes for the children turned away for the lack of a qualified teacher. There are no classes for 200,000 children denied nursery places. And there is certainly no class in a government that for the last decade has sold our children and our future short.'

Example 20

In the second extract she was discussing her education at a State School and later at the Royal Academy of Dramatic Art:

'And forty years later I stand here addressing conference. Yet without state education it's doubtful I'd be addressing envelopes.'

My final example of deliberate ambiguity is taken from *The Money Programme*.[33] Once again the hearer cannot fully understand the speaker's intention without **simultaneously** entertaining the two meanings of the word *bank*.

Example 21
The speaker is referring to the Swiss city of Geneva:

'It's a city where "The banks along the river" has a different meaning from usual.'

1.4 Utterance meaning: the first level of speaker meaning

When in interaction we have resolved all the ambiguities of sense, reference and structure — when we have moved from abstract meaning (what a particular sentence could mean in theory) to what the speaker actually does mean by these words on this particular occasion — we have arrived at **contextual meaning** or **utterance meaning**.[34] Utterance meaning can be defined as 'a sentence-context pairing' (Gazdar 1979) and is the first component of **speaker meaning**.

1.4.1 Importance of utterance meaning

Now, you may feel, and with some justification, that (except, of course, for story book detectives deciphering baffling clues!) in everyday interaction people do not normally go around straining their interpretative faculties trying to determine sense and reference. Although it is certainly the case that the majority of sentences, taken out of context, are, at least from the point of view of the hearer,[35] potentially multiply ambiguous, in real life we rarely have difficulty in interpreting them correctly in context. In fact, more often than not, we fail to notice ambiguities of sense and reference at all, unless some misunderstanding occurs or unless, as in jokes or word-play, our attention is deliberately drawn to their existence.

But, as we have already seen with the example of the Demjanjuk trial, problems really do occur in assigning sense and reference and there are cases where correctly assigning sense and reference can, quite literally, be a matter of life and death. An example of this can be found in the transcript of a controversial English murder trial, which was held in 1952. A youth of nineteen, Derek Bentley, was charged jointly with a sixteen-year-old, Christopher Craig, with having committed the then capital offence of murdering a police officer. It was never disputed that it was Craig who fired the fatal shot; Bentley was unarmed and had, in fact, already been caught and was being restrained by a policeman at the time the shot was fired. The case against Bentley hinged on the allegation that he had shouted, *Let him have it, Chris!* At Bentley's trial, the prosecution argued that this meant *Shoot the policeman*, which in turn was construed as 'deliberate incitement to murder'. An alternative interpretation proposed later in Bentley's defence[36] was that *it* referred to *the gun*, *him* referred to *the police officer* and that far from telling Craig to shoot his pursuer, Bentley was recommending Craig to hand over the gun. This second interpretation was rejected by the court and Bentley was found guilty and hanged. Craig, who had actually fired the shot, was still a minor and was sentenced only to youth custody.[37]

It is generally true that law courts (at least in Britain) exhibit an extreme reluctance to take account of anything other than the dictionary meaning of particular expressions. A particular source of irritation to me is the use of so-called 'expert witnesses' in legal cases involving the use of obscene or abusive (often racist) language. In such cases the defence invariably bring in to court some cobwebby philologist who will testify, for example, that to shout *Bollocks!* is not offensive because it 'means' *little balls*.[38] It seems that the only linguistic evidence admissible in these cases is the etymology of a word or phrase (and frequently the 'etymology' is wholly spurious) — no account is taken of the circumstances in which the word is used nor of the speaker's intention in uttering it. In another court case,[39] the defendant was charged with four offences against the owner of a Chinese restaurant. One was that he had called the restaurant owner a *Chinky bastard*, but this charge was dismissed because an 'expert' testified that the expression 'meant' *'wandering parentless child travelling through the countryside in the Ching Dynasty'* and was in no way offensive.[40] Courts seem incapable of taking on board the fact that the original lexical meaning of an expression is not a good guide to the speaker's intention in employing that expression.

1.5 Force: the second level of speaker meaning

In the previous section we saw that there was a crucial dispute about the meaning of Bentley's words (utterance meaning). More importantly, however, there was a disagreement about Bentley's **intention** in making the alleged utterance: was Bentley urging Craig to commit murder or recommending him to surrender? The psychologist, Miller, writing in 1974, was one of the first people to point out the significance of this level of analysis:

> Most of our misunderstandings of other people are not due to any inability to hear them or parse their sentences or understand their words ... A far more important source of difficulty in communication is that we often fail to understand a speaker's intention.

In pragmatics we use the term **force** to refer to the speaker's communicative intention. Force, a concept introduced by the philosopher, J. L. Austin, is the second component of speaker meaning. Imagine someone says to you: *Is that your car?* And suppose further that because of the context in which the question is asked, there are no ambiguities of sense or reference, that the word *that* indicates a unique entity (your car) and *your* refers to you. So, although you have no problem in understanding the utterance meaning (the first level of speaker meaning), yet still you might not understand the force behind the question. Is the speaker expressing admiration or expressing scorn? Is it a complaint that your car is blocking the drive? Is the speaker requesting a lift into town? These are all examples of the different pragmatic forces which the same utterance might have.

In the sections which follow we shall examine how utterance meaning and force, the two components of speaker meaning, interrelate. There are four possible permutations in understanding utterance meaning and force, which we shall explore in sections 1.5.1–1.5.4.

1.5.1 Understanding both utterance meaning and force

To understand both utterance meaning and force is probably the most common state of affairs. This was illustrated in example 1. Although the sentence *What's wrong with the cat?* was ambiguous, in practice the hearers had no problem whatever in understanding what the speaker meant. The *cat* in question was the *cat-o' nine-tails* and the speaker's intention was to advocate the reintro-duction of corporal punishment as a legal sanction.

1.5.2 Understanding utterance meaning but not force

Probably the second most common situation is when we understand the meaning of a speaker's utterance, but not the force. This was illustrated well in an article about Barry Manilow.[41] The writer was discussing the singer's feelings of insecurity:

> **Example 22**
> He suspects compliments. He sifts them for snide subtext. Conditioning has taught him this. Bob Dylan stopped him at a party, embraced him warmly, told him: 'Don't stop doing what you're doing, man. We're all inspired by you.' He knew not what to make of the encounter. Nearly two years later, it haunts him still.
>
> 'Who knows?' he says, shrugging the shrug of one who has shrugged much. 'It seems so odd that Bob Dylan would tell me this. I wasn't exactly sure what he meant. He may have been laughing out of the other side of his mouth while he said it, but it didn't seem like it. I mean, he looked me dead in the eye. But maybe he says that to everybody who walks by. He may have had one drink too many. You know, people give me jabs all the time — but not to my face ... I sort of left the party for a minute because I wasn't sure, I thought, "Well, maybe ..." '

It was not the meaning of the utterance *Don't stop doing what you're doing* which caused Manilow problems, but what Dylan **meant** by those words. Was he being sarcastic, sincere, flattering Manilow? As Miller pointed out, it is this level of communication which is often so difficult to understand.

1.5.3 Understanding force but not utterance meaning

To understand the force of what is said without understanding the meaning of that utterance is rather more unusual, but it does happen. In example 8, we saw that although Alan fails to under-stand the exact meaning of the word *chased*, yet he understands the force of his girlfriend's utterance — she is **praising** her father. Here are two further examples, the first was said to me the first day I arrived in Australia by a man who had taken me to the University restaurant. The second I heard in the United States, and was spoken by one teenager to her friend, who was getting into a panic:

Example 23
It's my shout.

Example 24
Don't have a cow!

I had never encountered either of these idioms, but in each case the context and circumstances were such that the intended force was perfectly clear.[42] The first meant *It's my treat* or *I'll pay* and clearly had the force of an offer; the second in British English would be something like *Keep your hair on!* and constituted a piece of advice.

1.5.4 Understanding neither utterance meaning nor force

A hearer who fails to establish the utterance meaning correctly or at all may fail to understand the force the speaker intended. I was once at a conference in Greece and a group of British and American linguists were discussing another linguist, who was not present. Speaker A (British) said:

Example 25
'Her work has become very popular.'

I already knew what he thought of the book in question, and correctly interpreted *popular* as meaning *non-academic*. I therefore correctly interpreted the intended force of the utterance as criticism. The Americans agreed that it was indeed popular, but they interpreted *popular* as meaning *well-received/having a lot of success*. They therefore incorrectly interpreted the intended force of the utterance as praise.

Again in the United States I overheard one woman say to another:

Example 26
'He says now I'm well down my personal corridor.'

I had no idea what was meant by *personal corridor* and, since

I didn't know whether being well down it was a good or a bad thing, I was completely unable to assign force to this utterance.

1.5.5 Interrelationship of utterance meaning and force

We have seen, then, that there are two components of **speaker meaning** — utterance meaning and force. It is frequently (but not invariably) the case that we derive force from utterance meaning but we can, for example, use paralinguistic features (such as intonation and tone of voice) or non-linguistic features (such as gesture) in order to work out the intended force. Or we may (as in example 8) rely mainly or entirely on context. On the other hand, if (as in example 25) we fail to understand the utterance meaning, we may well fail to understand the force or if (as the Bentley example on page 18 illustrated), we cannot agree on utterance meaning, we are unlikely to be able to agree as to the intended force. From this we can see that the two components of speaker meaning are closely related, but not inseparable and it would be a mistake to conflate or confuse them. It is precisely this mistake which I criticized in section 1.2.

1.6 Definitions of pragmatics (revisited)

It is extremely easy, with the benefit of hindsight, to pick holes in earlier approaches to the study of pragmatics. In the discussion which follows it is important to bear in mind that the 'pioneers' in the area of pragmatics were reacting against an approach to linguistics which was strongly biased towards meaning in abstract rather than meaning in use.[43] But disciplines evolve and our definitions, theories and methodologies must also change in order to respond to new concerns and insights.

1.6.1 Speaker meaning

In section 1.2 I criticized the fact that the term 'speaker meaning' obscures the fact that there are two aspects or levels of speaker meaning — utterance meaning and force. There are two reasons why writers who, explicitly or implicitly, have used this definition have not needed or wanted to make the distinction. In the first place (reasonably enough, given the approach to linguistics they were reacting against), this group of writers was really only interested in the second level — force — and in the factors (particularly the social factors) which lead a speaker to formulate an utterance in a particular way. For example, they were interested in **why** a speaker might use an indirect rather than direct form of request, complaint, criticism, etc. In the second place — and this now seems a rather serious weakness in their approach — this group of writers was concerned primarily or exclusively with **speaker intention** and focused on the speaker or producer of talk to the near exclusion of the hearer or receiver of talk. It must be obvious that **for the speaker** ambiguities of sense, reference or structure rarely, if ever, exist. For example, the person who wrote the *out of order* sign which I found knew exactly what was meant. For him or her there was no ambiguity; the ambiguity only existed for me, the reader.

1.6.2 Utterance interpretation

In contrast, the broadly cognitive approach claimed by those who operate the *utterance interpretation* definition of pragmatics focuses almost exclusively on the process of interpretation from the point of view of the **hearer**. This approach does seem potentially to offer a rather good account of disambiguation at level one. But their focus on the way in which hearers reach a particular interpretation is accompanied by a refusal to take account of the social constraints on utterance production, and it is this which severely limits the explanatory power of their account at level two. It is clearly more difficult to interpret the force of a person's utterance, if you are not interested in **why** he or she is speaking in a particular way.

1.6.3 Pragmatics: meaning in interaction

In this book I shall be working towards a definition of pragmatics as *meaning in interaction*. This reflects the view that meaning is not something which is inherent in the words alone, nor is it produced by the speaker alone, nor by the hearer alone. Making meaning is a dynamic process, involving the negotiation of meaning between speaker and hearer, the context of utterance (physical, social and linguistic) and the meaning potential of an utterance.

I was recently doing some examining at another university. Members of staff from several different departments were gathering for the meeting when one, greeting someone he hadn't seen for some time, said: *How are things, Scott?* Now the **meaning**

potential of this utterance was not unlimited. For example, the words themselves could not reasonably have been interpreted as an invitation to dinner, or a request to feed the goldfish or as a proposal of marriage. And in the particular **context** of an examiners' meeting, with its clear social constraints on the sorts of questions that could appropriately be asked, it would not have been reasonable for Scott to have interpreted the question as a request to expatiate about his private life, bodily functions, etc. (note that these would have been perfectly reasonable interpretations of the same utterance at a counselling session or at a doctor's surgery). But even when these interpretations had been excluded, there still remained a range of perfectly reasonable interpretations. The hearer could have chosen to take it as a purely phatic greeting, or as a question about how he liked his new job, an expression of anxiety about a particular student, etc. In fact he chose to say: *I've sold the house,* and the two of them discussed property in the area for a while. From the range of possible utterance meanings and speaker meanings the hearer developed a topic which was appropriate to the circumstances and (in this instance) congenial to both participants. And this is a fairly typical state of affairs. As we shall see in the chapter which follows, it is comparatively rare for a speaker to formulate an utterance so that the hearer has absolutely no room for manoeuvre.

1.7 Summary

In this chapter we have discussed the relative strengths and weaknesses of different definitions of pragmatics (and the underlying assumptions which these definitions presuppose). I shall be referring to these approaches very frequently as I review the development of pragmatics in the remaining chapters of this book, but by the end of the book I shall present a view of pragmatics as *meaning in interaction,* since this takes account of the different contributions of both speaker and hearer as well as that of utterance and context to the making of meaning.

Notes

1.   See, for example, the work of G. Fauconnier (1985).

2. See, for example, Leech (1983a) (also the review in Levinson (1983: 17)).

3. For example, Sperber and Wilson (1986).

4. Although many writers now would contend that the work of Leech and Levinson, for example, is not sufficiently grounded within any social theory. See, for example, the work of Fairclough (1989), Mey (1985) and Mey and Talbot (1989).

5. You may also come across the terms **decontextualized meaning**, **lexical meaning**, **semantic meaning** or **linguistic meaning** used to refer to the phenomenon which I am here calling **abstract meaning**.

6. Ruth Rendell (1980 [1979]) *Make death love me*. Arrow Books, London, p. 29.

7. The definitions are taken from *Longman's dictionary of contemporary English* 1987.

8. Umberto Eco, (1984 [1980]) *The name of the rose*. Pan Books, London, p. 209.

9. Where appropriate, the terms *speaker* and *hearer* or *addressee* should be understood to include *writer* and *reader* respectively. In a more advanced book, *The dynamics of discourse*, I have refined the use of all these terms.

10. All the examples given in this book are authentic and naturally-occurring unless otherwise stated.

11. The term **polysemy** refers to situations where a word has different, but clearly related meanings. Thus the *neck of a bottle* and the *neck of a giraffe* refer to very different entities, but nevertheless contain related concepts. The term **homonymy**, on the other hand, refers to words which have different and completely unrelated meanings, such as *(cricket) bat* and *(vampire) bat*.

   In practice, it can be very difficult to sustain the distinction between polysemy and homonymy (cf. Hurford and Heasley 1983: 123–6 or Jackson 1988: 127–8). For example, *wing* (of a bird) and *wing* (of a plane) are obviously related, but would we want to claim the same of *wing* in the sentence *Sinn Fein, the political wing of the IRA*? Since such distinctions are not important for my purposes in this book, from now on I shall only use the term homonymy.

12. John Demjanjuk was a naturalized American citizen of Ukrainian origin. It was alleged that he was 'Ivan the Terrible', a guard who had committed appalling crimes against prisoners at the Treblinka concentration camp during the Second World War and in February 1987 he was extradited to Israel, where he was put on trial. In April 1988 he was found guilty and sentenced to death. This verdict was overturned on appeal and in 1993 he was released.

13. I owe this example to Miriam Schlesinger.

14. The example is taken from Nigel Rees (1984) *Graffiti 1*, Unwin Paperbacks, London. I am grateful to Neil Johnston for drawing my attention to this and to other examples.

15. Reported in *The Guardian*.

16. Ruth Rendell (1980 [1979]) *Make death love me*. Arrow Books, London, p. 41.

17. In April 1995 (in W. H. Smith in Milton Keynes), I observed a genuine example of switching signs in this way: someone had taken a notice which read *True Crimes* from its original location and propped it against a pile of Mrs Thatcher's memoirs, *The Downing Street years*.

18. They are also known (particularly in philosophy) as **indexical expressions**.

19. See Levinson (1983: 89–94).

20. Colin Dexter 1987 [1986] *The secret of annexe 3*. Pan Books Ltd, London, p. 10.

21. The possible meanings they consider are (in this order): *Polonius thinks Hamlet is in love with Hamlet's daughter, Polonius thinks Polonius is in love with Polonius's daughter* or, (the interpretation which the player intended), *Polonius thinks Hamlet is in love with Polonius's daughter*.

22. Tom Stoppard (1967) *Rosencrantz and Guildenstern are dead*. Faber and Faber, London, p. 50.

23. *Othello* Act 4, Scene 1.

24. *Pick of the Week*, BBC Radio 4, 26 October 1990.

25. See, for example, the entry for 21 February 1666, where reference is made to *the Duke*. The duke in question on this occasion was James, Duke of York, brother of King Charles II. In other entries (e.g. for 23 June 1666) *the Duke* refers to the Duke of Abermarle.

26. BBC Radio 4 news.

27. Anecdote related at Brian Johnston's memorial service, St Paul's Cathedral, 17 May 1994.

28. Second son of Queen Elizabeth II. Cf. the Duke of York referred to in note 25, which referred to the brother of King Charles II.

29. *Any Questions*, BBC Radio 4, 4 July 1985.

30. A good example of this is to be found in Henry Reed's poem, *Naming of Parts*. The word *spring* is used twice in the third stanza: the first time with reference to a part of a rifle, the second time with reference to the season of the year. In the fourth stanza the word *spring* carries **both** meanings at the same time.

31. The expression *double entendre* referring expressly to the two meanings conveyed.

32. Part of a speech at the Labour Party Conference in Brighton, 30 September 1991.

33. BBC Radio 4, 14 November 1986.

34. The terms *contextual meaning* and *utterance meaning* can be used interchangeably. I used the term *contextual meaning* at the beginning of the chapter as it is easier to understand. However, the term *utterance meaning* is used much more widely within pragmatics and so this is the term I shall use from now on.

35. For a more detailed examination of this argument — albeit using slightly different terminology — see Burton-Roberts (1994).

36. Bentley himself always denied having uttered the words at all.

37. Account based on reports given in *The Times* of the 10 and 11 December, 1952.

38. Evidence given during the trial of the pop group, 'The Sex Pistols' for obscenity for releasing a record entitled *Never mind the bollocks!*

39. Case before Edinburgh Magistrates' Court, December 1993. Televised in the BBC series *The Trial*. This was the first (and, to

date, only) occasion on which television cameras were allowed into a British law court.

40. Another charge against this same defendant was that he had urinated on the steps of the restaurant. It was noticeable that no medical expert was called in to testify that urinating is a perfectly normal, necessary and entirely innocuous physiological function. Instead, the jury members were left to decide for themselves the accused's intention in performing the action — had he urinated in public out of dire necessity (a minor misdemeanour) or with the intent of affronting decency (a criminal offence)? In British courts it seems that ordinary people are deemed capable of judging the interpersonal significance of physical actions, but not of verbal ones.·

41. Bill Zehme (1991) 'When your name is a punchline you live in Hell'. *Observer Magazine*, p. 28.

42. Some people have suggested to me that in each of these examples the hearer simply *constructs* an utterance meaning. Clearly there are instances where this may occur (although not, in my view, in the particular examples I have given) but equally clearly there are cases where hearers understand the force of the utterance without understanding the utterance meaning. Here is one such example, given me by a friend who loves opera:

In the British theatre, before an actor goes on stage (particularly on a First Night), the other actors say *Break a leg!* As everyone in the theatre world knows, the force of the utterance is to wish the other party **good luck**. In the opera there is a similar convention, but instead of saying *Break a leg!* they say (or write) *Toi toi*. I have yet to meet anyone, including opera singers, who could tell me what the **words** mean, but they all perfectly understand the force.

43. For a good overview of this see Leech (1983a: 1–5).

CHAPTER 2

Speech acts

2.1 J. L. Austin

Austin is the person who is usually credited with generating interest in what has since come to be known as pragmatics. It is not altogether clear to me why Austin's ideas on language should have been taken up so enthusiastically within linguistics, when the work of others with not dissimilar views (e.g. the ideas of the philosopher G. E. Moore and Wittgenstein's later work) has not had anything like the same impact. However, there are four factors which, taken together, may explain why the influence of Austin's work has been so great. The appearance of the most influential collection of Austin's papers (*How to do things with words*, published posthumously in 1962) was very timely, coinciding as it did with a growing frustration within linguistics with the limitations of **truth conditional semantics** (this will be explained in section 2.3 below). Secondly, Austin's writing is admirably clear and accessible and, thirdly, although over the years he refined and modified his ideas considerably, his work represents a consistent line of thought.[1] And finally, what continues to make the study of Austin's work so rewarding is that it foreshadows many of the issues which are of major importance in pragmatics today. Whatever the explanation, it is a source of mild pride that the 'father of pragmatics' should have been born here in Lancaster (I can see the street where he lived from my window as I write!).

Austin was not a linguist at all (although he himself foresaw that it would be within an expanded science of linguistics that his work would be developed[2]) but a philosopher, working at Oxford University in the 1940s and 1950s. Austin, his almost equally influential pupil H. P. Grice and a group of like-minded philosophers working at Oxford and elsewhere[3] came to be known as 'ordinary language philosophers'.

Austin's ideas on language were set out in a series of lectures which he gave at Oxford University between 1952 and 1954; and he delivered a version of these talks as the William James Lectures at Harvard in 1955. After Austin's sudden death in 1960, the lectures were brought together in book form by J. O. Urmson, based on Austin's own (not always complete) lecture notes and recordings of his lectures. *How to do things with words* is therefore a rather informal book, very easy to read and well worth reading. However, as Levinson (1983: 231) notes, you really need to read the book from cover to cover, because Austin developed and modified his position considerably as the series of lectures progressed. The same is true of this chapter: distinctions introduced early on will be shown to be untenable by the end, but it will help you to understand the key issues in pragmatics if you work your way through the arguments carefully.

2.2 Ordinary language philosophy

In order to understand the significance of ordinary language philosophy you need to understand what Austin and his group were reacting against. Since the early years of the twentieth century, Oxford-based philosophers such as G. E. Moore and Bertrand Russell had been concerned with the relationship between philosophy and language. But whereas Moore was interested in what he termed 'the language of common sense', Russell and others[4] took the view that everyday language is somehow deficient or defective, a rather debased vehicle, full of ambiguities, imprecision and contradictions. Their aim was to refine language, removing its perceived imperfections and illogicalities, and to create an ideal language.

The response of Austin and his group was to observe that ordinary people manage to communicate extremely effectively and relatively unproblematically with language just the way it is. Instead of striving to rid everyday language of its imperfections, he argued, we should try to understand how it is that people manage with it as well as they do.

2.3 Logical positivism and truth conditional semantics

Let us explore a little further the basis of the disagreement between the ordinary language philosophers and logical positivist philosophers of language (such as Russell). Logical positivism is a philosophical system which maintains that the only meaningful statements are those that are analytic or can be tested empirically. Logical positivist philosophers of language, therefore, were principally concerned with the properties of sentences which could be evaluated in terms of *truth* or *falsity*. Within linguistics this approach was adopted within an area known as **truth conditional semantics**. Consider the following:

> *There are seven words in this sentence.*

You can count the words for yourself and judge whether the sentence is *true* or not. For our purposes a much more important tenet of logical positivism is that unless a sentence can, at least in principle, be verified it is strictly speaking meaningless.[5] According to this view, a sentence such as *the King of France is bald*, in a world in which there is no King of France, cannot be judged to be true or false, but merely meaningless. Logical positivist philosophers of language and truth conditional semanticists expended a great deal of energy debating the status of invented examples of this nature. Let us look instead at some real data and consider whether, if you encountered such utterances in the real world, you would judge them to be *false*:

Example 1
An invisible car came out of nowhere, hit my car and vanished.[6]

Example 2
Everyone hates Aileen Elkinshaw because she's so popular.[7]

Example 3
I sleep all the time, doctor.[8]

If we examine examples 1 and 2 in relation to their underlying propositions they will be seen to be false: cars are not invisible and cannot come 'from nowhere'; there is an internal contradiction in example 2 (it is not possible to be both popular and hated by everyone). Example 3 is anomalous in a different way: the speaker was clearly awake while talking to her doctor. And yet we would all recognize in these three examples the sort of language use we encounter daily in casual conversation — do we in real life judge them to be 'false' or 'meaningless', or do we try to make sense of them, in spite of the fact that they are illogical?

It was often alleged by Austin's critics that he thought that 'ordinary language' was in some way sacrosanct. This is not true — there were two reasons why Austin was interested in the way ordinary people use language in everyday life. The first reason does not really concern us at the moment, but I mention it for completeness, and because it foreshadows in a very interesting way an approach to linguistics in general and to pragmatics in particular which now, in the mid-1990s, is of major concern.[9] It is generally accepted that one of the main tasks of philosophy is to make distinctions, and Austin believed that one good way to identify which distinctions are important or relevant is to examine how ordinary people do this in everyday language:

> ... our common stock of words embodies all the distinctions men have found worth drawing, and the connexions they have found worth marking in the lifetimes of many generations.

(Austin 1961 [1946]: 129-30)

Thus if ordinary language makes a distinction between *commanding, ordering, requesting* and *inviting* (which all have in common that the speaker (S) is using language to get the hearer (H) to do something (X)), then there is a good chance that these distinctions are important to the users of that language. Note, however, that it would be a mistake to think that *all* the distinctions a society wishes to make in the realm of *getting H to do X* are captured by the different verbs available in a given language. Nor are such distinctions by any means restricted to verbs.[10]

More important for the present discussion was Austin's belief that there is a lot more to a language than the meaning of its words and phrases. Austin was convinced that we do not just use language to *say* things (to make statements), but to *do* things (perform actions). It was this conviction which eventually led him to a theory of what he called **illocutionary acts** (see section 2.5 below), a theory which examines what kinds of things we do when we speak, how we do them and how our acts may 'succeed' or 'fail', but he began exploring his ideas by way of the (soon to be abandoned) **'performative hypothesis'**.

2.4 The performative hypothesis

So why waste time looking at a distinction which Austin himself was soon to abandon? There are two main reasons why it is worthwhile examining the performative hypothesis: it shows how Austin's ideas developed and it demonstrates neatly the distinction between a truth-conditional approach to meaning and Austin's view of 'words as actions' (in other words, it illustrates very clearly how and why pragmatics came into being). A third reason is that performatives constitute a very interesting (if very restricted) subset of illocutionary verbs — performatives are fun!

Austin's first step in *How to do things with words* was to show that some utterances — in fact, as he later came to see, most utterances — have no truth conditions.[11] In fact, Austin claimed, they are not statements or questions but actions, a conclusion he reached through an analysis of what he termed '**performative verbs**'. To understand what is meant by a performative verb, compare these four sentences:

(i)   I drive a white car.
(ii)   I apologize.
(iii)   I name this ship *The Albatross*.
(iv)   I bet you £5 it will rain.

Syntactically the four sentences are similar: all are in the first person, declarative (rather than, say, interrogative), indicative (as opposed to the subjunctive, for example), active (rather than passive) and in the simple present tense. Pragmatically, the first sentence is very different from the other three. Sentence (i) is a statement (what Austin called 'constative') and it is a simple matter to establish empirically whether or not the statement is true. In fact my car is a rather pleasing metallic grey colour, and if you discovered this fact and heard me utter sentence (i), you could contradict me by saying: 'That is not true, your car is silver'. In the case of the sentences (ii)–(iv) it makes no sense at all to respond to them by saying: 'That is not true'. This is because the verbs in sentences (ii)–(iv) do not make statements (which can be judged true or false) but belong instead to a class of utterances called 'performatives', which (according to Austin) cannot be judged true or false, but are best understood as performing an action. In uttering the words *I apologize* I do not make a statement, I perform an act, the act of apologizing. One useful (but not infallible) test for a performative verb is to see whether you can meaningfully insert the adverb *hereby* between subject and verb:

> I **hereby** apologize
> I **hereby** name this ship *The Albatross*
> I **hereby** bet you £5

but not

> ★I **hereby** drive a white car.

As you may already have observed, although (ii)–(iv) are all instances of performatives, yet they are not quite the same in nature. Sentence (ii) is probably the least problematic: once I have uttered the words *I apologize* no one can deny that I did apologize (even though you may suspect that my apology is insincere). But what if I sneak up on the cruise ship *The Queen Elizabeth II* at dead of night as it lies in dry dock and, in a fit of republican passion, smash a bottle of Guinness against the hull and re-name it *The Albatross*? Must it henceforward be known by everyone as *The Albatross*? In the sections which follow, I shall discuss three different categories of performatives. Austin himself noted that there are different sorts of performatives and I have tried to systematize, simplify and in a few cases expand upon Austin's original categories. The names for the different types of performatives are mine.

2.4.1 Metalinguistic performatives

These are the most straightforward examples of performatives. Like all performatives they are self-referential (the verb refers to what the speaker of the utterance is doing), self-verifying (they contain their own truth conditions) and non-falsifiable (they can never be untrue). In any language there is probably a fairly small and certainly finite set of metalinguistic performatives. Examples in English include:

I say	I withdraw (my complaint)
I protest	I declare (the meeting open)
I object	I plead (not guilty)
I apologize	I vote (to abolish vivisection)
I deny	I move (that exams be abolished)
I promise	I thank (the audience for their attention)

Now compare the following pairs of sentences (the performatives appear in boldface):

(i)a **I say** that John is a liar
(i)b John is a liar

(ii)a **I plead** not guilty
(ii)b I am innocent

(iii)a **I move** that fox-hunting be abolished
(iii)b I believe that fox-hunting should be abolished

(iv)a **I object** to the licensing hours being extended
(iv)b I do not want the licensing hours to be extended

(v)a **I apologize** for deceiving the auditors
(v)b I'm sorry I deceived the auditors

Sentence (i)a is different from (i)b. *John is a liar* has truth conditions. If, in the real world, it can be shown that John is a liar, then sentence (i)b is true. Strictly speaking sentence (i)a is self-verifying. Whatever words follow *I say that* cannot, in strictly logical terms be untrue: all the speaker is doing is making a statement about what he or she is saying.[12] However, this strictly logical analysis seems to run counter to our intuitions about the way in which people really do use such utterances, and I shall return to this point in section 2.4.8.

Sentences (ii)a and (ii)b are identical to sentences (i)a and (i)b in terms of their truth conditions. Sentence (ii)a must always be true, sentence (ii)b is true if and only if in the real world the speaker has not committed the crime of which he or she is accused. This time, however, if we look at the way in which people use these forms in real life, you will find that meta-linguistic performatives are often used in precisely this way, even by speakers who are completely naïve linguistically: *I plead not guilty* is regularly (and legally and truthfully) used by people who know full well that they are guilty as charged. To say *I plead not guilty* is different from saying, *I am not guilty*. In the first case you are merely saying something about your plea (saying something about what you are saying), in the second you are making an actual claim about your innocence. In the light of the legal status of performative utterances, I often wonder about the declaration made by Judge Clarence Thomas before a committee of the

United States Senate, established to approve his nomination to the Supreme Court:[13]

> I deny that I had conversations of a sexual nature or about pornographic material with Anita Hill, that I ever attempted to date her ...

Sentences (iii)*a* and (iv)*a* and (iii)*b* and (iv)*b* are identical in terms of their truth conditions to the first two pairs of sentences. All the *a* sentences are self-verifying, all the *b* sentences are subject to truth conditions. We would expect (iii)*b* and (iv)*b* to be produced by speakers who are opposed to fox-hunting/the extension of licensing hours. All we can say for sure about the speakers of (iii)*a* and (iv)*a* is that they have formally opposed something. We cannot necessarily draw conclusions concerning their personal feelings about so-called blood sports or late-night drinking (they could, for example, be M.P.s or lawyers objecting on behalf of constituents or clients, even though they do not share their views).

In a similar way people seem intuitively to respond differently to (v)*a I apologize* ... and to (v)*b I'm sorry that I* ... During the miners' strike in Britain (1984/5), the miners' leader, Arthur Scargill, was ordered to apologize to the court or face sequestration of union funds. He was interviewed afterwards and asked whether he regretted his actions (in refusing to tell the auditors where his Union's funds were located). With a smile he replied: 'I said *I apologize*, I didn't say I was sorry!' I have shown this response to a number of native speakers of English and most seem to agree that *I apologize* often sounds like something one says for form's sake, that it is less sincere than *I'm sorry*.[14] These findings are neatly illustrated by quotations from two successive pages of Mary Wesley's novel, *A sensible life*.[15]

Example 4
The speaker is Angus, a belligerent man, who is haranguing Miss Green, a mild-mannered elderly guest in his house. The third speaker is Angus's wife, Milly.

'Then vote, Miss Green; denounce as I do these impossible Bolshie foreigners building palaces of peace in Geneva with your money, or never come to my house again.'

'I shan't', said Miss Green quietly.

'Angus! Apologize,' Milly's voice cut through the gale. 'At

once!'

'I apologize,' said Angus, unapologetically.

Example 5
But by the end of the meal Angus is genuinely sorry for his rudeness and says:

'You must forgive me, Miss Green.'

Although, as I have already noted, **all** performatives are self-verifying, there is a difference between metalinguistic performatives and the rest. Metalinguistic performatives as well as always being true, are, in addition, always **felicitous** or **successful**. They do not appear to depend on any external conditions for their success.[16] The following example illustrates beautifully the unfalsifiability of metalinguistic performatives:

Example 6
Norman Tebbit, Conservative Secretary of State for Employment, made the following utterance:

'I predict that unemployment figures will fall by one million within a year.'

Roy Hattersley, deputy leader of the Labour Party, commented later on BBC Radio:

'Notice he said "I predict they will fall" and not "they will fall". That means when next year comes and they haven't fallen, he will have a let out!'

2.4.2 Ritual performatives

The same automatic guarantee of successfulness does not apply to 'ritual' performatives, nor to my third category, '**collaborative performatives**'. In section 2.4 above, I raised the question of my unilaterally deciding to rename the *QE II*, *The Albatross*. Austin observed that although it would make no sense to respond to such an act of renaming by saying: 'That is not true!' yet it would be perfectly reasonable to say: 'You have no right to do that!' And nobody would feel they had to be bound by what I had done. Austin observed that although performatives are not subject to truth conditions, yet they can 'go wrong'. If the '**felicity conditions**' are not observed (as in the case of my renaming the ship), the performative may be **infelicitous** (or they may 'fail' or be 'unsuccessful'). Felicity conditions apply particularly to performatives associated with various rituals or very formal events. Unlike metalinguistic performatives (which seem to operate in broadly the same way in all languages and cultures and which apparently[17] have no felicity conditions) what I have called 'ritual performatives' are highly culturally dependent. Examples of such ritual performatives are:

(i)   I sentence you to ten years' ...
(ii)   I absolve you from your sins
(iii)   I baptize you ...
(iv)   I name this ship ...

Each of these can only appropriately and successfully be uttered by a specified person in a specified situation (e.g. (i) by a judge in a court of law, (ii) by a priest, etc.)

2.4.2.1 Felicity conditions
Austin stated his felicity conditions as follows (1962: 14–15):

A: (i)   there must be a conventional procedure having a conventional effect.
     (ii) the circumstances and persons must be appropriate.

B: The procedure must be executed (i) correctly, (ii) completely.

C: Often

     (i)   the persons must have the requisite thoughts, feelings and intentions and
     (ii) if consequent conduct is specified, then the relevant parties must do it.

Let us take each felicity condition in order.

Condition A
(i)   In a given culture (or sub-culture) there will probably be a conventional procedure for a couple to get married. In Britain this involves a man and a woman, who are not debarred from marrying for any reason, presenting themselves before an authorized person (minister of religion or registrar), in an authorized place (place of worship or

registry office), at an approved time (certain days or times of day are excluded) accompanied by a minimum of two witnesses. There they must go through a specified form of marriage: the marriage is not legal unless certain declarations are made and unless certain words have been spoken. The following extract illustrates a situation in which a marriage appears to be invalid because the minister of religion had not been properly authorized:

Example 7

This is a passage from a play by J B Priestly, When we are married. *The story concerns three couples who had all been married on the same day at the same ceremony. They are preparing to celebrate their silver wedding when they are shown a letter from the minister who officiated at the wedding which reveals that they had not been properly married:*[18]

... Although I was only temporarily at Lane End [chapel] I could not forget it for there I was guilty of the most culpable negligence. I went to Clecklewyke straight from college, and during those first few months I did not realise that there were various forms I ought to have signed, and had witnessed by church officers, so that one may be recorded as an authorised person to perform the ceremony of marriage. The result was, I was not then an authorised person. Fortunately during that short period I was only called upon twice to marry people, but the first time there were no less than three hopeful young couples who imagined — poor souls — that I was joining them in holy wedlock, when I was completely unauthorised to do so.

(ii)   The condition that 'the circumstances and persons must be appropriate' explains why my naming of *The Albatross* was unsuccessful or infelicitous — I was not the person mandated by the shipping company to perform the launching ceremony, nor were the time and place appropriate.

Condition B
(i)   The procedure must be executed correctly. At a marriage ceremony (in Britain), for example, (at least in theory) the words have to be the precise ones laid down — a rough approximation will not do:

Example 8[19]

Vicar: Will you take this woman ...?
Groom: Absolutely! I mean, I will.

Note that something which means the same as *I will*, will not do. Those precise words have to be used.[20]

(ii)   The procedure must be executed completely. Part of the procedure under English law is that the person conducting the wedding and the couple getting married must sign the register before witnesses. At a wedding I attended when I was at University, the priest (who was very distracted) and the couple somehow forgot this part. Hours later (in fact, when the couple had already gone to bed) the priest came banging on their door, telling them their marriage wasn't legal!

Condition C

(i)   This is one of the more problematic of Austin's felicity conditions and one about which people tend to disagree. A straightforward example would be in the case of a marriage where one party has been forced to marry under duress — 'shotgun weddings' are not legally binding. A more tendentious case would be when one party claims (sometimes years after the marriage took place) to have had 'mental reservations'.[21]

(ii)   It is hard to find many convincing examples where *subsequent conduct* is specified. 'Subsequent conduct' in the case of a marriage would be that the marriage must be consummated. If this condition is not met, the marriage is annulled.[22] It was on the grounds of non-consummation that Henry VIII's fourth marriage (to Anne of Cleves) was declared null. Anne quietly maintained that their marriage had never been consummated, while the ever-chivalrous Henry asserted that on their wedding night he had been: '... struck to the heart by her ugliness and ... left her as good a maid as I found her.' I noticed a rather more up-to-date example in which 'subsequent conduct' was specified in an episode of the American police series *NYPD Blue* but, while it made a good storyline, I cannot vouch for its authenticity. In the episode in question, a police officer (a Catholic) confessed to having murdered a mobster and his driver.

The priest gave her absolution on condition that she 'turn herself in' (which she did).[23]

2.4.2.2 Explicit reference to felicity conditions

It is interesting to note that speakers may make explicit reference to their reasons for speaking in a particular way (this is something which often happens in pragmatics, see chapter 7). Often speakers make reference to the felicity conditions which allow them to perform a particular act. In the following example the act in question is 'naming', a ritual performative restricted (to the best of my knowledge) to the British House of Commons:

Example 9
The then Speaker of the House of Commons, Mr Bernard Weatherill, banned the Scottish M.P. Mr Tam Dalyell from the House for refusing to withdraw an 'unparliamentary' description of Mrs Thatcher:

I have no alternative but to exercise the power invested in me and order the honourable member from the chamber for the remainder of the session. I name Mr Dalyell.

2.4.3 Collaborative performatives

Some writers have observed (see, for example, Hancher 1979) that some performatives do not have felicity conditions in the sense that a specified person must utter the words in particular circumstances, but nevertheless their success is not guaranteed. They require, for their success, the 'collaboration'[24] or particular uptake of another person, as in the following example:

Example 10
Menzies Campbell, an opposition M.P., had challenged the Minister of Defence using the performative 'I bet you ...'. His intervention was reported that evening in the following way:

Menzies Campbell offered to bet Mr Riftkind £100 that the Rosythe Naval Support Base would close within two years, but a cautious (or perhaps knowledgeable) Mr Riftkind declined to take up the bet.[25]

As the report makes clear, a bet or wager is only successfully made when the other person accepts it (for a fuller discussion of this see Fotion 1981). At first glance, collaborative performatives seem to be rather few in number (but see section 2.4.7.2 below and chapter 7), but here are some clear examples:

> I bet/wager you five pounds …
> I challenge you to pistols at dawn
> I bequeath you my gerbil

As with a bet, a challenge is only successfully made when the other person accepts the challenge. And, in English law (it might well be different under other legal systems), a bequest is only successfully made if the legatee accepts the bequest (otherwise I could leave you something extremely nasty — such as all my debts — and you would have no option but to accept).

2.4.4 Group performatives

Some performatives[26] are either commonly or necessarily produced by more than one person, e.g. a communiqué from a summit conference, a report from a committee and, most obviously, a verdict from a jury (in the high court the judge responds to the statement by the foreman or forewoman of the jury by asking: 'And is that the verdict of you all?'). Group performatives may fall into any of the three preceding categories. Below are examples of a group metalinguistic, ritual and collaborative performative. Note that the performative in example 12 is **only** successful when performed on behalf of the entire committee — the views of one member of the committee would carry no weight; unlike example 11, example 12 can only be successfully performed by the group.

Example 11
'We three Fossils … vow to try and put our name in history books because it's our very own and nobody can say it's because of our grandfathers.'[27]

Example 12
This example is taken from the findings of the General Medical Council Disciplinary Committee:[28]

We do not judge you to be guilty of professional misconduct.

Example 13
The following example is taken from a letter which I received from British Telecom plc, 18-7-94:

We agree to hire the Equipment to you on the following terms and conditions ...

Please check all the details. If you are happy with them, simply sign both copies of the Agreement, keep the white copy and send the blue copy back to us in the return envelope.

As the final sentence makes clear, British Telecom cannot agree to the hire unilaterally. It only becomes an agreement when I indicate consent.

2.4.5 Overlap of categories

As you will probably have observed by now, not all the categories are as neat or as self-contained as I have implied. For example, it would be possible to argue that many 'ritual' performatives are also 'collaborative' in nature. Performatives such as 'I baptize you ...' are arguably only successful if the person concerned (or at least his or her representatives) is willing to accept the baptism. Similarly, some 'collaborative' performatives also fall within the category of 'ritual' performatives (*bequeathing*, for example). And the argument could be extended: can an announcement be made if there is no one there to hear it? Can S be said to have apologized if H refuses to accept the apology (i.e. is there not a 'collaborative' element to some metalinguistic performatives)? And consider the following letter:[29]

Example 14
<u>Sunday 4th Day of August</u>

To whom it may concern

I Thomas Benjamin Swift, now on this day of Sunday in the year of our Lord, 1901, do hereby confess to the murder of Molly Brown, maid of this establishment.

We had meetings, and she threatened to reveal that she had conceived. This I could not allow. Now I cannot live with the burden of my guilt any longer ...

The letter was written in 1901, but was hidden under the floorboards in the maid's room and not found until June 1994.

Ms Brown was never reported missing, no body was ever found, Mr Swift was never charged with anything. Can we seriously accept as a genuine confession a letter which was seen by no one until 93 years after the murder was committed? It seems that *confessing* can only succeed if at least one person hears and understands what has been said or written. In fact, as we shall see in chapter 7, the majority of speech acts require some degree of hearer uptake in order to succeed (and can thus be seen as 'collaborative').

2.4.6 Cross-cultural differences in the use of performatives

In each of the categories I have outlined above we can find cross-cultural differences in the range and the use of performatives. This is particularly so in the case of performatives relating to culturally-specific rituals. Obviously, if you live in a country/culture which does not have baptism, there will be no performative form *I baptize you* ... Or the verb may exist, but cannot be used performatively. This is the case with the verb *to divorce*: in Britain divorce exists, and we have a verb *to divorce*, but (no matter what your religion) you cannot felicitously use the utterance *I divorce you* to separate yourself legally and permanently from your spouse. And even in countries where Sharia law operates, its interpretation may vary. The following events were reported to have occurred in Pakistan but, I am told, would not have been dealt with in the same way in other Islamic states:[30]

> **Example 15**
> A terrible tangle has arisen in Pakistan over a local soap
> opera. Soap star Usman Pirzada divorced his television wife
> in traditional Muslim style, pronouncing *Talaq* — I di-
> vorce thee — three times. The trouble was that his TV
> spouse was played by his real wife, Samina. Now the
> ulemas are saying that the divorce is binding, even though
> the formula was spoken in the interests of art. Their decree
> maintains that the Prophet ordained that in three matters
> (marriage, divorce and the freeing of slaves) words uttered
> unintentionally or even in jest cannot be withdrawn.
> Divorced they are and divorced they must remain.

This example also illustrates the fact that a performative which in one language/culture is subject to felicity conditions (e.g. the requirement that the performative be uttered with serious intent) in another language/culture may be subject to no such conditions.

2.4.7 Collapse of Austin's performative hypothesis

By means of the performative hypothesis Austin had been able to demonstrate that people do not use language just to make statements about the world; they also use language to perform actions, actions which affect or change the world in some way. The effect may be very small (A offers to make B a cup of tea) or it may be cataclysmic (country A declares war on country B). The effect of Austin's insight revolutionized the way people look at language and led directly to the development of pragmatics as an area of linguistic investigation. And the performative remains a very clear, *par excellence* example of 'how to do things with words'. However, the notion that *only* performative verbs could be used to perform actions was untenable. Austin's performative hypothesis collapsed for a number of rather different sorts of reasons:

(i)   There is no formal (grammatical) way of distinguishing performative verbs from other sorts of verbs.

(ii)   The presence of a performative verb does not guarantee that the specified action is performed.

(iii)   There are ways of 'doing things with words' which do not involve using performative verbs.

2.4.7.1 The grammatical distinctiveness of performatives
It was not long before Austin saw that the grammatical basis on which he had initially tried to distinguish between performatives and other sorts of utterances (see section 2.4) could not be sustained. Performatives, as we have already noted, can be plural as well as singular (see section 2.4.4). They can also be written as well as spoken, as in examples 16 and 17:

Example 16
I hereby resign as Chief of Staff to the President of the United States of America. Respectfully yours, Donald T. Regan.[31]

LIBRARY, UNIVERSITY OF SHEFFIELD

Example 17
The author asserts the moral right to be identified as the author of this work.[32]

Performatives do not, Austin realized, have to be in the first person (example 18 performs the act of finding an accused person not guilty just as well as example 12 does):

Example 18
This example is taken from a naval court martial, rather than a civilian court.[33]

The court finds the accused not guilty.

Nor is it essential for a performative to be in the active mood:

Example 19
Your employment is hereby terminated with immediate effect.[34]

Nor do they have to be in the simple present tense:

Example 20
A radio journalist is interviewing the Chairman of Railtrack during a strike by signalworkers:[35]

A: Are you denying that the Government has interfered?
B: I am denying that.

Example 21
This example is taken from a naval disciplinary hearing, known as 'Captain's Table', which is roughly equivalent to a hearing in a civilian magistrates' court.

You are being discharged on the grounds of severe temperamental unsuitability for service in the Royal Navy.

2.4.7.2   Do performatives always perform actions?
We have already seen that 'ritual' and 'collaborative' performatives may 'fail' because the requisite **felicity conditions** do not exist. However, it also became apparent that the supposedly self-verifying 'metalinguistic' performatives may also fail. Take the following example:

Example 22

I promise I'll come over there and hit you if you don't shut up!

This utterance certainly performs an action, but not the one specified by the performative verb. In or out of context it is difficult to see how this could be taken as other than a *threat*, in spite of the *promise* explicitly mentioned in the utterance. In chapter 4 I show how Searle attempted to resolve this problem, although not satisfactorily, in my opinion.

2.4.7.3 How to do things without performative verbs

The most important reason for the collapse of Austin's performative hypothesis was the realization that Austin had (at least tacitly) equated 'doing things with words' with the existence of a corresponding performative verb. This is clearly erroneous: there are many acts performed using language where it would be impossible, extremely odd or very unusual to use a performative verb. Consider those acts for which English has no performative verb, such as 'letting the cat out of the bag', 'incriminating oneself', 'putting one's foot in it', 'treading on someone's corns'. People do not say: *I hereby let the cat out of the bag, I hereby tread on your corns*, and yet these are (unfortunately) very common actions performed by means of language. Consider the following example:

Example 23

Notice on the door of a second-hand furniture shop. The last element had been added in handwriting in very large letters.[36]

> **Pine Trade Shop**
> **Serious Enquiries Only**
> **Please ring bell for service**
>
> *NO MOOCHERS!*

It is clear what this notice is doing: it is strongly discouraging casual passers-by from dropping into the shop. There would be no way of accomplishing this act using a performative, as no such performative exists in English (and I doubt whether it exists in any other language).

Language is frequently used to insult, but (outside surrealist comedy) it would be impossible to say: *I (hereby) insult you!* We readily use language to invite, but in English it is not usual to use the words *I invite you* to perform the act of inviting. And the same is true for many extremely common acts: *offering, hinting, boasting, divulging, expressing an opinion*, are all instances of acts for which it would be most odd to use a performative verb (but note that in reporting the act you would readily say: *She invited me ..., He hinted that ..., They boasted that ...*). There are literally hundreds of examples like this. It was in the light of counter-examples of this kind that in chapter six of *How to do things with words*, Austin briefly introduced a distinction between **primary performatives** (which, following Levinson 1983 I shall call **explicit performatives**) and **implicit performatives**.

2.4.8 Explicit and implicit performatives

An explicit performative (of the *I hereby* ... kind which we have looked at so far) can now be seen to be a mechanism which allows the speaker to remove any possibility of misunderstanding the force behind an utterance. Compare:

(i)   We remind you that all library books are due
        to be returned by 9th June.
(ii)   This is to remind you that all library books are due to
        be returned by 9th June.
(iii)   You are reminded that all library books are due to be
        returned by 9th June.
(iv)   All library books are due to be returned by 9th June.

We can see that sentences (i), (ii), (iii) and (iv) all perform the same action — that of reminding borrowers to return their books by the due date. But whereas utterance (i) uses an explicit performative to perform the act of reminding, (ii)–(iv) do so using different sorts of non-performative utterances. While it is certainly true to say, as Austin does, that there are no substantial distinctions in meaning between explicit and implicit performatives, yet (before we abandon the distinction altogether) it is worth exploring the difference in the way in which a performative utterance and its non-performative counterpart are used. Some situations (typically very formal or ritual situations) require that a specific form of language be used (cf. example 8), while others imply a stylistic difference (e.g. in the degree of formality conveyed) or imply a difference in emphasis. Here are some examples:

(i)   I apologize
(ii) I'm sorry

Sentence (i) seems more formal than sentence (ii) (but see also note 14).

(iii) I assure you, I did send in the application on time
(iv) I did send in the application on time

Sentence (iii) seems more forceful that sentence (iv)

(v)   I swear I love you
(vi) I love you

In this case, the performative form would only seem to be necessary in a situation where there seems to be a degree of doubt in the mind of the loved one. It might also be a second attempt at reassuring someone — we often find that a speaker will first try an implicit performative and move onto an explicit performative only if the first attempt fails. People often avoid using an explicit performative since in many circumstances it seems to imply an unequal power relationship or a particular set of rights on the part of the speaker. As Alston (1980: 130) observes, to use an explicit performative involves a degree of risk:

> [its use] ... changes one's normative status in a certain way; one sticks one's neck out or goes out on a limb.

This is illustrated nicely by the following example. The first speaker is King Arthur — notice how King Arthur uses first an implicit performative and then, only when that has failed, moves on to the explicit form. Unfortunately, the second speaker is an anarcho-syndicalist peasant who does not recognize the existence of monarchs, and so the performative does not have the desired effect (once again we see the importance of uptake):

Example 24
King Arthur [A] is talking to anarcho-syndicalist peasant [B].[37]

A: Be quiet!
B: [Peasants continue talking]

A: Be quiet! I order you to be quiet!

B: Order eh? Who does he think he is?

A: I am your King.

B: Well I didn't vote for you.

A: You don't vote for kings.

B: Well how do you become King, then?

A: The Lady of the Lake, her arm clad in the purest shimmering samite held aloft Excalibur from the bosom of the water, signifying by Divine Providence that I, Arthur, was to carry Excalibur. That is why I am your king.

B: Listen, strange women lying in ponds distributing swords is no basis for a system of government. Supreme executive power derives from a mandate from the masses, not from some farcical aquatic ceremony.

2.5 Utterances as actions

In chapter eleven of his book, Austin abandons completely the original distinction between 'constatives' (statements) and all forms of performative utterance. Statements, too, are seen to have a performative aspect, and what is now needed is to distinguish between the truth-conditional aspect of what a statement is and the action it performs; between the meaning of the speaker's words and their **illocutionary force**.

2.5.1 Locution, illocution, perlocution

Utterances, as we saw in the Bentley example in chapter 1, not only have sense (did Bentley's words mean *Shoot him!* or *Hand over the gun!*?) but also force (*inciting* Craig to murder, or *advising* Craig to give himself up). Austin, in fact, made a three-fold distinction:

Locution	the actual words uttered
Illocution	the force or intention behind the words
Perlocution	the effect of the illocution on the hearer

For example, I might say: *It's hot in here!* (locution), meaning: *I want some fresh air!* (illocution) and the perlocutionary effect might be that someone opens the window. Generally speaking there *is* a close and predictable connection between locution and perlocutionary effect as in the following example:

Example 25

The speakers are Lord Peter Wimsey, ace amateur detective, and Bunter, his butler:[38]

'If, Bunter, you do not immediately sit down here and have your supper, I will have you drummed out of the regiment …'
Bunter [drew] up an obedient chair.

Bunter correctly interprets the illocutionary force of Lord Peter's utterance as an *invitation* or *request* (in the form of a mock *threat*) to join his employer for supper.[39] All competent adult speakers of a language can predict or interpret intended illocutionary force reasonably accurately most of the time — human beings simply could not operate if they had no idea at all how their interlocutor would react, although, of course, things can go wrong, as in the following example:

Example 26

A man and a woman enter an art gallery. The man is carrying a plastic carrier bag. The woman goes to buy the admission tickets, while her husband has gone ahead into the gallery.

Official: Would the gentleman like to leave his bag here?
Woman: Oh no, thank you. It's not heavy.
Official: Only … we have had … we had a theft here yesterday, you see.

The illocutionary force of B's first utterance is to *request* A's husband to leave his bag, but A interprets it as an *offer*. Part of the problem stems from the fact that the same **locution** could have a different **illocutionary force** in different contexts. E.g. *What time is it?* could, **depending on the context of utterance** mean any of the following:

The speaker wants the hearer to tell her the time;
The speaker is annoyed because the hearer is late;
The speaker thinks it is time the hearer went home.

2.5.2 Speech acts

Austin originally (1960: 52) used the term **'speech act'** to refer to an utterance and the 'total situation in which the utterance is issued'. Today the term 'speech act' is used to mean the same as 'illocutionary act' — in fact, you will find the terms **speech act, illocutionary act, illocutionary force, pragmatic force** or just **force**, all used to mean the same thing — although the use of one rather than another may imply different theoretical positions.

Just as the same words can be used to perform different speech acts, so different words can be used to perform the same speech act. The following utterances illustrate different ways of performing the speech act of *requesting someone to close the door*:[40]

> Shut the door!
> Could you shut the door?
> Did you forget the door?
> Put the wood in the hole.
> Were you born in a barn?
> What do big boys do when they come into a room, Johnny?

2.6 Conclusion

In this chapter we have seen how utterances perform actions, how **speakers** can mean considerably more than their words say. In the next chapter we shall address the question of **how** hearers get from what is said to what is meant.

Notes

1. Cf. Wittgenstein, who changed his views completely after the publication of his *Tractatus*.

2. See Urmson in Fann (1969: 82).

3. Moore, Ryle, Strawson and Urmson are among the better known.

4. Such as Carnap, Davidson and Tarski.

5. To explore further the area of truth-conditional semantics, the reader is referred to Lyons (1977: 167–73) or to Hurford and Heasley (1983).

6. Statement given to police officer following a road accident.

7. This example is actually taken from a short story (*La belle dame sans thinguy* by Liz Lochhead, broadcast on BBC Radio 4, 24 September 1991), but I overheard an almost identical example at a linguistics summer school in Morocco in 1983: *No-one goes to her lectures any more because they're too crowded.*

8. Patient to Consultant at Lancaster Royal Infirmary.

9. I am speaking here of 'Prototype Theory', a topic which is developed in detail in my forthcoming book, *The dynamics of discourse*.

10. Of course, the distinctions which a given society finds it important to make will change over time. Good examples are to be found in the area of kinship terms.

11. In fact, Austin had first introduced the distinction between statements which can be judged as true or false and those which cannot in 1946 in a paper entitled 'In other minds'.

12. If you were of a very casuistic turn of mind and wanted never to utter another untruth in your life, you could preface everything you said with *I say*, and then it would always be true! In everyday life, this type of linguistic behaviour would be totally unacceptable, but note that it is the sort of thing which occurs regularly in Parliament and sometimes in courts of law.

13. U.S. Senate Committee hearing, October 1991.

14. Of course, there are other differences, including the fact that *I apologize* is often used in more formal situations. Some informants said they would use it when *I'm sorry* seemed too weak.

15. Mary Wesley (1991 [1990]) *A sensible life*. Black Swan, London, pp. 161 and 162.

    There is another nice example of an insincere apology later on in the same book (p. 216). The speaker on this occasion is Milly, who is pleased her children have not woken up in time to see off a visitor whom Milly considered to be 'beneath' them socially. This apology is actually a barely-veiled insult: 'I apologize for their lack of manners. They must still be snoring. It takes something they think really important to rouse them in the mornings.'

16. But see section 2.4.5 below.

17. It will be shown, however, that some 'metalinguistic' performatives (such as *promising*) are, in fact, governed by felicity conditions of a sort.

18. James Boynton Priestly (1938) *The plays of J. B. Priestley*, Vol. II. Heinemann, London, p. 171.

19. Ben Travers, *A cuckoo in the nest*. BBC Radio 4 production.

20. Ironically, Austin himself got this example wrong. He says that the bride and groom have to say: *I do*.

21. An example in the Catholic church would be when one party claims that when they contracted the marriage they secretly never intended to have children. This escape clause operates mainly for the rich and famous.

22. NB It is not a question of a divorce being granted — a null marriage is one which was <u>never</u> valid, whether because of a deliberate act on someone's part (as in the case of bigamy) or because of a situation of which no one was aware (e.g. a man unwittingly marrying his half-sister).

23. The episode entitled *Guns 'n rosaries*, broadcast in U.K. on 11 June 1994, on Channel 4.

24. I use this term in preference to 'cooperation' (cf. Hancher 1979) only because it seems a little odd to talk of 'cooperation' in relation say, to a challenge to fight or a declaration of war.

25. *Today in parliament*, BBC Radio 4, 21 July 1994.

26. See Hughes (1984).

27. From: Noel Streatfield (1936) *Ballet shoes*. Dent, London, p. 31.

28. Reported in *File on Four*, BBC Radio 4, 2 July 1994.

29. Reported *Daily Mail*, 18 June 1994.

30. Report in *The Guardian*, 5 November 1987.

31. Reported 27 February 1987.

32. You will find this in the front of many novels published in the U.K. in recent years. Under the Copywright, Designs and Patents

Act 1988 certain protections obtain only if the author has made this assertion. It appears to be an example of a brand new performative (perhaps it should be patented!).

33. For the information on courts martial, I am grateful to Lieutenant Commander S. R. M. Crozier, R.N., Barrister-at-Law.

34. Letter from trustees to a woman who had worked as a foster mother for 25 years (reported on *Face the facts*, BBC Radio 4, 16 June 1994).

35. *Today*, BBC Radio 4, 18 July 1994.

36. Observed outside 'Country Pine', Chipping Campden, Gloucestershire 25 June 1994. Chipping Campden is a village in the Cotswolds popular with tourists. It should be noted that on the other shops the signs said: *You are welcome to come in and look around — no obligation!*

37. From *Monty Python and the Holy Grail*.

38. Dorothy L. Sayers (1937) *Busman's honeymoon*. Victor Gollancz, London, pp. 60-1.

39. The difficulty of specifying precisely the illocutionary force will be discussed in chapter 7.

40. Adapted from Levinson (1983).

CHAPTER 3

Conversational implicature

3.1 Introduction

In chapter 2 I discussed the relationship between **sense** and **force**, between what speakers say and what their words mean. In this chapter I want to explore this relationship further. Consider these three examples:

Example 1

The following incident, which occurred at a seaside resort in Kent, was reported in several national newspapers in July 1994.

Kent Coastguard reports that a girl, drifting out to sea on an inflatable set of false teeth, was rescued by a man on a giant inflatable lobster.[1]

Example 2

'We must remember your telephone bill', she said, hinting that Louise had talked long enough. 'Goodbye', said Louisa, ringing off. It takes the rich to remind one of bills, she thought.[2]

Example 3

Late on Christmas Eve 1993 an ambulance is sent to pick up a man who has collapsed in Newcastle city centre. The man is drunk and vomits all over the ambulanceman who goes to help him. The ambulanceman says:

'Great, that's really great! That's made my Christmas!'

In example 1 the reporter has written exactly what he means, neither more nor less. The speaker in example 2 means more than her words say; in uttering the words: *We must remember your telephone bill*, she is hinting that she wants to close the telephone conversation. In example 3 the ambulanceman means exactly the opposite of what his words say. None of these situations is linguistically unusual; the most casual observation of people talking (and to be good at pragmatics you must become a committed eavesdropper!) will produce similar examples. There are times when people say (or write) exactly what they mean, but generally they are not totally explicit. Since, on the other occasions, they manage to convey far more than their words mean, or something quite different from the meanings of their words, how on earth do we know, on a given occasion, what a speaker means? For we do, on the whole, communicate very successfully. In this chapter I am going to look at the work of Paul Grice, who attempted to explain how, by means of shared rules or conventions, competent language-users manage to understand one another.

3.2 H. P. Grice

H. P. Grice had worked with J. L. Austin at Oxford in the 1940s and 1950s and his work on the Cooperative Principle (see section 3.4) and its related conversational maxims (see section 3.5) arises from the same tradition of ordinary language philosophy. Like Austin before him, Grice was invited to give the William James lectures at Harvard University, and it was there in 1967 that he first outlined his theory of implicature (a shorter version of which was published in 1975 in a paper 'Logic and conversation'). In papers published in 1978 and 1981 Grice expanded upon this earlier work, but he never fully developed his theory — there are many gaps and several inconsistencies in his writings. Nevertheless it is this work — sketchy, in many ways problematical, and frequently misunderstood — which has proved to be one of the most influential theories in the development of pragmatics. In chapter 2 we saw how Austin made the distinction between what speakers say and what they mean. Grice's theory is an attempt at explaining how a hearer gets from what is said to what is meant, from the level of expressed meaning to the level of **implied meaning**.

3.3 Implicature

The additional or different meanings which we observed in examples 2 and 3 are conveyed by means of **implicature**. Grice distinguished two different sorts of implicature: **conventional implicature** and **conversational implicature**. They have in common the property that they both convey an additional level of meaning, beyond the semantic meaning of the words uttered. They differ in that in the case of conventional implicature the same implicature is always conveyed, regardless of context, whereas in the case of conversational implicature, what is implied varies according to the context of utterance.

3.3.1 Conventional implicature

There are comparatively few examples of conventional implicatures; Levinson (1983: 127) lists four: *but, even, therefore* and *yet* (to these we might add some uses of *for*, as in: *She plays chess well, for a girl*). Consider the following example:

Example 4
... she was cursed with a stammer, unmarried but far from stupid.[3]

Notice that although it is not actually asserted that unmarried people (or, perhaps, people who stammer) are stupid, the word *but* definitely implies that this is the case. The word *but* carries the implicature that what follows will run counter to expectations — this sense[4] of the word *but* **always** carries this implicature, regardless of the context in which it occurs ('My friends were poor, but honest',[5] 'He is small, but perfectly formed'). And, in everyday life, people readily respond to such conventional implicatures, as the following extract illustrates:

Example 5
The American actress, Kathleen Turner, was discussing perceptions of women in the film industry:[6]

'I get breakdowns from the studios of the scripts that they're developing ... and I got one that I sent back furious to the studio that said "The main character was thirty-seven but still attractive." I circled the *but* in red ink and I sent it back and said, "Try again!" '

3.3.2 Conversational implicature

This contrasts with the implicature generated in example 3. It would be absurd to argue that saying 'Great, that's really great! That's made my Christmas!' always generated the implicature that the speaker was furious because someone had just vomited over him! On other occasions a person producing this utterance might be genuinely expressing delight over a gift or event, or anguish because the dog has eaten the turkey. This type of implicature, which Grice termed (particularized) **conversational implicature** arises only in a particular context of utterance.[7]

3.3.3 Implicature and inference

Before I go further into Grice's theory of conversational implicature, I want to interpolate a discussion of the difference between implicature and inference, implying and inferring. There are two reasons for doing this. The most important is that it is the confusion of these two levels of interpretation which is at the root of some misunderstandings of Grice's theory. The second is that in Britain, if not in other parts of the English-speaking world, there is widespread misuse of the terms themselves — people frequently say *inferring* when they really mean *implying*.[8] To imply is to hint, suggest or convey some meaning indirectly by means of language. We have seen how this operates in example 2, where the speaker hints or indicates indirectly that she wants to finish the telephone conversation; an implicature is generated intentionally by the speaker and may (or may not) be understood by the hearer. To infer is to deduce something from evidence (this evidence may be linguistic, paralinguistic or non-linguistic). An inference is produced by the hearer. Let us begin with a simple example:

Example 6
The following extract is taken from a children's book, set in Holland under William the Silent, during the wars with Spain. Maurice was a boy caught up in the events; Theo was his manservant:[9]

Tears filled his eyes; he cried easily in these days, not having full control of himself, and Theo's fate caused him great grief. The Duchess had told him that she had been able to discover nothing, and therefore it was assumed that he had been released as entirely innocent. Maurice was convinced that nothing of the kind had happened, and

assumed that the Duchess had found out that Theo was
dead and had invented the agreeable solution in order not
to distress him. He could not do anything about it and had
accepted the statement in silence, but he fretted a great deal
over Theo's death.

This extract illustrates neatly the distinction between implicature and inference. The Duchess implied that Theo was all
right. Maurice understood what she had implied, but nevertheless inferred the opposite (that Theo was dead). The next
example is slightly more complicated:

Example 7
*Some years ago, I went to stay with my brother and his family,
including his son, aged about 5. I had with me an electric toothbrush, into which I had recently put new batteries. My brother
asked to see the toothbrush, but when he tried to operate it, it would
not work.*

Me: That's funny. I thought I put in some new
            batteries.
Nephew: *[Going extremely red]:* The ones in my engine
            still work.

Let us look at these two utterances from the point of view
of both the speakers and the hearers. My remark had been a
genuine expression of surprised irritation, addressed to the family
at large and I did not expect any response, except perhaps
sympathetic murmurings about the poor quality of batteries and
this is how the adults understood it. My nephew, however,
misinterpreted the force of my utterance as an accusation and
inferred (wrongly) that he was a suspect. We can spell out the
interpretation of the boy's contribution as follows:

Step 1   As we saw in chapter 2, the hearer's first step is to assign sense
            and reference to his words. In this case, this was not difficult;
            the boy was asserting that he had batteries in the engine of his
            toy train which were in working order.

Step 2   The hearer works out the speaker's intention in uttering those
            words; we all understood him to have implied that he was not
            responsible for the fact that my batteries were flat. The
            pragmatic force of his utterance was to deny guilt.

Step 3   Nevertheless, everyone present inferred from the evidence
          (from our knowledge of how little boys behave, from the fact
          that he blushed, from the attempt to deflect attention from his
          toy and, indeed, from the fact that he spoke at all) that he had
          in fact switched the batteries.

Grice's theory is designed to explain how hearers get from
level 1 to level 2, from what is said to what is implied. Steps one
and two fall within the realm of pragmatics; the third step
depends on more than just linguistic factors and needs to be
explained within a more general theory of social interaction.[10] Let
us take another example:

Example 8
Throughout July 1994 a minor controversy was rumbling on in the
British House of Commons. For five or six years investors (known
as 'Names') in the huge company of insurance underwriters,
Lloyd's of London, had incurred massive losses and many had gone
bankrupt. A number of Conservative M.P.s are Lloyd's Names
and if M.P.s are declared bankrupt they must resign their seat. Peter
Hain (a member of the opposition Labour Party) was conducting a
one-man campaign to show that these M.P.s had been moved (with
or without their knowledge) from the most loss-making syndicates,
to avoid being declared bankrupt, having to resign their seats and
(since there had been a spate of by-elections around this time and the
Conservatives had lost every one) possibly precipitating a General
Election. In the House of Commons Peter Hain **said***:*

'Lord Wakeham, the Leader of the House of Lords, and
other leading Conservatives in 1988 were taken off selected
Lloyd's syndicates which later suffered three years of cata-
strophic losses.'

I chose this example because Peter Hain's speech was
widely reported, and so I can say with some confidence that all
the political commentators were agreed that what Hain had
implied was that knowledgeable insiders at Lloyd's had improp-
erly tipped off Conservative sympathizers so that Conservative
M.P.s could switch (or be switched) to different syndicates. But
although everyone understood what Hain was implying, different
listeners **inferred** a variety of different things, depending on their
political persuasion, background knowledge, etc. Here is a small
selection of the interpretations I came across in the days following
Peter Hain's speech:

The M.P. was trying to expose dubious and possibly illegal practice.

The M.P. was trying to cause trouble for the Government.

The M.P. was trying to draw attention to himself.

Conservative M.P.s cannot be trusted in financial matters.

It was very clear what the Prime Minister, Mr Major, inferred from the speech; it was that Mr Hain could not have much evidence, or he would have gone to the police or to the newspapers instead of confining his attack to Parliament (where he could make his accusations without risking a libel action). In relation to the points put by Mr Hain, Mr Major, said:

> 'I have to say to you that inferences that are clearly under-
> lying your question today under the privilege of Parliament
> is not a way that most people would regard as the right way
> to raise these matters.'[11]

[Note that Mr Major's use of the word *inferences* here is incorrect. He should have said *implications* or (more technically) *implicatures*. This is precisely the error I criticized in the first paragraph of this section.] There are two important things to bear in mind from the discussion of these two examples. The first is that a speaker may imply something he or she knows to be untrue and hearers may understand exactly what a speaker has implied, without in any sense believing it. The second is that Grice's theory attempts to explain how people get from the level of expressed meaning to the level of implied meaning. Many misunderstandings of Grice's work stem from the fact that people wrongly assume that he was trying to explain how inferences are formed, rather than how implicatures are generated and inter-preted. In the sections which follow, I shall outline Grice's theory of how this process operates.

3.4 The Cooperative Principle

In order to explain the mechanisms by which people interpret conversational implicature, in 'Logic and conversation' Grice introduced four conversational maxims and the Cooperative Principle (CP). The CP runs as follows:

> Make your contribution such as is required, at the stage at

which it occurs, by the accepted purpose or direction of the talk exchange in which you are engaged.

Already we have a problem. The fact that Grice expressed the CP in the imperative mood has led some casual readers of his work to believe that Grice was telling speakers how they ought to behave. What he was actually doing was suggesting that in conversational interaction people work on the assumption that a certain set of rules is in operation, unless they receive indications to the contrary. In all spheres of life we make similar assumptions all the time. A useful analogy is driving a car. When we drive, we assume that other drivers will operate according to the same set of regulations as we do (or, at the very least, that they know what those regulations are). If we could not make such assumptions the traffic system would rapidly grind to a halt. Of course, there are times when we do have indications that another driver may not obey the rules (a learner, a drunk, a person whose car is out of control, an ambulance or fire tender with its lights flashing and siren blaring) or that they may be following a different set of rules (a car with foreign number plates) and on these occasions we re-examine our assumptions or suspend them altogether. And, of course, there are times when our assumption that others are operating according to the same set of rules is misplaced, and then an accident may occur.

The same is true of conversation. Within a given community,[12] when we talk we operate according to a set of assumptions and, on the whole, we get by. There will be times when we may suspend our assumption that our interlocutor is operating according to the same conversational norms as we are: we may be talking to a young child who has yet to acquire our community's conversational norms, to a drunk, to someone in pain or distress. Or we may be talking to a person whom we have reason to think may have different conversational norms from our own (a member of a different cultural or linguistic community). And there will be times when our assumptions are wrong and then mistakes and misunderstandings occur, or when we are deliberately misled by our interlocutor. For, in setting out his Co-operative Principle, Grice was not (as some commentators have erroneously assumed) suggesting that people are always good and kind or cooperative in any everyday sense of that word. He was simply noting that, on the whole, people observe certain regularities in interaction and his aim was to explain one particular set of regularities — those governing the generation and interpretation of conversational implicature. Consider the following example:

Example 9

The speaker has accidentally locked herself out of her house. It is winter, the middle of the night and she is stark naked:

A: Do you want a coat?

B: No, I really want to stand out here in the freezing cold with no clothes on.[13]

On the face of it, B's reply is untrue and uncooperative, but in fact this is the sort of sarcastic reply we encounter every day and have no problem at all in interpreting. How do we interpret it? According to Grice, if A assumes that, in spite of appearances, B is observing the Cooperative Principle and has made an appropriate response to his question, he will look for an alternative interpretation. Grice argues that without the assumption that the speaker is operating according to the CP, there is no mechanism to prompt someone to seek for another level of interpretation. The observation that the speaker has said something which is manifestly untrue, combined with the assumption that the CP is in operation sets in motion the search for an implicature. The four **Conversational Maxims** help us establish what that implicature might be.

3.5 The four conversational maxims

In 'Logic and conversation' Grice proposed four maxims, the maxims of Quantity, Quality, Relation and Manner, which were formulated as follows:

Quantity: Make your contribution as informative as is required (for the current purpose of the exchange).
Do not make your contribution more informative than is required.

Quality: Do not say what you believe to be false.
Do not say that for which you lack adequate evidence.

Relation: Be relevant.

Manner:	Avoid obscurity of expression.
	Avoid ambiguity.
	Be brief (avoid unnecessary prolixity).
	Be orderly.

3.5.1 Observing the maxims

The least interesting case is when a speaker observes all the maxims as in the following example:

> **Example 10**
> Husband: Where are the car keys?
> Wife: They're on the table in the hall.

The wife has answered clearly (Manner) truthfully (Quality), has given just the right amount of information (Quantity) and has directly addressed her husband's goal in asking the question (Relation). She has said precisely what she meant, no more and no less, and has generated no implicature (i.e. there is no distinction to be made here between what she says and what she means, there is no additional level of meaning).

3.5.2 Non-observance of the maxims

Grice was well aware, however, that there are very many occasions when people fail to observe the maxims. There are five ways of failing to observe a maxim:

> Flouting a maxim
> Violating a maxim
> Infringing a maxim
> Opting out of a maxim
> Suspending a maxim

People may fail to observe a maxim because, for example, they are incapable of speaking clearly, or because they deliberately choose to lie. I shall discuss each of these possibilities in order, but the most important category by far, the one which generates an implicature, is the first, and I shall devote an entire section to **flouting**.

3.6 Flouting a maxim

The situations which chiefly interested Grice were those in which a speaker **blatantly** fails to observe a maxim, not with any intention of deceiving or misleading, but because the speaker wishes to prompt the hearer to look for a meaning which is different from, or in addition to, the expressed meaning. This additional meaning he called 'conversational implicature' and he termed the process by which it is generated 'flouting a maxim'.

A flout occurs when a speaker **blatantly** fails to observe a maxim at the level of what is said, with the deliberate intention of generating an implicature. I shall give examples of flouts of each of the maxims in turn and at the same time review Grice's discussions of the reasons for flouting a maxim.

3.6.1 Flouts necessitated by a clash between maxims

A speaker flouts the maxim of Quantity by blatantly giving either more or less information than the situation demands.

> **Example 11**
> *The speaker is Rupert Allason (author, M.P. and expert on the British intelligence services). He is discussing the identity of the so-called 'Fifth Man':*[14]
>
> It was either Graham Mitchell or Roger Hollis and I don't believe it was Roger Hollis.

According to Grice, such a response would set in motion a process of informal reasoning which would lead the listeners to derive an additional piece of information. This might work in the following way:

(i)   Rupert Allason has blatantly given more information than required (he could simply have said 'The Fifth Man was Graham Mitchell'). Allason appears to have breached the maxim of Quantity.

(ii) However, we have no reason to believe that Allason is being deliberately uncooperative (i.e. that he is failing to observe the Cooperative Principle (CP)).

(iii) We must conclude that his failure to observe the maxim of Quantity is due to his wish to observe the CP in some other way. We must work out why the CP should lead Allason to give more information than was requested.

(iv) The failure to observe the maxim of Quantity can be explained if we assume that Allason also wished to observe the maxim of Quality. We conclude that for some reason he is confronted with a clash between these two maxims (either he tells the truth or he gives just the right amount of information).

(v) His reply is a compromise, which leads us to deduce that whilst he strongly believes that Mitchell was the spy, he doesn't have sufficient evidence to assert this as a fact. He has signalled that his belief may not be accurate.

As we have seen, Grice's explanation for the non-observance of the maxim of Quality in this instance is that the speaker was faced with a clash of maxims. In this instance the speaker found himself unable simultaneously to observe the maxims of Quality and Quantity, signalled his dilemma by flagrantly failing to give the right amount of information and prompted his interlocutor to look for an implicature. A similar explanation might be offered for the following instance of non-observance of the maxim of Quantity. In this case, the second speaker gives less information than the situation demands:

Example 12
A is asking B about a mutual friend's new boyfriend:

A: Is he nice?
B: She seems to like him.

B could simply have replied: 'No' — this would give the maximum amount of information possible in the situation. Instead, B gives a much weaker and less informative response. It would be possible to argue that his failure to do so stems from a clash between the maxims of Quantity and Quality (B cannot say for certain whether the new boyfriend is nice or not, and speaks only on the basis of the evidence he has). But this explanation is rather implausible. It is better explained by what Grice terms 'exploiting' the maxims.

3.6.2 Flouts which exploit a maxim

According to Grice's theory, interlocutors operate on the assumption that, as a rule, the maxims will be observed. When this expectation is confounded and the listener is confronted with the blatant non-observance of a maxim (i.e. the listener has discounted the possibility that the speaker may be trying to deceive, or is incapable of speaking more clearly, succinctly, etc.), he or she is again prompted to look for an implicature. Most of Grice's own examples of flouts involve this sort of 'exploitation'.

3.6.2.1 Flouts exploiting maxim of Quality

Flouts which exploit the maxim of Quality occur when the speaker says something which is blatantly untrue or for which he or she lacks adequate evidence. In the 'ambulanceman' example I gave (example 3), an implicature is generated by the speaker's saying something which is patently false. Since the speaker does not appear to be trying to deceive the listener in any way, the listener was forced to look for another plausible interpretation. According to Grice, the deductive process might work like this:

(i) The ambulanceman has expressed pleasure at having someone vomit over him.

(ii) There is no example in recorded history of people being delighted at having someone vomit over them.

(iii) I have no reason to believe that the ambulanceman is trying to deceive us in any way.

(iv) Unless the ambulanceman's utterance is entirely pointless, he must be trying to put across some other proposition.

(v) This must be some obviously related proposition.

(vi) The most obviously related proposition is the exact opposite of the one he has expressed.

(vi) The ambulanceman is extremely annoyed at having the drunk vomit over him.

The following example works in much the same way, but this time involves what Grice terms 'generating a conversational implicature by means of something like a figure of speech'.

Example 13
The speaker was Lady Lucinda Lambton and she was talking about John Patten, who at the time was Secretary of State for Education:[15]

'I lived in the same house as that man for three years and he's the man I hate most in all the world. In all my greasy past, he is the biggest grease spot.'

(i)   It is patently false that John Patten is a grease spot.

(ii)   Lucinda Lambton does not appear to be trying to make us believe that John Patten is a grease spot.

(iii) Unless her utterance is entirely pointless, she must be trying to put across some other proposition.

(iv)   This must be some obviously related proposition.

(vi)   The most obviously related proposition is that, like grease spots, John Patten is a bane.

Here is one final example of a flout which exploits (or apparently exploits) a maxim. Often an individual will try to deflect unwelcome attention by giving an improbable or obviously untrue response. For example, if someone asks you your name and you don't want to tell them, you might say: 'I'm the Queen of Sheba'.

Example 14
B was on a long train journey and wanted to read her book. A was a fellow passenger who wanted to talk to her:

A: What do you do?
B: I'm a teacher.
A: Where do you teach?
B: Outer Mongolia.
A: Sorry I asked!

Outer Mongolia is seen as somewhere impossibly remote, so that B's improbable response prompted the hearer to look for an implicature (in this case that his attentions were unwelcome).

The funny thing about this example was that B really did teach in Outer Mongolia, but A was nevertheless correct in assuming that B was trying to give him the brush off![16] I shall return to these examples in chapter 4 (section 4.2.1).

3.6.2.2 Flouts exploiting the maxim of Quantity

A flout of the maxim of Quantity occurs when a speaker blatantly gives more or less information than the situation requires. We have already seen one instance (example 12) of a person giving less information than required by the situation, and the following examples operate in the same way:

Example 15
A: How are we getting there?
B: Well *we're* getting there in Dave's car.

B blatantly gives less information than A needs, thereby generating the implicature that, while she and her friends have a lift arranged, A will not be travelling with them.

Example 16
Petruchio has come to ask Baptista for his daughter's hand in marriage:[17]

Pet: And you, good sir! Pray, have you not a daughter
         Call'd Katherina, fair and virtuous?

Bap: I have a daughter, sir, call'd Katherina.

By confirming that he has a daughter called Katherina, but omitting any mention to her fairness or virtue, Baptista implies that she does not possess these qualities to any marked degree.

Examples in which more information is given than is required by the situation are also common, as the following example illustrates:

Example 17
The speaker was a BBC continuity announcer:[18]

At the time of recording, all the cast were members of the BBC Drama Group.

The apparently superfluous information in the first clause generates the implicature that by the time the play was broadcast, one or more of the cast had left the BBC Drama Group.

3.6.2.3 Flouts exploiting the maxim of Relation

The maxim of Relation ('Be relevant') is exploited by making a response or observation which is very obviously irrelevant to the topic in hand (e.g. by abruptly changing the subject, or by overtly failing to address the other person's goal in asking a question). Examples of flouting the maxim of Relation by changing the subject (example 18) or by failing to address the topic directly are encountered very frequently, and the examples which follow are typical:

> **Example 18**
> *Geoffrey is a vicar, trying hard to curry favour with his bishop. The speaker is Susan, his wife, who couldn't care less about the church, religion (or, for that matter, for Geoffrey). The emphasis is mine:*[19]
>
> We were discussing the ordination of women. The bishop asked me what I thought. Should women take the services? So long as it doesn't have to be me, I wanted to say, they can be taken by a trained gorilla. 'Oh yes,' Geoffrey chips in, 'Susan's all in favour. She's keener than I am, aren't you, darling?' '**More sprouts anybody?**' I said.

It would be tedious once again to work through all the steps in the informal deductive process — so let us just say that the bishop is likely to come to the conclusion that Susan is not interested in the subject of women's ordination and wishes to change the subject. Again, Grice's theory fails to address a very important issue, *viz.* why does Susan choose to indicate only indirectly that she is bored or uninterested? After all, if the bishop was a particularly insensitive person, there is the risk that he might ignore Susan's hint and pose the question again. Susan could have avoided that possibility by saying: 'I couldn't care less!'. In the 1970s and 1980s much effort in the field of pragmatics has been put into developing theories of **politeness** (see, for example, Brown and Levinson 1978 [1987] and Leech 1983a) which, proponents argue, 'rescue' Grice's theory by explaining the social constraints governing utterance production and interpretation (see chapter 6).

> **Example 19**[20]
> I finished working on my face. I grabbed my bag and a coat. I told Mother I was going out ... She asked me where I was going. I repeated myself. 'Out.'

In this example the speaker, Olivia, makes a response which is truthful, clear, etc., and which does answer her mother's question (unlike Susan's response in example 18). What it does not do is address her mother's goal in asking the question: her mother can see that Olivia is going out, what she wants to know is where she is going. Example 19 could also be analysed as a flout of the maxim of Quantity, in that Olivia has given less information that the situation requires. I shall take this point up in the next chapter (section 4.2.4).

3.6.2.4 Flouts exploiting the maxim of Manner
The following is an example of a flout of the maxim of Manner.

Example 20
This interaction occurred during a radio interview with an un-named official from the United States Embassy in Port-au-Prince, Haiti:

Interviewer: Did the United States Government play any part in Duvalier's departure? Did they, for example, actively encourage him to leave?

Official: I would not try to steer you away from that conclusion.

The official could simply have replied: 'Yes'. Her actual response is extremely long-winded and convoluted and it is obviously no accident, nor through any inability to speak clearly, that she has failed to observe the maxim of Manner. There is, however, no reason to believe that the official is being deliberately unhelpful (she could, after all, have simply refused to answer at all, or said: 'No comment').

The hearer must therefore look for another explanation and, once again, there is nothing in Grice's theory to help us explain her flouting of the maxim of Manner. In this case, it is not a clash of maxims which has caused her to flout the maxim of Manner in this way. Rather it is occasioned by a clash of **goals**: the desire to claim credit for what she sees as a desirable outcome, while at the same time avoiding putting on record the fact that her government has intervened in the affairs of another country. In fact, this exchange was widely reported and the implicature spelt out in news broadcasts later the same day: 'Although they have not admitted it openly, the State Department is letting it be known that the United States was behind Jean-Paul Duvalier,

"Baby Doc's", decision to quit the island.' The desire 'to say and not say' something at the same time is lucidly discussed by Dascal (1983).

The important thing to note in each of the foregoing cases is that it is the very blatancy of the non-observance which triggers the search for an implicature.

Grice made clear that there are many occasions on which speakers fail to observe the maxims, even though they have no desire to generate an implicature. These categories are discussed in the next section and seem to cover all possible instances of non-observance.

3.7 Other categories of non-observance of the conversational maxims

In his first paper (1975: 49) Grice listed three ways in which a participant in a talk exchange may fail to fulfil a maxim: the speaker may **flout** a maxim, **violate** a maxim or **opt out** of observing a maxim. He later added a fourth category of non-observance: **infringing** a maxim. Several writers since Grice have argued the need for a fifth category — **suspending** a maxim. Having made all these distinctions, it is extremely irritating to note that Grice himself does not always use the terms consistently and remarkably few commentators seem to make any attempt to use the terms correctly. The distinctions Grice originally made are important for a full understanding of his theory. We have already examined flouting in detail and I shall now take each of the others in turn.

3.7.1 Violating a maxim

Many commentators incorrectly use the term 'violate' for all forms of non-observance of the maxims. But in his first published paper on conversational cooperation (1975), Grice defines 'violation' very specifically as the **unostentatious** non observance of a maxim. If a speaker violates a maxim s/he 'will be liable to mislead' (1975: 49).

Let us take as an example an extract from a fictional interaction between Martin and his wife, Alice.[21]

Example 21

*Alice has been refusing to make love to her husband. At first he
attributes this to post-natal depression, but then he starts to think she
may be having an affair:*

'Allie. I've got to ask you this.'
He stopped.
'Ask me then—'
'Will you give me a truthful answer? However much you
think it'll hurt me?'
Alice's voice had a little quaver.
'I promise.'
Martin came back to his chair and put his hands on its back
and looked at her.
'Is there another man?'
Alice raised her chin and looked at him squarely.
'No,' she said. 'There isn't another man.'
And then Martin gave a long, escaping sigh, and grinned at
her and said he thought they had better finish the cham-
pagne, didn't she?

It is later established that Alice's assertion that she is not
having an affair with another man is true, but not the whole truth
(she is, in fact, having an affair with a woman). But there is
nothing in the formulation of Alice's response which would allow
Martin to deduce that she was withholding information. This
unostentatious violation of the maxim of Quantity generates the
intentionally misleading implicature that Alice is not having an
affair with anyone.

The next example is authentic (naturally-occurring examples are quite difficult to come by because, of course, you do not
generally find out that you have been misled):

Example 22

*An English athlete, Dianne Modahl, the defending Commonwealth
Games 800 metres champion, pulled out of her opening race and
returned to England. Caroline Searle, press officer for the England
team, said:*[22]

'She has a family bereavement; her grandmother has died.'

The next day it was announced that Ms Modahl had been
sent home following a positive test for drugs. What Ms Searle had
said was true, but the implicature (that the reason for Modahl's

returning home was a bereavement) was false.

Pragmatically misleading (or potentially pragmatically misleading) utterances of this sort are regularly encountered in certain **activity types** (see chapter 7), such as trials, parliamentary speeches and arguments. So regularly do they occur, in fact, that they could be seen as the norm for this type of interaction, and be interpreted in that light by participants. I return to this point in section 3.7.4.

At first blush, it might appear that violating a maxim is the exact opposite of flouting a maxim. In example 21, Alice says something which is 'true' (as far as it goes) in order to imply an untruth. In the case of a flout (as in example 3), the speaker blatantly fails to observe the maxim of Quality at the level of what is said, but nevertheless implies something which is true. All the examples of flouts which Grice himself gives are of this order. However, there is no principled reason to expect that an implicature will be 'true' — speakers can imply a lie as easily as they can say one (as in example 7).

3.7.2 Infringing a maxim

A speaker who, with no intention of generating an implicature and with no intention of deceiving, fails to observe a maxim is said to 'infringe' the maxim. In other words, the non-observance stems from imperfect linguistic performance rather than from any desire on the part of the speakers to generate a conversational implicature. This type of non-observance could occur because the speaker has an imperfect command of the language (a young child or a foreign learner), because the speaker's performance is impaired in some way (nervousness, drunkenness, excitement), because of some cognitive impairment, or simply because the speaker is constitutionally incapable of speaking clearly, to the point, etc.

3.7.3 Opting out of a maxim

A speaker opts out of observing a maxim by indicating unwillingness to cooperate in the way the maxim requires. Examples of opting out occur frequently in public life, when the speaker cannot, perhaps for legal or ethical reasons, reply in the way normally expected. On the other hand, the speaker wishes to avoid generating a false implicature or appearing uncooperative. Examples of such cases could include a priest, counsellor or even an investigative journalist refusing to relay information given in confidence, or a police officer refusing to release the name of an accident victim until the victim's relatives have been informed. Here is a typical example from a British M.P.:

Example 23
The Conservative M.P., Teddy Taylor, had been asked a question about talks he had had with Colonel Gadaffi:[23]

'Well, honestly, I can't tell you a thing, because what was said to me was told me in confidence'.

Another reason frequently given for 'opting out' is that giving the requested information might hurt a third party (example 24) or put them in danger (example 25):

Example 24
Ruth Rendell, a famous crime novelist, was being interviewed by an equally famous psychiatrist, Professor Anthony Clare. Clare asked Rendell about her husband:[24]

AC: You married him twice. You've been interviewed many times, but I've never seen a satisfactory explanation for that very interesting fact.

RR: Well *[pause]* I don't think I can give you one. That is not to say that I don't know it but I do know it but I cannot give it. I don't think that to give it would be a very good idea, particularly for my husband.

Example 25
The first speaker is a caller to a radio chat show. The second speaker is the host, Nick Ross:[25]

Caller: ... um I lived in uh a country where people sometimes need to flee that country.
Ross: Uh, where was that?
Caller: It's a country in Asia and I don't want to say any more.

When speakers expressly opt out of observing a maxim in this way, they make explicit reference to the way in which speakers normally attend to the maxims, which in turn offers support for Grice's contention that interactants have a strong expectation that, *ceteris paribus* and unless indication is given to the contrary, the CP and the maxims will be observed.

3.7.4 Suspending a maxim

Several writers have suggested that there are occasions when there is no need to opt out of observing the maxims because there are certain events in which there is no expectation on the part of any participant that they will be fulfilled (hence the non-fulfilment does not generate any implicatures). This category is necessary to respond to criticisms of the type made by Keenan (1976) who proposed as a counter-example to Grice's theory of conversational implicature the fact that in the Malagasy Republic participants in talk exchanges:

> ... regularly provide less information than is required by their conversational partner, even though they have access to the necessary information.

> (Keenan 1976: 70)

Keenan's example does not falsify Grice's theory if it is seen as a case where the maxim of Quantity is suspended. There is no expectation at all on the part of interactants that speakers will provide precise information about their relatives and friends, in case they draw the attention of evil spirits to them. Although the Malagasy speaker may appear to be underinformative at the level of what is said, the uninformativeness is nevertheless systematic, motivated and generates no conversational implicature for members of that community. Here are two further examples, taken from a novel set on a Navajo reservation, which make explicit reference to the suspension of a maxim:

Example 26
The speaker in this example and the next is the daughter of a murdered man. She is talking to Officer Jim Chee of the Navajo Tribal Police:[26]

'Last time you were with that FBI man — asking about the one who got killed,' she said, respecting the Navajo taboo of not speaking the name of the dead. 'You find out who killed that man?'

Example 27

'... they told him he could not be cured,' Bistie's Daughter
said in a shaky voice. She cleared her throat, wiped the back
of her hand across her eyes. 'That man was strong,' she
continued. 'His spirit was strong. He didn't give up on
things. He didn't want to die. He didn't hardly say anything
at all. I asked him. I said, "My Father, why —" ' She stopped.

Never speak the name of the dead, Chee thought. Never
summon the *chindi* to you, even if the name of the ghost is
Father.

In examples 26 and 27 the speaker fails on three occasions
to observe the maxim of Quantity. On the first occasion she
refers vaguely to 'the FBI man', thereby generating the (true)
implicature that she does not know his name. Then she refers in
a similarly vague fashion to 'the one who got killed' and 'that
man'. Normally this would generate exactly the same implicature
(that she does not know the name of the man). However, among
the Navajo this implicature would not be generated in the case of
a person who had died a violent or premature death, because to
mention his or her name in these circumstances is taboo. In this
case the non-observance of the maxim of Quantity generates no
implicatures because all the participants know that it is suspended.

Suspensions of the maxims may be culture-specific (as in
Keenan's example and in examples 26 and 27) or specific to
particular events. For example, in the acting community in
Britain (but not among the population at large) people refrain
from uttering the name of Shakespeare's play *Macbeth* because to
do so is supposed to bring bad luck. They refer instead to 'The
Scottish Play', thereby failing to observe the maxim of Quantity.
Similarly (but less obviously, perhaps), as I observed in section
3.7.1, in most cultures the maxim of Quantity appears to be
selectively suspended in, for example, courts of law, Committees
of Inquiry or indeed in any confrontational situation where it is
held to be the job of an 'investigator' to elicit the truth from a
witness. The witnesses are not required or expected to volunteer
information which may incriminate them, and no inference is
drawn on the basis of what they do not say. (This is in direct
contrast to the implicatures drawn in example 21. A man could
reasonably expect his wife to answer fully — he should not have
to wheedle every piece of information out of her, as if they were

in a court of law.) We find similar instances of the suspension of the maxim of Quality in the case of funeral orations and (until recently) in the case of obituaries,[27] of the maxim of Manner in the case of poetry, of the maxim of Quantity in the case of telegrams, telexes and some international phone calls and of all three maxims in the case of jokes. It is hard to find any convincing examples in which the maxim of Relation is suspended (see section 4.2.4).

3.8 Testing for implicature

The distinction between what a speaker's words mean and what they imply should by now be clear. In 'Logic and conversation' Grice discussed six 'tests' for distinguishing semantic meaning from implied meaning, and I outline them below as a useful way of summarizing the material covered in chapters 1–3. Grice (1975) listed six distinct properties of implicatures, but I have condensed them into four.

3.8.1 Non-detachability and non-conventionality

Some aspects of meaning are semantic and can be changed or removed by **relexicalization** or **reformulation** (replacing one word or phrase with another closely related one, but lacking the supposedly unpleasant connotation). Here are three examples where one participant overtly relexicalizes:

Example 28

Speaker A is a newly-widowed woman who finds living with her interfering mother a strain:[28]

A: I wish you wouldn't creep up on me, Mother.
B: I don't creep, dear. I merely refrain from making gratuitous noise.

Example 29

John Stanley, M.P., was defending the Government's new policy of questioning social security claimants closely about their availability for work:[29]

' "Methods of interrogation" was the phrase you used. I think we would call it "questioning" '.

Example 30
A radio interview with Jim Morgan, of the management of Rail-track Southwest, during the eighth week of a signalworkers' strike:[30]

Int: Some will obviously, and indeed already have, accused you of trying to bribe staff to cross the picket lines.

J.M.:   Well, it's not a bribe to staff to cross picket lines, it's an offer.

In the case of 'creep', 'methods of interrogation' and 'bribe', the unpleasant associations are part of the meaning of the lexical item. Replacing the offending lexical item with a synonym which does not have such negative connotations removes the unpleasantness.[31] This is not possible with implicature. No matter how much you reword an utterance, the implicature remains. For example, my cats are on the large size. A visitor looked at one of them and said, 'Underfed, isn't he?' implying, thereby, that the animal was fat (when, in fact, he is merely big-boned). The same implicature would be maintained however the utterance had been relexicalized and regardless of whether or not the chosen adjective had positive or negative connotations: Frail/puny/ skinny/delicate/light-on-his-feet/slimline, isn't he? — all carry the implicature that the cat is fat.

The distinction between semantic meaning and implicature-generated meaning cannot always be made so clearly. What begins as a conversational implicature may become *the* meaning of a lexical item. This may take place very slowly, as in the case of the word *goodbye*, the use of which has altered over the years while the form has changed to such a degree that its original meaning has become obscured. *Goodbye* is a contraction of *God be with you* and in the Middle Ages was widely used among Christians in a variety of ways and conveying a variety of implicatures, including being used as a salutation on meeting or valediction on parting. By Shakespeare's time it had become restricted to a farewell formula and has remained so ever since, while gradually changing its form:

1558:   God be wy you.[32]

1668:   To Mr Wren, to bid him 'God be with you'.[33]

1818:   And so your humble servant and good-b'ye![34]

Today, often contracted in British English to *bye-bye* or just *bye*, it is used solely as a farewell formula by people of all religions and of none and the vast majority of people are almost certainly completely unaware of its original (religious) meaning.

Sometimes the movement from a phrase conveying a conversational implicature, via conventional implicature to semantic meaning can occur very quickly. During the 1980s the term 'creative accounting' came to mean 'cheating' and now means nothing else, as in the following example:[35]

Example 31
Because of 'creative accountancy' used by high-spending boroughs, the GLC failed to take into account about £140 million.

The same was true in the following case but on this occasion 'being economical with the truth' came to mean 'lying' within days of being uttered by Sir Robert Armstrong and now it is used to mean nothing else:

Example 32
In November 1986 Mrs Thatcher was trying to prevent the publication in Australia of <u>Spycatcher</u>, a book by a former agent of MI5. Sir Robert Armstrong, who at that time was head of the British Civil Service, had admitted that a letter he had written to the Australian High Court might have 'given a misleading impression':

Judge: How does 'given a misleading impression' differ from lying?

R.A.:   Lying is saying that which is untrue. Giving a misleading impression is being economical with the truth.

3.8.2 Implicature changes

Implicatures are the property of utterances, not of sentences and therefore the same words carry different implicatures on different occasions. Consider the sentence: *How old are you?* and how it is used in the three following examples:

Example 33
A young boy is talking to a colleague of his father:

A: It's my birthday today.
B: Many happy returns. How old are you?

A: I'm five.

Example 34
This example is taken from a novel. Speaker A is talking to his son:[36]

A: How old are you, George?
B: I'm eighteen, Father.
A: I know how old you are, you fool.

Example 35
A psychiatrist is talking to a woman patient:[37]

A: What do you do?
B: I'm a nurse, but my husband won't let me work.
A: How old are you?
B: I'm thirty-nine.

In each case the semantic meaning of *How old are you?* is the same, but the implicature is different. In example 33 it is a straightforward request for information; in example 34 the father is implying that the son's behaviour is inappropriate for a person of that age (more precisely, he is implying that it is time his son got a job) and the psychiatrist in example 35 is probably trying to prompt the patient to consider whether, at thirty-nine, she isn't old enough to make up her own mind about whether or not to work.

The following extract from a detective novel[38] also illustrates well the point that I am trying to make:

Example 36
The villagers in the story are hiding a fugitive suspected of murder. The conversation is between a villager and a rich incomer:

'What news of Alan Fenny now?'
'None, Mr Harding. Nobody knows anything.'
'I'll bet they don't,' said Thomas …
[2 lines omitted]
'Food and drink and shelter. He must have those, mustn't he? Somewhere.'
'That's right,' said Gladys. 'But he hasn't been near his mother, that I do know.'
'I'll bet he hasn't,' said Thomas warmly.

In the third and the final lines the speaker uses virtually the same words. On the first occasion the expression was used ironically (the speaker knows full well that the villagers are hiding Alan), on the second occasion it was spoken in all seriousness (the villagers have told Alan that the police are watching his mother's house and he has given it a wide berth).

3.8.3 Calculability

As we have seen, the same words may convey, in different circumstances, very different implicatures. The implicature conveyed in one particular context is not random, however. It is possible to spell out the steps a hearer goes through in order to calculate the intended implicature. These are the steps which I described in section 3.6.2.1, in relation to examples 3 and 13.

3.8.4 Defeasibility

This is the most important difference between semantic meaning and implied meaning. The notion of 'defeasibility' means that an implicature can be cancelled. This allows the speaker to imply something, and then deny that implicature. We saw how this worked in example 24 when Ruth Rendell said 'I don't think I can give you one', then realized that she could have been understood to have implied that she didn't know the reason; she cancels that unwanted implicature by saying 'I do know it'. Here are three more examples in which, for a variety of reasons, an implicature is cancelled:

Example 37
A: Let's have a drink.
B: It's not one o'clock yet.

An hour or so later:

B: Let's have a gin and tonic — it's after one o'clock.
A: I didn't say that you could drink after one o'clock. I said that you couldn't drink before.

In this example, speaker A may be held to have implied that B could have a drink after one o'clock. However, in her second contribution she cancels that implicature. Notice that the implicature can be cancelled, without making complete nonsense of the first contribution.

Example 38

A and B are sisters. A is getting ready for a job interview:

A: Did you get your velvet jacket back from the clean-
     ers?

B: You're **not** borrowing it.

A: I don't want to borrow it. I just wondered if you'd
     got it back.

B: You just wondered!

A: Well, I haven't got anything decent to wear!

In this case we see that A does deny the implicature of her first question, but not very plausibly. When challenged she backs down and instead offers a justification for her implied request.

Example 39

The following is a newspaper report of a court case:[39]

At this interruption Mr Findlay for the prosecution asked
Churchill if he was denying that he had deliberately set his
dog on Police Constable Lloyd. 'Yes, Sir', replied the defendant, 'I do deny it. When PC Lloyd walked into the
club, I just said, "Oh look, Rambo, a copper" and the dog
sort of made up his own mind.'

Here we have an even more improbable denial of an im-
plicature, but what is important is that it *can* be denied. Nobody can prove that Findlay intended to set his dog on the police officer — he could, as he suggested, have simply been exchanging pleasantries with his pet.

Example 40

*A letter to a newspaper shortly before Mrs Thatcher resigned as
Prime Minister in November 1990:*[40]

For the sake of the country the PM should hold on until
the summer.

This is no time of year for street parties.

In this case the writer has deliberately generated a false implicature (that she regrets that Mrs Thatcher may resign), which her second sentence immediately cancels. This sort of 'set 'em up and knock 'em down' technique is regularly used to generate humour, and is used quite effectively here to make a political point.

As will be seen in chapter 5, the possibility of cancelling or denying an implicature is the most important reason why people choose to use it.

3.9 Conclusion

In this chapter we have explored one approach to explaining how people interpret indirectness. In chapters 5 and 6 we shall consider *why* people use indirectness in the first place — why don't they just say what they mean?

Notes

1. Reported in *The Guardian* 20 July 1994.

2. Mary Wesley (1983) *Harnessing peacocks*. Black Swan, London, p. 57.

3. Mary Wesley (1990) *A sensible life*. Black Swan, London, p. 160.

4. *But* has other, rarer, meanings as in: 'He's not only a fool but a blackguard' and 'You can but try'.

5. William Shakespeare, *All's well that ends well*, Act I, Scene iii.

6. Kaleidescope Feature ('When I'm bad I'm better'). BBC Radio 4, 27 August 1994.

7. Grice also introduces the concept of **generalized conversational implicature**. This refers to utterances such as: *He ran over a dog*. The use of the indefinite article implies that the dog in question was not his own. The notion of generalized conversational implicature is of peripheral concern here and is also problematical. For good discussions of the issues see Levinson (1983: 126–7) or Green (1989: 94–5).

8. In semantics *imply* is used differently from the way it is used in pragmatics. In semantics it is used of a formal relation between propositions, e.g. 'She lives in London' implies 'She lives in England'.

9. Violet Needham (1948) *The boy in red*. Collins, London, pp. 236–7.

10. This is discussed in greater detail in my forthcoming book, *The dynamics of discourse*.

11. Report in *The Guardian*, July 1994.

12. Note that there is enormous cross-cultural variation.

13. From the film *Splash*. I owe this example to Samantha Oakes.

14. Allason writes under the pen-name of Nigel West. Speaking on BBC Radio 4, *Today*, 13 June 1986. During the years after the war a group of four men, highly placed in British Intelligence, had been exposed as spies. It was always suspected that there was a 'Fifth Man', still unmasked. A few years after this interview Allason was proved wrong: a man called Cairncross was exposed as the 'Fifth Man'.

15. Reported in *The Daily Mail*, 21 July 1994, but the incident took place in January of that year.

16. I am grateful to Dorothy Bond for this example.

17. William Shakespeare, *The taming of the shrew*. Act II, scene 1.

18. BBC Radio 4, 13 June 1986.

19. Alan Bennett (1988) *Talking heads*. BBC Enterprises, London, p. 32.

20. Elizabeth George (1994) *Playing for the ashes*. Bantam Press, London, p. 91.

21. Joanna Trollope (1989) *A village affair*. Black Swan, London, p. 157.

22. The reported events occurred at the Commonwealth Games in Victoria, Canada, 25 August 1994.

23. BBC Radio 4, 9 June 1991.

24. *In the psychiatrist's chair*. BBC Radio 4, 31 July 1994.

25. *Call Nick Ross*, BBC Radio 4, November 1991.

26. Tony Hillerman (1990) *Skinwalkers*. Sphere Books Limited, London, pp. 63 and 144.

27. Since about 1968 some newspaper obituaries (e.g. in *The Times*), have started to contain criticisms or unflattering observations of the deceased. The following extract from the obituary of Sir Robert Helpmann (*The Times*, 29 September 1986, p. 14) is a very untypical, but particularly striking, example of this:

    'A homosexual of the proselytizing kind, he could turn young men on the borderline his way. He was also capable of cutting a person down in public without mercy.'

28. Taken from the BBC sit. com., *After Henry*.

29. BBC Radio 4, *Today*, 30 October 1985.

30. Interview on BBC Radio 4, *P.M.*, 1 August 1994.

31. By chance I came across a very old reference condemning the practice of relexicalization in a sermon given by Archbishop Latimer to King Edward VI in 1549: 'Nowe a dayes they call them *gentle rewardes*, let them leaue their colourynge, and cal them by their Christian name *Brybes*.'

32. William Shakespeare, *Love's labour's lost*, Act III, scene i.

33. Samuel Pepys, 6 August 1668.

34. Byron, *Don Juan*.

35. *The Times*, 27 July 1985.

36. V. S. Pritchett (1951) *Mr Beluncle*. Chatto and Windus, London.

37. Taken from Labov and Fanshel (1977).

38. Catherine Aird (1994 [1967]) *A most contagious game*. Chivers Press, London, p. 108.

39. Report in the *Marylebone Mercury*, 6 May 1991.

40. Letter to *The Guardian*, 16 November 1990.

CHAPTER 4

Approaches to pragmatics

4.1 Introduction

In chapters 2 and 3 we saw how Austin and Grice attempted to explain the process of performing speech acts and of generating implicature by means of 'informal reasoning'. I have already noted problems associated with Austin's work. In this chapter I discuss some of the problems which are associated with Grice's informal approach and then go on to examine Searle's more formal approach to speech act theory. I shall conclude by comparing formal and informal approaches to the description of speech acts.

4.2 Problems with Grice's theory

There are a number of problems associated with Grice's theory. However, a detailed discussion of all the issues would take us beyond the scope of an introductory book. I have outlined them briefly. The main problems are:

• Sometimes an utterance has a range of possible interpretations. How do we know when the speaker is deliberately failing to observe a maxim and hence that an implicature is intended?

• How can we distinguish between different types of non-observance (e.g. distinguish a violation from an infringement)?

• Grice's four maxims seem to be rather different in nature. What are the consequences of this?

• Sometimes the maxims seem to overlap or are difficult to distinguish from one another.

• Grice argued that there should be a mechanism for calculating implicature, but it is not always clear how this operates.

4.2.1 When is non-observance intentional?

According to Grice, a flout is so blatant that the interlocutor is supposed to know for certain that an implicature has been generated (even if we are not always quite sure what that implicature is) but, as we saw with the 'Outer Mongolia' example (example 14 in chapter 3) this is not always the case. There are times when it is really very difficult to determine whether a non-observance is intentional and hence to know whether any implicature is intended at all. I once showed a group of students an extract from a poem by Thomas Hood.[1] The poem is devoted to boyhood reminiscences and begins as follows:

> **Example 1**
> I remember, I remember
> The house where I was born,
> The little window where the sun
> Came creeping in at morn.
>
> The lilacs where the robin built
> And where my brother set
> The laburnum on his birthday —
> → The tree is living yet!

We could not agree whether the last line observes all the maxims and simply makes a statement of fact (that the tree is still alive) or whether it is a flout of the maxim of Quantity, implying that the brother is dead.

We have already noted that an utterance frequently has a range of possible interpretations; Grice, however, did not discuss the possibility that more than one **implicature** might be intended. If it were indeed the case that an utterance can have only one implicature (an assumption which will be challenged in chapter 7) how do we know which is the intended implicature? Sometimes although the hearer perceives (and is perhaps amused by) possible alternative interpretations, the context of utterance is such that one interpretation is very much more probable than another. This is the case with my next example:

Example 2
The following was part of a speech made by the King of Matabeleland to Queen Victoria:

'I am but the louse on the edge of Your Majesty's blanket.'

The most obvious interpretation of this utterance is that the King of Matabeleland was 'generating an implicature by means of … a figure of speech' (see section 3.6.2.1) and that he was implying that he considered himself as nothing compared with Queen Victoria. However, there is an unfortunate presupposition contained in this utterance (namely, that the Queen's bedding was verminous) — could the King also have been implying that Queen Victoria's personal hygiene left something to be desired? Given the nature of the event (official exchange of greetings between heads of state), this was almost certainly not the case. In this instance, the context in which the utterance was made allows us to determine which of the possible implicatures was likely to have been intended, but this is not always so. There are times when it can be very difficult to decide from a range of possible implicatures which was the one intended. Consider the following example:

Example 3
This note was sent by the head of a University department to all members of her department:[2]

To all staff:

The window cleaners will be in the building during the weekend 28th/29th November.

Please clear your windowsills and lock any valuables away.

It is now three years since I was first shown this note, and I still cannot decide whether the sender was deliberately implying that window cleaners are dishonest, or whether this is simply an unfortunate inference which some readers might draw. Within Grice's theory there is no way of explaining in cases like this which implicatures are intended.

4.2.2 Distinguishing between types of non-observance

Closely connected with the previous point is the problem that we do not always know whether a non-observance is intentional and when this occurs it is not possible to distinguish a flout from other types of non-observance. The examples of flouting I gave in section 3.6.2 were *par excellence* illustrations, the clearest and least problematical I could find; in those cases there could really be no doubt at all that a maxim was being flouted. But many examples are less clear-cut than these and the question then arises as to how we know which type of non-observance is involved (flout, violation or infringement) which in turn raises once again the issue of what the speaker has implied. Grice does not explain how an interlocutor is supposed to distinguish between (say) a flout, a violation (possibly intended to mislead) and an infringement, not intended to generate any implicature. Consider the following example:

> **Example 4**
> *Bluey, a married woman, has become friendly with James and has indicated that she would like to start a sexual relationship with him. James doesn't want to become more deeply involved with Bluey, but neither does he want to hurt her feelings:*[3]
>
> 'You can't refuse just to come and have a drink with me,' Bluey said to James.
> → 'I don't want to refuse,' James said.
> She had tried not to build on this, not to take his five words apart, unpicking them over and over, and then stitching them together, again and again, to see if they couldn't be made to come out larger, more significant. If he said he didn't want to refuse to come, then surely that meant he wanted to come very much, which surely, in its turn, meant that he wanted to be alone with her, which surely ... Or perhaps he just meant, I don't want to disappoint you as clearly this means a lot to you. Did that then mean that coming wouldn't mean as much to him as he knew it would to her?

Bluey was unable to determine the status of James's utterance: *I don't want to refuse.* Was it an unintentional infringement or was he deliberately flouting a maxim with the intention of generating an implicature? If the non-observance was deliberate, precisely **what** was he implying?

4.2.3 Different nature of maxims

This point is closely connected with the previous one: not all Grice's maxims are of the same order. The maxim of Quality is the most straightforward, its operation is generally yes/no — someone is either telling the truth or is not, and (in the case of a flout) it is usually pretty easy to tell which is which. The maxims of Quantity and Manner, on the other hand, can be observed to a greater or lesser degree — it is rarely possible to give **precisely** the right amount of information or to speak with perfect clarity; usually it is a question of 'more or less the right amount', or 'more or less clear'. Compare the two examples which follow:

> **Example 5**
> The final night of the budget debate featured at its beginning and end the first public performance of the new Lawson/ Tebbit axis, the most principled alliance of its kind since the Aesthetically Handicapped Sisters put the squeeze on poor Cinderella.[4]

> **Example 6**
> *I once arrived at a Lancaster hospital for a meeting I was scheduled to attend, and the chairman said to me:*
>
> It's really very kind of you to come.

Example 5 is so convoluted that the non-observance of the maxim of Manner is clearly deliberate (although I never fully fathomed what the writer was trying to imply), whereas in example 6 I really could not work out whether the maxim of Manner was being flouted or not. The welcome seemed **slightly** effusive for a meeting which had been organized principally for my benefit, but was not so 'over the top' that I could say with certainty that the chairman was being sarcastic (I spent most of the meeting wondering whether or not he was implying that I had arrived late).

4.2.4 Maxims may overlap

It is not always possible to determine which maxim is being invoked — the maxims of Quantity and Manner, in particular, seem to overlap and to co-occur, as in the following example:

Example 7
A: What did you have to eat?
B: Something masquerading as chicken chasseur.

In this example B appears to be giving more information than required (she could just have said: *chicken chasseur*), while the *masquerading* seems to constitute a flout of the maxim of Manner. In section 3.6.2.3, in relation to example 19, I noted the problem of overlap between the maxim of Quantity and the maxim of Relation. The following example, in which Polonius is talking to Hamlet,[5] is very similar:

Example 8
Polonius: What do you read, My Lord?
Hamlet: Words, words, words.

In this dialogue Hamlet deliberately gives less information than is required by the situation (or, rather, less information than is required by Polonius) and so flouts the maxim of Quantity. But he also deliberately fails to address Polonius's goals, thereby flouting the maxim of Relation. Two issues arise from this example. The first is that the requirement of the Cooperative Principle to 'make your contribution such as is required …' may well be different for speaker and hearer; what is 'enough' information for Hamlet may not be 'enough' for Polonius. The second problem is that the maxim of Relevance **always** seems to be in operation — unless you assume that a contribution is in some way relevant to what has gone before, you will not begin to look for an implicature.[6]

4.2.5 Problems of calculability

Another important issue which Grice's theory (at least as originally formulated) fails to address is why in some cases (as in example 13 in chapter 3) we are expected to seek **a comparison** between grease spots and John Patten, in others (as in example 3 in chapter 3) we must look for a proposition which was **the exact opposite** of the one expressed by the ambulanceman, while in others still (as with the interpretation of 'Outer Mongolia' in example 14 in chapter 3) the hearer has to look for an implicature which is **in no way related**.

4.3 Grice's informal approach

It is now more than 25 years since Grice first put forward his ideas concerning the conversational maxims and his work continues to serve as the basis for much (probably most) work in pragmatics. Grice can claim credit for asking a lot of very exciting questions, which have led linguists to think about language in a completely new way. But in the end, what we are left with is a set of very informal procedures for calculating conversational implicature, which cannot really withstand close scrutiny and, as we have seen, the theory is full of holes, some of which have yet to be plugged.

4.4 J. R. Searle

John Searle, like Grice, studied under Austin at Oxford. In his philosophical writings (notably in his 1969 book *Speech acts: an essay in the philosophy of language*) Searle distinguishes between 'propositional content' and 'illocutionary force' (cf. Austin's 'locution' and 'illocution' and Grice's 'what is said' and 'what is meant') and in a later work (1975b) proposes a detailed classification of the major categories of speech acts; most important of all, he points out the necessity of taking into account in the analysis of a speech act the social institution within which it was produced. The aspects of his work which concern me here, however, are two of his early contributions to work in pragmatics: his theory of **indirect speech acts** (Searle 1975a), which I shall deal with very briefly in the next section, and his attempt to establish a set of rules for speech acts (1969). It is this second area which will be my main focus here because, although Searle's search for rules leads us, in my view, into a blind alley, the attempt raises important issues for pragmatic theory.

4.4.1 Indirect speech acts

An indirect speech act, in Searle's terms, is one performed 'by means of another' (1979: 60). Consider the following example:

Example 9
This notice is displayed in the changing rooms at the swimming pool at the University of Warwick:[7]

Would users please refrain from spitting.

What we have here (in Searle's terms) is a directive (*Don't spit!*) performed by means of an interrogative.[8] However, all speech acts (except explicit performatives) are, as Austin and Grice demonstrated, indirect to some degree (for a discussion on degrees of indirectness see chapter 5) and are performed 'by means of another speech act (e.g. in making the **assertion** *It is going to charge!* I perform the speech act of *warning* (Austin 1962: 74)) and to this extent Searle's introduction of the new term seems an unnecessary refinement. Moreover, for our present purposes,[9] Searle's (1979) account of how to calculate the meaning of indirect speech acts is so similar to Grice's method for getting from 'what is said' to 'what is meant' (see chapter 3) that it would be tedious to rehearse the argument here (but for a good, clear summary see Mey 1993: 142-5).

4.4.2 Searle's conditions for speech acts

Where Grice put forward a series of maxims and principles (informal generalizations) to explain how a speech act 'works', Searle tried to establish a set of rules.[10] In other words, Searle attempted to systematize and formalize Austin's work. In chapter 2 (example 21) I discussed the following (fabricated) utterance: *I promise I'll come over there and hit you if you don't shut up!* We saw that this example is problematic because, although it is an utterance which contains a performative verb and which performs an action, the action it performs is not the one specified by the speech act verb (*promise*); instead it is a *threat*. Searle set out a series of conditions which, properly applied, should exclude such anomalous utterances from the category of promising. Here are Searle's rules for promising:

Propositional act	Speaker (S) predicates a future act (A) of Speaker (S)
Preparatory condition	S believes that doing act A is in H's best interest and that S can do A.
Sincerity condition	Speaker intends to do act A.
Essential condition	S undertakes an obligation to do act A.

Let us see how this might work in practice. Suppose that Francis says to Helen: *I'll cook you a curry for dinner tonight.*

Propositional act	The speaker (Francis) says something about a future act (cooking a curry tonight) which the speaker himself will perform.
Preparatory condition	Francis believes that cooking a curry for Helen is to Helen's benefit (something which Helen will enjoy).
Sincerity condition	Francis truly intends to make a curry for Helen.
Essential condition	In uttering the words *I'll cook you a curry* Francis undertakes an obligation to make a curry for Helen.

Searle's rules would indeed explain why *I promise I'll come over there and hit you if you don't shut up!* is infelicitous: the preparatory condition (S believes that doing act A is in H's best interest) is not met. So far so good. According to Searle, the issues he raises in relation to promising are of general application and so it should, in principle, be possible to establish rules of this nature for every speech act. He offers (1969: 66-7) eight further examples of rules for speech acts: *requesting, asserting, questioning, thanking, advising, warning, greeting* and *congratulating*. However, four interrelated sets of problems arise from this work:

- It is not always possible to distinguish fully between one speech act and another (partly because the conditions specified by Searle tend to cover only the central or most typical usage of a speech act verb).

- If we attempt to plug all the gaps in Searle's rules we end up with a hopelessly complex collection of *ad hoc* conditions.

- The conditions specified by Searle may exclude perfectly normal instances of a speech act but permit anomalous uses.

- The same speech act verb may cover a range of slightly different phenomena and some speech acts 'overlap'; Searle's rules take no account of this.

4.4.2.1 Distinguishing speech acts

It is not always possible, using Searle's rules, to distinguish among speech acts which, although in some sense 'related' to one another, are by no means interchangeable. I talk of some speech acts as being 'related' in the sense that they share certain key features. For example, *ask, request, order, command, suggest,* all typically involve an attempt by the speaker (S) to bring about an action (A) on the part of the hearer (H). Searle himself notes that in order to distinguish *order* or *command* from *request* it is necessary to introduce some additional preparatory rules (he does not show us how to distinguish *order* from *command*):

> *Order* and *command* have the additional preparatory rule that
> S must be in a position of authority over H ... Furthermore
> in both, the authority relationship infects the essential
> condition because the utterance counts as an attempt to get
> H to do A *in virtue of the authority of S over H.*

Searle's additional preparatory rule in fact applies to many other speech acts; an understanding of the nature of the power relationships which obtain between speaker and hearer in order to interpret the illocutionary force of many utterances. In the following example, it is his understanding of the power relationship between himself and the police officer which enables Dillow to interpret the officer's words, which express no explicit order whatsoever:

Example 10
Police officer to butler:[11]

'Thank you, Dillow.'

The phrase constituted dismissal to a butler and Dillow left them.

But even with the additional preparatory condition, Searle's rules can only cope with the most stereotypical uses of *order* and *command*. In examples 11 and 12, where the power relationship between the interactants is contested, there is no guarantee that the *order/command* will be successful (in other words, as we shall discuss further in chapter 7, the speech act does not work in and of itself):

Example 11

*Commander Dalgliesh from Scotland Yard has come to a convent
in order to interview a nun, the sister of a woman who had died in
suspicious circumstances. The first speaker is the Mother Superior:*[12]

…with a little nod she said: 'I'll send Sister Agnes to you.
It's a lovely day, perhaps you would care to walk together in
the rose garden.'

It was, Dalgliesh recognized, a command not a suggestion
…

In this example it would be difficult to say who is in
authority. The Mother Superior is rather a formidable woman
and is certainly in charge of the convent. Dalgliesh, on the other
hand, is a very senior police officer, who has the right (within
reason) to interview a witness when and where he pleases (he
could have required her to come to the police station, for
example). Dalgliesh recognizes that the Mother Superior *intends*
her utterance to be a command, but he does not accept that she
has any authority over him. On this occasion, however, he
chooses not to assert his authority and does as she wishes.

Example 12

*In the next extract, set in the Philippines at the turn of the century,
the three speakers are all surgeons. Carriscant is the chief surgeon,
but Wieland and Cruz are several years older than he is. The speech
act verbs I want to focus on are underlined:*[13]

Wieland rose to his feet, the studied neutrality all gone. His
eyes were heavy with resentment and distaste. 'I demand to
know what you said to the Governor.'

'And I order you to tell him,' Cruz added.

Carriscant felt his jaw muscles knot and his shoulders
bunch … They had just handed him the advantage with
their hectoring pomposity; they no longer unsettled him.

'That must remain a confidential matter between me and
the Governor. The Governor requested that our discussion
of Dr Wieland's merits, or otherwise, be conducted under
such conditions …'

Notice that the *order* from Carriscant's colleague, Cruz,
carries less weight than a mere *request* from the U.S. Governor of

the Philippines, and nothing in Searle's conditions (including the additional preparatory conditions) can adequately explain this.

In practice, many of Searle's sets of conditions could apply to any number of speech acts and it is difficult to see what additional preparatory conditions could be introduced to distinguish *request* unproblematically from *invite*, *demand*, many uses of *ask*, etc., or *question* from *examine*, *inquire*, *quiz* or (other uses of) *ask*,[14] even though most native speakers intuitively recognize that these speech act are different from one another in important respects.

In the case of other speech acts, it is only the final (essential) condition which distinguishes one speech act from another, totally unrelated one. For example, *congratulate* could only be distinguished from *compliment* by modifying the final (essential) condition:

Propositional act	Some event, act, etc., E related to H.
Preparatory condition	E is in H's interest and S believes E is in H's interest.
Sincerity condition	S is pleased at E.
Essential condition	Counts as an expression of pleasure at E *[congratulate]*.
	Counts as a commendation of E or tribute to H *[compliment]*.

There is a further problem here in that when we look at the essential condition we often find that Searle is relying on our existing understanding of the meaning of the speech act verb to describe that speech act verb (you must already understand the meaning of *expression of pleasure* or *commendation/tribute* if you are to grasp the distinction between *congratulate* and *compliment*) and to this extent, it has been argued that many of Searle's rules are circular.[15]

4.4.2.2 Plugging the gaps in Searle's rules
The argument so far is that Searle's rules are circular (which Searle disputes), that they fail to distinguish between speech acts and that they cover only paradigm cases of speech acts. In a recent publication (1991: 85) Searle acknowledged this last criticism:

Of course, this analysis so far is designed only to give us the bare bones of the modes of meaning and not to convey all of the subtle distinctions involved in actual discourse. It is important to emphasize this because, in various ways, Bennett, Habermas and Apel all object that this analysis cannot account for all the richness and variety of actual speech acts in actual natural language. Of course not. It was not designed to address that issue.[16]

The fact that Searle's rules fail to capture the nuances of even the commonest of speech acts does not in itself provide grounds for dismissing a rule-governed approach: it could simply be an argument for improving those rules. A far more serious criticism is that although Searle **claims** to be setting out rules for speech acts, all he is really doing is describing the semantics of speech act **verbs**. Be that as it may, the question which concerns us here is whether it is **possible** to extend Searle's conditions to cover at least some of the subtleties of a speech act. In the section which follows I have tried to establish a set of Searlian conditions for a slightly more complicated example than those I have given so far — the speech act of *apologizing* (these rules are modelled closely on Searle's (1969: 67) rules for *thanking*).

4.4.2.3 The speech act of *apologizing*: a case study

Propositional act	S expresses regret for a past act A of S.
Preparatory condition	S believes that A was not in H's best interest.
Sincerity condition	Speaker regrets act A.
Essential condition	Counts as an apology for act A.

Let us again see how this might work out with a concrete example: Pat says to Michael: 'I'm sorry I broke your nose.'

Propositional act	The speaker (Pat) expresses regret for a past act (breaking Michael's nose) which the speaker herself performed.
Preparatory condition	Pat believes that breaking Michael's nose was not in Michael's best interest.

Sincerity condition   Pat is sorry she broke Michael's nose.

Essential condition   In uttering the words *I'm sorry I broke your nose* Pat apologizes to Michael.

Once again, Searlian rules could cope well with the example I have given. But my example was a very simple, paradigm case; we do not have to look very far to find perfectly ordinary examples of apologies which do not fit these rules. Let us take the conditions one at a time and see how they handle the sort of instances of apologizing which we encounter in everyday life:

Propositional act

Does the act have to have been performed by the speaker? In many cultures[17] it is possible to apologize on behalf of someone or something else: for someone close to you or for whom you have responsibility (spouse, children, pets, the family car); for an institution with which you are associated (e.g. the company or college for which you work). It is not unusual to hear people apologizing for things over which they have no control whatsoever, such as the behaviour of their compatriots.[18] In Britain you will frequently hear people saying sorry when someone bumps into them, or apologizing to overseas visitors for the weather!

Does the act have to be a **past** act? Can you apologize for a present act — *I'm sorry about the noise*? Or a future act — *I'm sorry but I shall have to report you* (can we describe as an *apology* the action of the executioner who seeks your forgiveness before chopping your head off[19])?

Does the speaker have to express regret formally/explicitly? There are circumstances (e.g. if a student arrives late at my seminar) when simply saying *The buses are on strike* could 'count' as an apology if I chose to accept it as such (Searle's work, like most early work in pragmatics, takes insufficient account of the role of the hearer). The following example, taken from the British TV series *Soldier, Soldier*,[20] illustrates some of these points well:

Example 13

The episode from which this exchange was taken was set in a British army base in Germany. The main character, Tucker, had been served with a paternity suit by a German woman. Tucker's wife (not surprisingly) was very upset and had decided to leave him and return to England. At the last moment, she changes her mind and goes back to her husband. Meanwhile, Tucker has undergone blood tests and has learnt that he is not the father of the child after all:

Tucker: It's not my baby, Donna.
Donna: Is that 'sorry'?

[Tucker nods his head shamefacedly.]

An important point arises from this example: Tucker's words have the **potential** to act as an apology; the words only 'become' an apology when Donna chooses to take them as such. I shall return to this example in chapter 7.

Preparatory condition
Does the speaker have to believe that the act was/is/will be to the hearer's disadvantage? I could apologize with perfect sincerity for inadvertently knocking to the floor your full fat double chocolate cheesecake with whipped cream, while privately thinking that you would be much better off not eating it. I have a friend from Japan who, knowing I love Japanese stationery, brings me some whenever she visits England; she routinely apologizes for her gift, even though she knows that I shall be delighted with it.[21]

Sincerity condition
People frequently say they are sorry when they are not. Does this mean that they have not apologized (see chapter 2, section 2.4.1 and note 15)?

Essential condition
As its name suggests, actually **saying** (or writing) that you are sorry seems to be the *sine qua non* of apologizing. But is it, in fact, absolutely essential to utter certain words (or any words at all) in order to apologize (cf. example 13 above)? Perhaps I could be extra nice to you for a while; clean your house; send you a bouquet (say it with flowers!); go around in sackcloth and ashes for forty days? At the time of writing there is an advertisement on British television[22] which begins: 'Why is this man giving his wife chocolates? ... Is it an apology?'

Without labouring the point too much, we rapidly see that such constitutive rules for *apologizing* fail to capture what we recognize as perfectly ordinary, instances of *apologizing*. In order to cope with the (far from exhaustive[23]) list of eventualities I have mentioned so far, our rules would have to start off like this:

Propositional act	The speaker expresses or implies or in some other way indicates regret for a past, present or future act performed by the speaker, or someone or something for which the speaker has responsibility or could be seen to have responsibility (but perhaps has no responsibility whatsoever).
Preparatory condition	The speaker may or may not believe that the act was, is or will be against H's best interests ... and so on.

When we attempt to expand Searle's rules to reflect the way in which the speech act of *apologizing* operates in everyday life, the conditions become hopelessly complex, vague and unworkable. Producing formal rules for the way in which speech acts operate is immensely appealing; unfortunately the rules only work in very restricted circumstances: not only do they exclude perfectly normal instances of speech acts, but they are also so general in their specification that they fail to eliminate anomalous use, as will be shown in the following section.

4.4.2.4 Over-generality of rules

So far I have discussed perfectly ordinary examples of given speech acts which Searle's rules cannot cope with; we can also find totally anomalous examples which his rules will not eliminate. The following is a case in point. Shortly before the British General Election in 1983 Neil Kinnock[24] (the then leader of the British Labour Party) issued a series of explicit 'warnings':

Example 14
If Margaret Thatcher wins on Thursday, I warn you not to be ordinary. I warn you not to be young, I warn you not to fall ill, and I warn you not to grow old.

Mr Kinnock's warnings to the electors are, on the face of it, extremely peculiar, but in fact Mr Kinnock observes all Searle's conditions for *warning* (1969: 67):

Propositional act	Future event or state, E.
Preparatory condition	H has reason to believe E will occur and is not in H's interest.

Sincerity condition   S believes E is not in H's best interest.

Essential condition   Counts as an undertaking to the effect that E is not in H's best interest.

In passing it is worth noting that the conditions specified for *warning* could apply equally to other related speech acts (*informing, advising, cautioning, counselling*) and also, arguably, to a series of completely unrelated speech acts (*putting a curse on someone*, for example).

On the face of it Searle has achieved the odd distinction of producing sets of conditions which are simultaneously over-specific and over-general — which exclude valid instances of a speech act and include invalid or anomalous ones. One reason for this is that Searle treats speech acts as if they were clearly-defined categories with clear-cut boundaries. In reality, as we have seen, the boundaries between, say, *commanding, ordering, requesting, asking* and *inviting* are blurred, overlapping and fluid: the same speech act verb may cover a range of slightly different phenomena, as is illustrated by the mini-case study of *warning* in the next section.

4.4.2.5   The speech act of *warning*: a case study

What Searle does not point out is that (in English) there are at least two different types of *warning*, with different grammatical forms and different conditions. 'Type 1' warnings relate to situations where you can do nothing to avoid the event itself, although it is sometimes possible, as in the case of flood, hurricane or other severe weather warnings (see example 15) to take steps to avoid some of the worst consequences of the event:

Example 15
… she wouldn't take a groom with her, although I warned her that the fog would come down later.[25]

In the case of other Type 1 warnings, which might include events such as delivering some sort of adverse medical prognosis or political prognostication, there is really nothing to be done except to steel yourself for the unpleasant event (see example 16).

Example 16
The speaker was Denis Healey, Chancellor of the Exchequer in the Labour Government:[26]

I warn you there are going to be howls of anguish from the

80,000 people who are rich enough to pay over 75% on the
last slice of their income.

In their direct form, Type 1 warnings often take the grammatical form of **declarative** ('The National Rivers Authority this
morning reiterated that in Devon and Cornwall the severe
weather warning remains in force, with risk of flooding in some
areas'[27]) or **imperative** ('Macbeth, Macbeth, beware Macduff!'[28]).
'Type 2' warnings are designed to avert the unpleasant event
altogether, as in the following example:

Example 17
… told him to go immediately to wherever it was this boy
lived and warn him that if he didn't stop the police would
be informed.[29]

This type of warning frequently appears in the form of a
negative imperative ('Do not lean out of the train window —
danger of decapitation!') or a conditional ('If you move, I'll shoot
you!'). In the case of Type 2 warnings, we would normally expect
an important additional preparatory condition: namely that it is
actually within the power of those warned to avoid future event
or state E.

In English the speech act verb *to warn* covers a wider range
of conditions than the analogous verb in other languages and
because of this Mr Kinnock (in example 14) was able deliberately
to combine elements of both variants, cautioning voters against
a series of events or states which no one can avoid at some stage
in their life. He issues a Type 2 warning but with Type 1
limitations. In this way, Mr Kinnock very skilfully **exploited** the
normal constraints on the first type of *warning* to produce a
powerful piece of political rhetoric.[30] Many (perhaps most)
languages have two different speech act verbs for the two types of
warning[31] and such a 'play on speech acts' would not be possible
(you can test this for yourself by seeing whether you can translate
Mr Kinnock's speech into any language you speak well without
either losing the sense or diminishing the rhetorical effect).

In English there are interesting cases where the two variants
of the verb *to warn* appear to overlap. The following example
offers an illustration of such an 'in-between case'. It is not clear
whether Jack has already eaten so many cakes that the result is
inescapable (Type 1), or whether, if he stopped guzzling now, he
could avoid being sick (Type 2):

Example 18
The following story was related by J. M. Barrie, author of Peter Pan, concerning one of his wards, Jack Llewelyn-Davies, and a friend:

When stuffing himself with cakes at tea, Sylvia had warned him, 'You'll be sick tomorrow.' 'I'll be sick tonight,' replied Jack cheerily.[32]

There are many examples in literature where at least the recipient of the warning appears to be unsure whether s/he is receiving a Type 1 or a Type 2 warning. The story of Oedipus is a case in point: the warnings given by the Oracle to Oedipus and his father led them to take steps to avoid the prophesied events, but, inevitably, things turned out as the Oracle had forewarned.[33]

As in literature, so in life: it is often the case in pragmatics that the most interesting effects are achieved when categories overlap or are blurred (such that one interactant can exploit the uncertainty) or are unclear to one of the participants. This applies not just in the case of speech acts, but to many other linguistic phenomena (such as **discourse roles** and **activity types**[34] (see chapter 7)) and it is a mistake to sacrifice the potential to exploit all the potential richness of meaning of speech acts for the sake of (the appearance of) a tidy system of rules.

4.5 Searle's formal approach to the categorization of speech acts

As we saw when we discussed the speech act of *apologizing* (section 4.4.2.2), the reasons for categorizing a particular locution as performing one speech act rather than another are complex. In real-time interaction we take account of more than just formal criteria (as in Searle's system of classification).

Let us look again at some examples from chapter 3 (in each of which one participant fails to tell the whole truth) and consider whether or not we would wish to classify the key speech act as *lying* and on what basis such a judgement would be made. In example 21 in chapter 3, Alice does not *formally* lie to her husband: i.e. she **says** nothing which is untrue. However, in the context (a husband asking his wife about something of major importance to their relationship) we could legitimately say that Alice's words **function** as a lie and that her **goal** in speaking as she did was to deceive her husband; in this type of event and in the context of an intimate relationship, anything other than the complete truth functions as a lie. If we consider example 22 in chapter 3, however (in which the England athletics team official said something which was true, but, once again, not the whole truth), we might be less inclined to classify the woman's utterance as a lie. Unlike Alice, the spokeswoman had nothing to gain personally from not revealing the whole truth and moreover it is part of her job to protect the interests of team members. For these reasons we are psychologically less disposed to condemn her. In example 32 in chapter 3 we noted that Sir Robert Armstrong was disinclined to categorize as *lying* his misleading words to the Australian court; here **affective** (emotional) factors come into play: we are less likely to classify in a negative way the behaviour of people we like or respect (including ourselves!).

There are certain **contexts** in which we do not expect the truth to be told: satirical comedy and funeral orations are two contexts in which we do not generally expect to hear the whole, unvarnished truth. Then again there are some culturally-specific situations in which the whole truth is not expected (e.g. in *mañana* cultures we do not classify as a liar the plumber or electrician who undertakes to turn up at a given time but then fails to appear: all parties involved have learnt that such promises must be taken with a pinch of salt). Finally there are times when a speaker does not tell the whole truth in order to avoid hurting the hearer's feelings or to avoid revealing something learned in confidence; would we necessarily classify these actions as *lies*?

Coleman and Kay (1981) in a most interesting article show that people's reasons for classifying something as *a lie* or *not a lie* are extremely complex. We not only take account of formal considerations (cf. Searle), but also of **functional, psychological** and **affective** factors; sometimes the way in which we classify a speech act may be influenced by considerations which are **culturally-specific** (or context-specific) or which relate to the speaker's **goal** in speaking in a particular way. We see then that a whole constellation of features contribute to the way in which **participants in interaction** (rather than analysts examining the data after the event) classify a speech act. The criteria they use are far richer and more complex than those which appear in descriptive frameworks of the type proposed by Searle, and include a range of different sorts of criteria.

Searle's rules, by his own admission, are capable of coping only with the most typical or central instances of a speech act and fail to distinguish adequately between one speech act and another.

In reality, as we have seen, the reasons for classifying a speech act in a particular way are complex and it is often impossible to assign a speech act to a clear cut category. However, my objection is not that Searle's rules can only cope with a few paradigm cases (this would simply be an argument for improving the rules) — rather, as I shall argue below, the whole approach to describing speech acts in terms of rules was misconceived.

Within linguistics there is a powerful push towards formalization; formalisms give an impression of intellectual rigour which, when applied to most areas of pragmatics, has proved to be almost entirely illusory. In the next section I shall discuss an alternative approach to describing speech acts, which captures some of their complexities without falling into the trap of establishing overly-restrictive rules.

From the example I gave of the speech act of *apologizing* it should be apparent that it is extremely difficult (if not impossible) to devise **rules** which capture satisfactorily the complexity of speech acts: too many different criteria and different types of criteria are involved. In the sections which follow I shall argue that it is necessary to recognize that speech acts can never be satisfactorily characterized in terms of rules but are better described in terms of principles.

4.6 Rules versus principles

As the following quotation (Searle 1969: 38) shows, Searle believed that it was possible to describe speech acts in terms of rules:

> ... *the hypothesis of this book is that speaking a language is a matter of performing speech acts according to systems of constitutive rules.*

In sections 4.4–4.5 I tried to show that Searle failed in his attempt to describe speech acts in terms of **'constitutive rules'** (see section 4.6.3, below). In this section I shall argue that not only did Searle not succeed, but that a rule-governed approach to the description of speech acts never could succeed. Searle was attempting to handle pragmatics in a manner appropriate to grammar. Pragmatics (as I shall show further in chapter 7) seeks different sorts of generalizations from those made within grammar (by which I mean phonology, syntax and semantics). Grammar is governed by rules, pragmatics is constrained by maxims or principles (these two terms can be used interchangeably). There are five basic differences between rules and principles (based on Leech 1983a: 8 and 21ff). I shall begin by stating rather starkly the differences between the two types of generalizations:

- Rules are all or nothing, principles are more or less.

- Rules are exclusive, principles can co-occur.

- Rules are constitutive, principles are regulative.

- Rules are definite, principles are probabilistic.

- Rules are conventional, principles are motivated.

4.6.1 Rules are all or nothing, principles are more or less

Rules are yes/no in their application — either a rule is in operation or it isn't: either you do apply the rule of subject-verb concord or you don't. You cannot apply it partially. Some Gricean maxims, on the other hand, as we saw in section 4.2.3, **can** apply in varying degrees: you can speak extremely clearly, fairly clearly or not at all clearly (Manner), you can give far too much information, slightly too much information or insufficient information (Quantity). And as we shall see in chapter 6, interpersonal principles/maxims can also be observed to different degrees — you can be extremely polite or moderately polite.

4.6.2 Rules are exclusive, principles can co-occur

Rules are exclusive in the sense that invoking one rule precludes invoking another. Consider the English pronominal system. When nouns are replaced by pronouns, the grammar of English requires that *he* is used to replace nouns referring to a male person (and some male animals), *she* is used to replace nouns referring to a female person (and some female animals), while *they* is the plural pronoun, referring to either animate or inanimate entities. Pronoun choice is problematical if you do not know the sex of the person concerned, e.g. *Someone's left [his? her? their?] briefcase in my room.* If you choose *their*, some self-styled 'purists' would consider that you have violated the rule of number concord; if you choose *his* you risk violating the rule of gender concord and may also cause confusion.[35] What you **cannot** do (and this is the key issue for the present argument) is to invoke both rules simultaneously: *Someone's left their his briefcase ...

In pragmatics, however, you **can** invoke two or more principles simultaneously: you can observe both the maxims of Manner and Quantity (by giving the right amount of information in a clear manner). And this is true even if those maxims 'clash' (see Leech 1983a: 82–3 and 137 and chapters 5 and 6 below). For example, you may find yourself in a situation where it is difficult to be both polite and truthful (to observe both the Politeness Principle and the Quality Maxim); it is, nevertheless, possible to do so by employing indirectness (see chapter 5), as in the following example:

Example 19
A is a waiter in a pretentious, but second-rate restaurant. B is a gourmet, who runs his own restaurant:[36]

A: Did you enjoy the lamb, Sir?
B: It was very interesting.

4.6.3 Rules are constitutive, principles are regulative

Constitutive rules **define** a system; regulative rules **regulate** a system. For example, a constitutive rule of chess is that a bishop can only be moved diagonally on its own colour. Of course, there is nothing which **physically** prevents you from moving your bishop straight up or down the board on whatever colour you please, perhaps knocking your opponents pieces to the floor for good measure. But if you broke the rules in this way, you would not be playing chess. A regulative rule of chess is that it is not generally a good idea to sacrifice your queen for a pawn. One type of rules defines the game, another describes how people play the game well (successfully) or badly.

Descriptive grammars provide constitutive rules, telling us what are/are not grammatically well-formed sentences in a given language;[37] a pragmatic description of that same language will include maxims/principles showing how people make choices from within the grammatical system in order to achieve their goals, behave appropriately, etc.

4.6.4 Rules are definite, principles are probabilistic

In grammar, the aim is to devise rules which have no (or very few) counter-examples. If a sufficiently powerful counter-example is found, the rule (see note 37) fails and has to be re-formulated. In pragmatics, we cannot say with absolute certainty what something means or what effect an utterance will have, the best we can do is to state with more or less certainty what is *probably* the case. This applies within all areas of pragmatics, including textual pragmatics (example 20), to speech acts (example 21):

> **Example 20**
> *This extract is taken from a novel by Sue Townsend in which Britain has been declared a Republic; the Queen and her family have gone to live on a council estate in the Midlands. King is the leader of a pack of street dogs, in which Kylie is the most desirable bitch. Harris is the Queen's corgi while Susan, another corgi, belongs to the Queen Mother. Harris is trying to ingratiate himself with the pack and urgently needs to gain some street-cred:*
>
> He was edging nearer to Kylie when King got to his feet and pricked his ears and stared at the far end of the Recreation Ground, where a strange dog could be seen in the distance. Harris recognized the intruder immediately. It was Susan, his half sister, running slightly ahead of Philomena Toussaint and the Queen Mother, who were strolling arm-in-arm, enjoying the spring sunshine. Harris had never liked Susan. She was a snob and, anyway, he was jealous of her fancy wardrobe ... Harris saw an opportunity to enhance his reputation with the Pack and he left the line and ran towards Susan, barking furiously. Susan turned tail and ran back towards the Queen Mother, but she wasn't a match for Harris, who easily caught up with her and bit her hard on her nose. The Queen Mother swiped at Harris with the walking stick she was carrying and shouted, 'Harris, you horrid little dog!'

From our knowledge of English grammar, we know that the pronouns *she* and *her* must have a female referent and in the sentence beginning *She was a snob ...* there is only one candidate — *Susan*; however, in the sentence beginning *Susan turned tail ...*, *she/her/her/her* are referentially ambiguous and (according to rules of grammar) could apply equally to *Susan* or to the *Queen Mother*.

Pragmatically, we know (for reasons external to the text) that the more likely candidate for being bitten on the nose is the unfortunate Susan (corgis are lower to the ground than dowager queens, which makes their noses more vulnerable). Both are possible referents, *Susan* is the more probable.[38]

> **Example 21**
> *The following extract is taken from a Colin Dexter novel. The setting is the coroner's inquest into the death of Matthew Rodway, an Oxford undergraduate, who had apparently committed suicide:*[39]
>
> Dr Felix McClure, one of Rodway's former tutors, was questioned about an obviously genuine but unfinished letter found in Rodway's rooms, containing the sentence 'I've had enough of all this'.
>
> Whilst he stoutly maintained that the words themselves were ambivalent in their implication, Dr McClure agreed with the Coroner that the most likely explanation of events was that Rodway had been driven to take his own life.

The sentence: *I've had enough of all this*, has, as McClure points out, a number of things (a complaint, a threat to a third party), but the jury is able to decide what it **probably** means.

4.6.5 Rules are conventional, principles are motivated

Rules are conventional (arbitrary), principles are motivated. It makes no sense to look at the following paradigm for tag questions and complain (as my Ukrainian students used regularly to do) that the *I*-form doesn't follow the pattern:

> You're coming, aren't you?
> He's coming, isn't he?
> *but* I'm coming, <u>aren't I?</u>

Am't I? they would argue, would be more logical than *aren't I?* and I would have to agree. But reason doesn't come into it. The point is that *am't I?* is not acceptable in standard English. For whatever reason, reversed polarity question tags have evolved in this way, the language is as it is and it is no good arguing for a more logical pattern.

Pragmatic principles, on the other hand, **are** motivated. If people find that they are more likely to achieve their aims if they speak politely, clearly and to the point they will do so. If, on the other hand, they find that their goals are best served by being rude, ambiguous and evasive (if they are a member of the Government, for example) then they will be just that.

The English pronominal system offers a useful illustration of motivation and of the division of labour between grammar and pragmatics: pronoun choice is covered by two sets of constraints — grammatical and social (pragmatic). Different sets of pronoun choices are available in different areas of the animal kingdom. When we refer to human beings we are almost always obliged to use gender-specific pronouns. It is not normally grammatically possible to use any pronouns other than *he/him/his* when referring to male human beings or to use any pronouns other than *she/her/hers* when referring to female human beings. Thus it is possible to say:

No, Peter is her son — her husband's name is John.

but we cannot say:

★No, Peter is her son — his/its husband's name is John.

Nor, as a rule, is it socially permissible to use other than gender-specific pronouns in relation to human beings. An exception to this norm is found in the case of unborn or very young children, in relation to whom some people find it appropriate to use the pronoun *it*, regardless of whether the infant's sex is known to them.

Example 22
He's unlikely to have died unbaptised, is he? I mean every infant was done in those days, wasn't it?[40]

Example 23
*Kay is talking to a man who claims to be her father. Both parties know the sex of the baby under discussion (in fact, Kay is speculating about **her own** birth):*

So let us say the child was conceived in early May 1903 ... It would have been born in January 1904. My date of birth is 9 January 1904.[41]

Another area of uncertainty is where the person is dead. In the following example the same speaker (Captain Bobby) uses both *him* and *it*, in respect of the same dead man:

Example 24
*Chief of police Captain Bobby has brought the surgeon Carriscant
to examine the body of a murdered soldier:*[42]

Carriscant slithered down the grassy bank behind Bobby
who was handed a hooded lantern by one of the soldiers.
'It's under the bridge,' Bobby said flatly ...
The body of the man had been propped against the stone
supports of the bridge's first arch, almost as if it had sat
down there for a rest and had fallen into a doze. It still had
trousers and boots ...
'Found at midnight,' Bobby said, his voice reverberating
beneath the vault of the bridge. 'He was on furlough ...'

Apart from these and a few other very special cases,[43] when
we are talking about human beings the choice of pronoun is
powerfully constrained by the grammar of English and cannot be
flouted without causing the gravest offence.[44]

At the other end of the evolutionary scale, when we talk
about insects we almost invariably use gender-neutral pronouns.
It would be unusual to refer to a bee as *she*, even if you were an
expert apiarist and knew the insect's sex. But in the vast area
between human beings and insects, and particularly when we are
dealing with other mammals, we do have considerable choice as
to which pronouns to use (and where there is grammatical
choice, there is pragmatic meaning). Compare the two examples
which follow, each of which concerns a cow (which is, by
definition, female):

Example 25
*The newsreader was referring to a cow, which had set off an IRA
booby trap bomb.*[45]

But the device was triggered by a cow when it walked onto
the trip mechanism.

Example 26
*This extract was taken from a BBC Radio 4 'soap opera'. The
speaker is a farmer:*[46]

It's the new heifer, she's kicked off her clusters and got her
legs tangled ...

Grammatically it is possible to refer to any of the so-called 'higher' animals by a gender-specific pronoun or the gender-neutral *it*. A variety of pragmatic factors govern the pronoun chosen. The most obvious one is whether or not the speaker **knows** the sex of the animal concerned (in the case of cows you do not have to be an expert stock keeper to work out the creature's sex, but with other animals, such as cats, it can be very difficult to tell). A second factor is professionalism — it is very unusual to hear people professionally involved with animals (farmers, breeders, stable hands, vets) use other than gender-marked pronouns — to do so marks them as members of an 'in-group'. Pet owners or people who have a sentimental attachment to an animal do the same. Even people who loathe animals (or babies!) and who privately refer to them as *it* refrain, out of politeness, from doing so in front of the owner (or parent).[47] The following example is slightly different — the pronoun *he* is used in reference to a drawing (rather than a photograph) of a dog. The intention is clearly to get us to identify with the animal more closely; to think of the dog as if it were our own pet:

Example 27
Notices in public car parks in the Lake District in summer. The signs have a picture of a dog shut in a car on a hot day:

He may be dead by the time you get back.

Thus we see that both grammar and pragmatics affect pronoun choice: the grammar of the language tells us what forms are available, while a variety of pragmatic factors (cognitive, psychological, social, affective and interpersonal) influence the choice we make.

4.7 Conclusion

In this chapter we have explored the concept of motivation principally in relation to textual pragmatics. In chapters 5 and 6 we shall explore the notion of motivation in relation to interpersonal pragmatics.

Notes

1. Thomas Hood (1826) 'Past and present'.

2. I owe this example to Liz Eyes.

3. Joanna Trollope (1992) *The men and the girls*. Black Swan, London, pp. 309-10.

4. Report in *The Guardian*, 20 March 1984.

5. William Shakespeare, *Hamlet*, Act II, scene ii.

6. A point well made in Dascal (1977).

7. Observed September 1994.

8. Note that the linguistic form of the message was interrogative, grammatically requiring a question mark, but it had none. I have often observed that people tend to punctuate for the pragmatic force of a message rather than the grammatical form. Could this indicate that the pragmatic force is in some sense prime?

9. Searle himself (1991: 85–9) argued that his emphasis on **Intentionality** constitutes a major difference between his approach and that of Grice.

10. 'Rules' are more powerful generalizations than are maxims/principles. On the distinction between 'rules' and 'principles' or 'maxims', see section 4.6 below.

11. Catherine Aird (1969) *The complete steel*. Macdonald, London, p. 149.

12. Taken from P. D. James (1994) *Original sin*. Faber and Faber, London, p. 271.

13. Taken from William Boyd (1993) *The blue afternoon*. Penguin Books, Harmondsworth, pp. 141-2.

14. Note that *ask* appears in both lists. A discussion of the way in which speech acts overlap is taken up in *The dynamics of discourse*.

15.   Searle argues (not very convincingly, in my view) that his concept of Intentionality (see note 9) gets round the problem of circularity (1991: 88):

'… that sort of circularity is always a danger … We have a notion of Intentionality which is prior to meaning, so there is no circularity in explaining meaning using Intentionality.'

16.   All three writing in E. Lepore and R. van Gulick (eds) (1991) *John Searle and his critics*. Basil Blackwell, Oxford.

17.   Note that there is considerable cross-cultural variation in perceptions of 'responsibility'. A Japanese friend reports being very upset by an incident which occurred in Australia, when the parents of a fellow student who had damaged her car offered no apology whatsoever for the incident. Presumably the Australian parents felt that their adult daughter was entirely responsible for her own actions.

In Germany you can be held legally, as well as morally, responsible if your cat digs up your neighbour's garden. In England, cats are held to be a law unto themselves and beyond anyone's control; you cannot be held responsible for the actions of your cat.

18.   When we (briefly) had a Minister for Sport in Britain, his principal occupation seemed to be to apologize for the behaviour of English football supporters overseas.

19.   At the execution of William Tyndale (credited with being the first translator of the New Testament from Greek into English) in 1536, the executioner (reportedly) said:

'For what I am about to do, I beg your forgiveness, Sir.'

20.   Episode entitled 'Stormy weather', broadcast 20th September 1994, ITV.

21.   It is important to note, however, that the speech act verb *to apologize* covers a very different range of illocutionary acts in Japanese and in English. For example, an act which in English would be accomplished using *thank you*, in Japanese may be accomplished using *I'm sorry* (see Okamura 1990). This is a topic which is taken up in *The dynamics of discourse*.

22. Advertisement for Bendinck's chocolate. December 1994.

23. For comprehensive studies which set out the true complexities of *apologizing* see, for example, Holmes (1990).

24. Speaking in Bridgend, two days before the British General Election in June 1983.

25. Pamela Bennets (1987) *Topaz*. Robert Hale Ltd, London.

26. Referring to forthcoming increases in the rate of taxation, during a speech at the Labour Party Conference, 1 January 1973.

27. BBC Radio 4 newsflash, 29 December 1994.

28. Apparition's warning to Macbeth in *Macbeth*, Act IV, Scene 1.

29. William Trevor (1976) *The children of Dynmouth*. Bodley Head, London.

30. Paradoxically, Mr Kinnock's words *did* operate as a warning, but not against the states or events specified in the speech acts. The overall meaning of Kinnock's words was a warning not to vote Conservative.

31. For example, Luganda would use *kujjukiza* or *kugamba* for the first type of warning and *kulabula* for the second type.

32. Andrew Birkin (1979) *J M Barrie and the lost boys*. Constable and Co., Ltd, London, p. 99.

33. Both Oedipus and his father, Laius, King of Thebes, were warned on separate occasions by the Oracle that Oedipus would kill his father. Laius tried to avoid his fate by exposing his baby son on the hillside (where he was found and adopted by Polybus, King of Thebes) and Oedipus by fleeing Thebes.

34. The issue of category overlap in both these areas is taken up in *The dynamics of discourse*.

35. There are, of course, a number of ways of avoiding the problem altogether. See, for example, Leech and Svartvik (1994 [1975]: 56–7).

36. *Pie in the sky*. BBC 1, 15 January 1995.

37. The grammar of most languages will, of course, contain a number of **variable** rules. These generally apply to sociolinguistic variables — different social groups, or regions may have different rules — but even in standard spoken English, the use of *a* or *an* before aspirated /h/ is a variable rule. Some speakers always say *a* hotel, some speakers always say *an* hotel, but many will vary as to which they say — the same individual may use both forms within one interaction.

38. It is more probable because of our 'physical prototype knowledge', one of nine 'knowledge types' discussed and developed in McEnery (1995).

39. Colin Dexter (1994) *The daughters of Cain*. Macmillan, London, p. 48.

40. Catherine Aird (1994 [1967]) *A most contagious game*, Chivers Press, London, p. 162.

41. William Boyd (1993) *The blue afternoon*. Penguin, Harmondsworth, p. 297.

42. William Boyd (1993) *The blue afternoon*. Penguin, Harmondsworth, p. 135.

43. Just occasionally, talking among themselves, male homosexuals might refer to other male homosexuals as *she*.

44. An example of this was widely reported in the popular press in November 1994 (it is too offensive for me to quote verbatim here). A transcript was made of a secret recording of a conversation which was alleged to have taken place between a footballer, Bruce Grobellar, and one of his former business associates. During the alleged conversation Grobellar repeatedly referred to a woman with whom he had engaged in casual sex as 'it', thereby reducing her (as the newspaper commentators pointed out) to the status of a 'thing'.

45. BBC Radio 4 news, 14 November 1990.

46. David Archer in *The Archers*, 11 November 1990.

47. Several people have commented to me that they will select a sex at random rather than refer to an unknown cat or dog as *it* in front of its owner.

CHAPTER 5

Pragmatics and indirectness

5.1 Introduction

In chapter 3 we looked at the mechanisms which allow the hearer to interpret indirectness — how a hearer works out what a speaker means by the words he or she utters. In this chapter I am going to explore indirectness further and discuss how and why it is used. As we have seen, indirectness occurs when there is a mismatch between the expressed meaning and the implied meaning. Indirectness is a universal phenomenon: as far as we know it occurs in all natural languages,[1] a fact which in itself requires some explaining.

5.2 Pragmatics and indirectness

There are four points which should be borne in mind in this discussion of indirectness:[2]

- We shall be concerned with intentional indirectness.

- Indirectness is costly and risky.

- We assume (unless we have evidence to the contrary) that the speakers are behaving in a rational manner and, given the universality of indirectness, that they obtain some social or communicative advantage through employing indirectness.

- For the purposes of this argument, we shall ignore the possibility that X cannot be expressed.

5.2.1 Intentional indirectness

Not all indirectness is intentional; some is caused by linguistic inadequacy, for example, when you do not know the correct word for some object in your own or a foreign language. This happened to me once in France, when I went into a shop to buy some coat hangers. It was only after I had attracted the attention of the shop assistant that I realized that I couldn't remember how to ask for them in French and I was forced to try to describe their use and appearance in a roundabout way. I was not trying to imply anything by my indirectness, nor was I trying to avoid an embarrassing topic, nor to spare my own or my hearer's feelings; I had simply forgotten the word. On other occasions we may have to use indirectness because of some performance error — for example, if you temporarily forget a word or, through fear, nervousness, excitement, etc., cannot get it out. The use of indirectness in these circumstances may lead the hearer to infer all sorts of things about you, but you cannot be said to have generated any implicatures. In pragmatics we are interested only in intentional indirectness (although, as we noted in chapter 4 (section 4.2.1), it is not always possible to say with certainty whether indirectness is intended or not).

5.2.2 Indirectness is costly and risky

In an excellent discussion Dascal (1983) makes the point that indirectness is costly and risky. It is 'costly' in the sense that an indirect utterance takes longer for the speaker to produce and longer for the hearer to process (a fact which has frequently been confirmed in psycholinguistic experiments). It is 'risky' in the sense that the hearer may not understand what the speaker is getting at. Consider the two interactions which follow:

Example 1
B (a non-native speaker of English) has been staying with A for several weeks. He has a passion for West Side Story *and has just played the film's sound track right through for the second time in one evening:*[3]

A: Would you like to listen to something else now?
B: No.

In order to avoid making a direct complaint to his guest, which could hurt his feelings, A suggests indirectly that he has had enough of *West Side Story*. However, his strategy fails; B interprets A's utterance as a genuine question and prepares to play the record for a third time!

Example 2
The following was related to me by Elite Olshtain and I have reconstructed the dialogue from memory. An American woman was visiting Israel; one evening she went to the flat of some friends and her host asked her what she would like to drink. She replied:

'Well, I've been on whisky all day.'

The American woman intended to indicate indirectly that, having been drinking whisky previously, she would prefer to stick with whisky. Unfortunately, the host misinterpreted her indirectness and thought she was saying that, as she had been on whisky all day, she didn't want any more to drink.

5.2.3 Assumption of rationality

You may think that assuming that your interlocutor is behaving rationally is a pretty big assumption to make! People do, of course, behave irrationally with tiresome frequency, but nevertheless we tend to assume, **until we have evidence to the contrary**, that people have reasons for behaving as they do. Let us begin with a non-linguistic analogy. When I first started working at Lancaster, I was sitting in my office when I noticed that everyone coming across the quadrangle made a detour at a certain point for no obvious reason. However hard I looked, I could not work out why they all avoided one particular area. I had no reason to think that they were all mad or that their behaviour was caused by some bizarre superstition, so I was forced to seek some other explanation. After a while another new member of staff came along, failed to make the detour, trod on a rocky paving stone and received a jet of filthy water up her legs. In this case there was a perfectly sensible explanation for the way the first set of people had behaved (they all knew the paving was loose). But what if it turned out that they had all made the detour because they believed an evil troll lived under that particular flagstone? If you genuinely believe that behaving in a certain way or performing a certain action (e.g. walking under a ladder) will bring you bad luck or cause you harm, it makes sense not to do it; given an irrational belief, the behaviour is rational.

So it is with language. You observe that everyone (or, at

least, everyone who is 'in the know') employs indirectness on certain occasions, even though to do so apparently costs them unnecessary effort. One possible conclusion is that they are all behaving irrationally, but, unless we have reason to think that this is indeed the case (and bearing in mind that the phenomenon of indirectness is universal), we are more likely to conclude that people obtain some advantage or avoid some negative consequence by employing indirectness. They may wish to avoid hurting someone else (as in example 1), or appearing 'pushy' (as in example 2) or to show how clever they are, as in the following example:

Example 3
He wouldn't stoop to a lie where a half truth would do!

Or people may employ indirectness because they are prey to some superstitions or are avoiding a taboo word or topic (as we saw in section 3.7.4). But whatever the underlying motivation for using indirectness (even if it is because of an irrational belief) the use of indirectness itself is perfectly rational, if it enables the speaker to achieve his or her goal or to avoid unpleasantness.

5.2.4 The principle of expressibility

I have said that for the purposes of this discussion we shall ignore the possibility that something (e.g. a concept or an emotion) cannot be expressed. Otherwise we could argue that instead of choosing to use indirectness, a speaker was forced to do so because what he or she wished to say was inexpressible. In pragmatics most people, with some reservations, subscribe to the **'principle of expressibility'**,[4] which states that 'anything that can be meant can be said'. This boils down to the belief that human beings can find a way of putting into words anything they need to say (this does not mean that any one individual can necessarily put into words everything he or she wishes to say).

I mentioned some reservations in accepting the principle of expressibility. In addition to the linguistic inadequacy or performance errors discussed earlier which might render us (temporarily or permanently) unable to express something, there are things which (arguably) **all** human beings find impossible to express. This could be because certain concepts are beyond our present understanding. For example, in July 1994 someone wrote into the 'Your Letters' slot on the BBC Radio 4 programme,

P.M., asking 'Does the present exist?'. For weeks afterwards listeners wrote in attempting to answer the question, but no one was able to define the concept without resorting to various forms of indirectness, including poetry or figures of speech such as metaphors and similes. The same applies to the expression of very powerful emotions, such as love.

5.2.5 Indirectness — an illustration

The following example illustrates how the issues I raised above work out in practice.

> **Example 4**
> *The following was a note sent by our Departmental Secretary to a research student one Friday afternoon:*
>
> Dear Beulah,
>
> A research student named *[name deleted]* from Zambia is arriving at Manchester tomorrow at 19.30. She's, got a room booked in County College and I don't know whether she will have any money or not. She can see me on Monday morning and we'll sort things out.

Several interesting points arise from this letter. The first is that everyone from my Department to whom I have shown this note has been in no doubt at all what Beulah was expected to do: to look out for the new student, to take her to her college, to lend her some money if necessary and to bring her into the Department on Monday. Yet none of this is explicitly stated. We saw in chapter 3 some of the processes which enabled people to interpret the writer's intention so accurately. The second question which arises is *why*, if that is what the secretary meant, did she not write precisely that? After all, the original version was twice as long as it needed to be to convey the message (**the propositional content**). Moreover, she risked being misunderstood — a few outsiders to whom I showed the note thought that Beulah was expected to travel to Manchester airport to meet the new student. So, if we assume that the writer is a rational being, we must also assume that she expected to obtain some social or communicative advantage from using indirectness. In this case the explanation is very simple: the secretary had no right to **tell** the student to perform these tasks, so she simply used a series of hints. In this case the writer judged with great skill the degree of indirectness required by the situation; the strategies she adopted worked very well and Beulah did what was wanted — an indirect approach succeeded where a direct order would certainly have failed.

5.3 How do we know how indirect to be?

We have seen that directness is universal in the sense that it occurs to some degree in all (natural) languages, but that does not mean that we always employ indirectness or that we all employ indirectness in the same way. Individuals and cultures vary widely in how, when and why they use an indirect speech act in preference to a direct one. Nevertheless, there are a number of factors which appear to govern indirectness in all languages and cultures. Note that I am emphatically **not** saying that all languages/cultures will employ indirectness in the same circumstances (an American may broach only indirectly a topic which in Britain would be tackled head-on, and vice versa). Nor am I saying that the form which the indirectness takes will be the same (we find systematic variation even across different varieties of English). The axes governing indirectness are 'universal' in that they capture the types of consideration likely to govern pragmatic choices in any language, but the way they are applied varies considerably from culture to culture. The main factors[5] are listed below, and I shall discuss each in order:

- The relative power of the speaker over the hearer

- The social distance between the speaker and the hearer

- The degree to which X is rated an imposition in culture Y

- Relative rights and obligations between the speaker and the hearer.

5.3.1 Power

The general point is that we tend to use a greater degree of indirectness with people who have some power or authority over us than to those who do not. You would probably be more indirect about conveying to your employer that you are annoyed by the fact that he or she always arrives late, than in conveying the same to your brother. This is partly because your employer can influence your career in a positive way (reward power) or a negative way (coercive power). These types of power are most apparent in obviously hierarchical settings, such as courts, the military, the workplace, although in the examples which follow the power depends not so much on the seniority/authority position of the interrogator, as his special power over a suspect in custody. Here are four separate extracts, taken from the interrogation of a naval rating by the S.I.B. (the Special Investigations Bureau of the Royal Navy, the military equivalent of the C.I.D.), which clearly illustrate coercive power.

Example 5

A is a senior N.C.O., B is a naval officer (both members of the S.I.B.). C is a naval rating, accused of drug dealing. The examples are taken from a ten-minute extract of a much longer interrogation:

1. A: You know what I'm going to do? I'm going to make sure you get locked away.

2. B: It's as simple as that. You're goin' to be pleased to [*sic*] punch when we start pulling matelots in from Nelson ... Then we'll, we'll mention your name just to see if they know anything about it ... Then there's the possibility that they'll think that you grassed on them.

3. B: It's not beneath me, you know. If you want to stitch me up, I'll stitch you up.

4. B: All I can say is stuff you because er I think You're a complete and utter shit. I really do, erm, if it means me making your life a misery before you go outside I will bloody do that, and that is no lie.
    C: I can't be more miserable than what I am here.
    B: Oh don't you believe it. Don't you believe it, you don't know misery yet, Smith.

I have noted on a number of occasions in this book how frequently speakers make explicit reference to their reasons for speaking as they do. This gives powerful support to the contention that certain pragmatic factors are consciously responded to by interactants. The next extract, in which explicit reference is made to coercive power, is a case in point (but in this instance the police lieutenant is telling a subordinate that, on this occasion, he does not have the power to force him to do something):

Example 6

The speakers are Lieutenant Leaphorn and Officer Chee of the Navajo tribal police. Leaphorn is about to resign his post, but is pursuing an investigation unofficially:[6]

'You want to stick with me a little longer on this Friedman-Bernal business?' he asked. 'If you do, I can arrange it with Captain Largo.'

Chee had hesitated, out of surprise. Leaphorn had identified the pause as indecision.

'I should remind you again that I'm quitting the department,' Leaphorn had interjected. 'I'm on terminal leave right now. I already told you that. I tell you now so if you're doing me a favor, remember there's no way I can return it.'

→ Which, Chee had thought, was a nice way of saying the reverse — I can't punish you for refusing.

Spencer-Oatey, in her discussion of reward power in relation to postgraduate students in Britain and China, focuses predominantly on students' perceptions of the reward power held by their academic supervisors. Reward power in these circumstances could relate to something as simple as lending books/ articles, pointing the students towards useful leads, etc. Or it could also relate to the students' belief that their supervisors have the power to influence their future job prospects, etc. However, there are many very obvious examples of reward power in most walks of life and some of the most explicit are to be found in job advertisements. The following[7] is very typical:

Example 7

... In return you can expect an attractive salary and benefits package, including 28 days' holiday, pension scheme, free life assurance and an interest-free season ticket loan.

Reward power and coercive power are the most 'naked' and the most obvious. However, power is present to a degree in all relationships, at least some of the time. Spencer-Oatey (1992) discusses different types and components of power at some length. I summarize her account very briefly here. In addition to the two categories already mentioned, we find:

Legitimate power	One person has the right to prescribe or request certain things by virtue of role, age or status.
Referent power	One person has power over another because the other admires and wants to be like him/her in some respect.
Expert power	In this case, one person has some special knowledge or expertise which the other person needs;

'Legitimate power', like reward power and coercive power, remains fairly constant within a relationship; it is the type of power most subject to cross-cultural variation. For example, teachers in some cultures can expect, by virtue of their role and status, that students will routinely perform certain tasks for them (carry their books, clean the boards, even run errands) while in another culture this would be unthinkable. As so often happens in pragmatics, we often encounter explicit reference to such power (e.g. 'I'm your mother, I have a right to know). In the following example, Kate makes it clear that she has the power to make Joss move, by virtue of being Joss's mother:

Example 8
Kate has been living with her lover for seven years; now she intends to move out and take Joss, her daughter, with her.[8]

'I don't want to,' Joss said. 'Right? You can do whatever bloody stupid thing you want, but you're not making me do it too. I'm not coming.'
'You have to,' Kate said. 'You're under sixteen and you're my daughter, and you have to come and live with me.'

Referent power is rather different from the other types of power, in that it is often not exerted consciously (you may be unaware that someone admires you from afar and emulates you!). In some societies, people in the public eye or with responsibilities for young people are assumed (rightly or wrongly) to have referent power and are placed under an obligation to act as a suitable role model; teachers, for example, may be required to behave, or even to dress, in a particular (invariably conservative) manner. It is the sort of power which pop stars and sports idols are alleged to have over the young.[9] The following press and TV reports of events during a Test Match between England and South Africa illustrate the importance of referent power in the eyes of cricketing enthusiasts:

> **Example 9**
> *Mike Atherton, captain of the English cricket team, was given out lbw on the first ball. He was judged to have 'shown dissent' because a television close-up showed him shaking his head as he walked back to the pavilion. He was fined £1,250:*
>
> Yesterday's fine appears to refer less to the sin than the need for Atherton to set an example ...[10]
>
> It is the duty of the captain of England to set a good example.[11]

We can only pray that there is no outbreak of head-shaking among the youth of England.

Expert power is, on the whole, more transient than the other types of power I have discussed. For example, if an individual has great expertise in, say, computing, he or she may have considerable (if temporary) power over someone who desperately needs to draw on that knowledge. But the computer expert may, in turn, have to defer to the person he or she was instructing earlier when it comes to finding out how to prepare a lemon soufflé.

5.3.2 Social distance

The term 'social distance' (Leech 1983a: 126) is the opposite of Brown and Gilman's (1960) 'solidarity factor'. It is best seen as a composite of psychologically real factors (status, age, sex, degree of intimacy, etc.) which 'together determine the overall degree of respectfulness' within a given speech situation. In other words, if you feel close to someone, because that person is related to you, or you know him or her well or are similar in terms of age, social class, occupation, sex, ethnicity, etc., you feel less need to employ indirectness in, say, making a request than you would if you were making the same request of a complete stranger.

> **Example 10**
> *The speaker wanted some change for the coffee machine. She first approached a colleague whom she knew very well, but, when he could not help, was forced to approach a complete stranger [a man*

considerably older than she was]:

Got change of fifty pence, DB?

Excuse me, could you change fifty pence for me? I need
tens or fives for the coffee machine.

It is sometimes difficult to distinguish between Power and
Social Distance and in fact some studies conflate the two. (See,
for example, the description of the questionnaire-design for the
Cross Cultural Speech Act Research Project, reported in Blum-
Kulka, House and Kasper (1989). When those involved (including myself) discussed the project, we identified power and social
distance as separate dimensions, but in practice we did not
maintain the distinction.) The reason they are so often confused
is that power and social distance very frequently co-occur — we
tend to be socially distant from those in power over us (e.g. in the
workplace). But this is by no means always the case; Aeginitou
(1995) clearly shows how in the language classroom students are
often close to their teachers, even though there is a marked
inequality of power. In the following example the interactants are
in an unequal power relationship, but are nevertheless quite close
to one another, as is revealed by the address forms used:

Example 11
*This is an extract from an (authentic) interview between a detective
superintendent and a detective constable of the Thames Valley
police:*

DS: … that's the way. Come back bloody fighting.
                 Let's have, let's have some grit about it.

DC: I know governor, now I've done that …

The detective constable is being disciplined and transferred
from the plain clothes to the uniformed division of the police
(which he regards as a demotion). For the first ten minutes of the
interaction the detective constable has used only very formal
language, although the detective superintendent addresses him by
his first name throughout; up to this point, the detective constable has addressed his superior officer as 'Sir' no fewer than eleven
times. Just before this extract begins, the detective constable has
started to cry, and the detective superintendent changes his tone
somewhat, speaking to him 'man to man', swearing ('bloody')
and using informal terms ('grit'). The detective constable

responded by addressing him as 'governor' which marks a close, but still subordinate relationship.

5.3.3 Size of imposition

When we talk about 'size of imposition' we mean how great is the request you are making? For example, you would probably use a greater degree of indirectness in asking to borrow £10 than you would in requesting to borrow ten pence. And you would probably use a greater degree of indirectness in requesting someone to translate an article for you than in requesting someone to pass you the newspaper. Here is an illustration:

> **Example 12**
> *The speaker was my mother. She made the two following requests to me within the space of a few minutes:*
>
> Shut the window, Jen.
>
> Do you think you could find the time to take those invitations to the printers?

Goffman's (1967) notion of 'free' and 'non-free' goods provides a useful framework within which to discuss the concept of 'size of imposition'. 'Free goods' are those which, in a given situation, anyone can use without seeking permission, for example, salt in a restaurant, peanuts at a bar (providing, of course, that you are having a drink at that bar and have not simply wandered in off the street). Requesting free goods (or 'free services', such as asking someone the time) requires a minimal degree of indirectness. Generally speaking, what an individual regards as free goods/services varies according to the relationship and the situation within which the interaction occurs. In one's own family or home, most things (food, drink, books, baths) are 'free goods'. In a stranger's house they are not.

Lakoff (1974: 27) has pointed out that free and non-free goods are not necessarily material — the concept can be extended to information. Clearly there are some topics that one may ask about freely and others that are 'none of your business' — that is, non-free goods. Again, what is considered 'freely available' varies according to the situation. Many British people would consider it intrusive to enquire directly about a stranger's income, politics, religion, marital status, etc., whereas in other countries such information can be sought freely and without circumlocution. In

Laos, so I am told, it is not unusual to ask strangers about their weight; in most western cultures it would be considered very impolite to do so (except in special circumstances, such as some medical consultations).

Closely related to the concept of 'free' and 'non-free' information are taboo topics. Taboos relate typically (but not exclusively) to sexual or religious topics or to bodily functions such as excreting, but they are by no means universal. As we saw in examples 26 and 27 in chapter 3, for the Navajo it is taboo to mention the name of a person who has died a violent death, in Britain it is not.

5.3.4 Rights and obligations

This dimension is needed in order to explain a situation in which a speech act involving a major imposition is performed with a minimal degree of indirectness. The first time I observed this was in an interaction involving two elderly women travelling on a country bus service. On country routes the driver stops only when requested to do so. The first woman wanted to get off at a scheduled stopping place, and as the bus approached it she simply called out: 'Next stop, driver!' Her companion wanted to get off where there was no official stop, and asked the driver, 'Do you think you could possibly let me out just beyond the traffic lights, please?' In this case, the parameters of power, social distance and size of imposition are all held constant. It cost the driver no more effort to stop at the traffic lights than at the bus stop. What changed was that in the first case the driver had an obligation to stop, in the second case he had no such obligation.

A policeman, speaking in his capacity as a police officer, could get you to move your car simply by saying: 'Move this vehicle.' But the same person, speaking in a purely private capacity, would have to use a much more indirect strategy to perform the same speech act. Again, what is important is whether or not the speaker has the right to make a particular demand and whether the hearer has the obligation to comply.

5.3.5 The negotiation of pragmatic parameters

It would be a mistake to believe that all the factors I have discussed above are 'given' (i.e. that they are determined in advance and would be accepted by all members of a community). There are frequently arguments about relative power, rights and obligations, etc. and people will use language in order to try to change the other person's perception of these dimensions. Examples 13 and 14 show the speaker trying to negotiate the size of imposition, while in examples 15 and 16 the speaker is trying to change the social distance between himself and his addressee.

Example 13

A is just going off to University. B is her mother.

A. Mum. You know those browny glasses.
B. Mm.
A. The ones we got from the garage.
B. Mm.
A. Do you use them much?
B. Not really, no.
A. Can I have them then?

You will notice that in each successive turn A systematically diminishes the 'value' of the glasses to B: they are not very attractive ('browny'), they did not cost anything in the first place ('from the garage'), they are, in a sense, family property ('the ones **we** got …') and finally she establishes that her mother doesn't use the glasses much. Notice that the actual form of the request is quite direct: 'Can I have them then?' This is because A has by this stage reduced the size of the imposition to such a degree that little indirectness is required.

Example 14

It is raining very hard and the driver (D), stops to offer a walker (W) a lift:[12]

D: D'you want a lift?
W: Well, if you're going near the campsite, yes please.

In example 14 the walker tries to reduce the degree of imposition on the driver by implying that he would only accept a lift to the campsite if the driver was going in that direction anyway.

Example 15

D is a visiting academic. He is meeting J for the first time.

J. Dr Galašinski?
D. Darek.
J. Darek.

In this example Dr Galašinski reduces the social distance between J and himself by changing the address form from Title + Surname to a diminutive form of his first name. In the following example the speaker does just the opposite, he emphasizes that he expects to be addressed by his Title + Surname:

Example 16
Basil Fawlty (B) has just been ordered out of his wife's hospital room very rudely by the Sister (S).[13]

S.   Out you go!
B.   Er, Fawlty's the name. **Mr** Fawlty

This brings out an important difference between pragmatics and sociolinguistics. While a sociolinguist would look at language use (e.g. at address forms) to see how it **reflects** social relations, a pragmaticist would look at the way people use language in order to change (or maintain) social relationships.

5.4 Measuring indirectness

I have talked a great deal about indirectness and about some utterances being more indirect than others, but what indirectness is, and how it is to be measured, are rarely discussed. On defining indirectness, the work of Dascal (1983), Dascal and Weizman (1987) and Weizman (1989) is very helpful. In a discussion which once again stresses the crucial importance of **motivation** in pragmatics, they talk of indirectness (Weizman 1989: 73):

> … not just as a lack of transparency, such as with the use of unusual words or ambiguous deictic references, but as lack of transparency *specifically* and *intentionally* employed by the speaker to convey a meaning which differed, in some way, from the utterance meaning. The key notion here is that of the *intended* exploitation of a *gap* between the speaker's meaning and the utterance meaning …

In fact, as we shall see, indirectness does not just refer to the utterance level and to the level of illocutionary force, but also to the directness with which the speaker achieves his or her illocutionary goal. In the pragmatics literature, people tend to deal with only two of the levels, but (as will become clear) for a complete understanding it is necessary to deal with all three.

Weizman (1985) discusses indirectness in terms of the relative transparency or opaqueness of meaning which can occur at utterance level ('propositional transparency/opacity') and at the level of what is implied ('illocutionary transparency/opacity'). Consider the following examples, all three of which were uttered by the same choirmaster on the same day,[14] and which illustrate the gradient from propositional transparency towards relative (but by no means total) propositional opacity:

Example 17
Rehearsing the choirboys at St Mary's Priory, Lancaster:

Stand!

Example 18
To adult members of the Lancaster University choir at a public carol concert:

Would you like to stand?

Example 19
To members of the public at the same carol concert:

I think we would sing better if we stood.

Here we have three examples of the same speech act, but the form of the utterance seems increasingly indirect in each case: first we have a direct, unmodified imperative (total propositional transparency), then a highly conventionalized polite request form (e.g. *can you, could you, will you, would you, would you like to*), requiring minimal processing by the hearers:

> ... the hearer is guided by some grammatical or semantic device, used conventionally for that purpose. For example, when interpreting the question 'Can you pass me the salt, please' as an indirect request, the speaker ... can exploit the grammatical structure of a 'can you/could you' question ... conventionally used to signal indirect requests, as cues for indirectness and as clues for the requestive interpretation.[15]

Example 19 is not a conventionalized form, but nevertheless the choirmaster's words contained (in Weizman's terms), 'sufficient indications as to the content of the act required' (i.e. to stand up) for the utterance to be considered propositionally transparent. Yet intuitively most people would agree that the third utterance seems less direct and to require more processing by the hearers. A paper by Wilson and Sperber (1981: 165-6) offers a useful approach to 'measuring' the degree of indirectness of an utterance.[16] They argue that there is a correlation between the degree of indirectness of an utterance and the amount of 'work' a hearer has to do in order to arrive at the propositional meaning. Imagine, for example, that Mr Collins has made his famous proposal to Elizabeth Bennet in Jane Austen's *Pride and prejudice* (chapter 19) and she refuses in one of the following ways:

(i)   No, I won't marry you.
(ii) I don't respect you and I could never marry a man I don't respect.
(iii) I could never marry a clergyman.
(iv) I refuse to marry a complete buffoon!

Each of the responses (i)–(iv) can be said to convey the following conclusion (v):

(v)   Elizabeth Bennet refuses to marry Mr Collins.

Reply (i) directly expresses (v) — it involves no indirectness. Reply (ii) does not directly express (v), but (v) can be logically deduced from it in the following way:

Elizabeth will not marry anyone she doesn't respect;
Elizabeth has stated that she does not respect Mr Collins;
Therefore Elizabeth will not marry Mr Collins.

Conclusion (v) cannot be deduced *directly* from reply (iii); we need an additional premise, one which, though unstated, is shared knowledge between Mr Collins and Elizabeth Bennet — that Mr Collins is a clergyman. Given that premise, we can proceed to conclusion (v) in the following way:

Elizabeth will not marry a clergyman;
Mr Collins is a clergyman;
Therefore Elizabeth will not marry Mr Collins.

The final response is more problematical. While it is shared knowledge between Elizabeth and Mr Collins that Mr Collins is a clergyman, it is not shared knowledge between them that Mr Collins is a complete buffoon. Mr Collins is required to establish the additional premise, before working through the deductive steps as before. In Wilson and Sperber's terms:

Utterance (i) **expresses** conclusion (v);
Utterance (ii) **logically implies** conclusion (v);
Utterance (iii) **directly pragmatically implies** (v);
Utterance (iv) **indirectly pragmatically implies** (v).

And the amount of 'work' required of Mr Collins in processing each utterance could (following Wilson and Sperber) be spelt out like this:

(i)   no work is required beyond establishing which proposition has been expressed by Elizabeth's utterance;

(ii)   to establish which proposition has been expressed by Elizabeth's utterance and then to make a deduction from the proposition he has established;

(iii)   to retrieve from memory the proposition that he is a clergyman and to draw a deduction from this retrieved proposition and the proposition expressed by Elizabeth's utterance;

(iv)   to **construct** (rather than retrieve from memory) the proposition that he is a complete buffoon, and to draw a deduction from this proposition, together with the proposition expressed in Elizabeth's utterance.

Wilson and Sperber's approach gives us an excellent basis for calculating the degree of indirectness of an utterance. However, I replaced Wilson and Sperber's more straightforward example ('Do you talk to Charles?') with my own in order to introduce some complications which they do not address. The first complication relates to the nature of the **activity type** in which the interactants believe themselves to be engaged (see chapter 7). Activity types have their own norms of interaction and participants have particular expectations, which constrain the possible range of interpretation of utterances and implicatures.

5.4.1 The role of context in interpreting indirectness

There are times when different participants have different

expectations of an activity type (or even believe themselves to be in different activity types). Mr Collins fondly imagines that he is engaged in some sort of flirtatious encounter, in which Elizabeth is bashfully rejecting his suit (but fully intends to accept the proposal later):

> 'I am not now to learn,' replied Mr Collins, with a formal wave of the hand, 'that it is usual with young ladies to reject the addresses of the man whom they secretly mean to accept, when he first applies for their favour; and that sometimes the refusal is repeated a second or even a third time. I am, therefore, by no means discouraged by what you have just said, and shall hope to lead you to the altar ere long.'

Mr Collins's belief is not totally irrational — there are many cultures in which a hearer is expected to reject an offer several times, before accepting with a show of reluctance. So even though he understands the proposition expressed by Elizabeth in (i) he believes that she is implicating the exact opposite. Mr Collins is firmly convinced that different conventions apply in this activity type and that although Elizabeth says 'no' she really means 'yes'. Even the most apparently straightforward reply can cause problems unless uttered against a background of shared norms and conventions.

5.4.2 The role of belief in interpreting indirectness

The next problem relates to Wilson and Sperber's 'indirect pragmatic implication', which is the most complicated, the most indirect and the most 'risky' of the strategies used. Mr Collins, it will be remembered, is required to **construct** (rather than retrieve from memory) the proposition that he is a complete buffoon. The risk, as Wilson and Sperber themselves note (1981: 167), is that, given Collins's hubris, stupidity and crass insensitivity, he will almost certainly construct the wrong proposition, his reasoning will run as follows and he will end up drawing a conclusion precisely the opposite of the one intended:

> Elizabeth will not marry a complete buffoon;
> I am not a complete buffoon;
> Therefore Elizabeth will marry me.

5.4.3 Background knowledge and interpreting indirectness

This point relates very closely to the previous one (indeed, the distinction between 'knowledge' and 'belief' is ultimately very difficult to sustain). What one person is able to retrieve from memory, another may have to construct, and this may sometimes be an immense or even impossible task. To give one very simple example. In the summer of 1993 I was visiting Japan, and I told a Japanese friend the following joke, which had been doing the rounds at work:

> **Example 20**
> Question: What's the difference between Oxford University and *Jurassic Park*?
> Answer: One's a theme park inhabited by dinosaurs, the other's a film by Stephen Spielberg.

Jurassic Park had not yet reached Japan and my friend could not see why this joke was supposed to be funny; I had the greatest difficulty trying to explain it. In order to begin to understand it you needed to be familiar with a very particular linguistic 'genre' — that of the 'what's the difference between …?' kind of joke (and to complicate matters, the norms of that genre are exploited here). You needed to know how certain aspects of Oxford are viewed from outside, the outline of the plot of *Jurassic Park* and (possibly) the identity of Stephen Spielberg. Without these elements of background knowledge and belief, it would be impossible to construct any propositions on which to base deductions.

5.4.4 The role of co-text in interpreting indirectness

The term '**co-text**' refers to the **linguistic** (rather than situational) context in which a particular utterance occurs. Both the original example furnished by Wilson and Sperber ('Do you ever talk to Charles?') and the one implied in my own example ('Will you marry me?') are 'Yes/No' questions, heavily constraining the possible interpretations of the replies. One example of co-text is the **adjacency pair** (Schegloff and Sacks (1974 [1973]: 238 ff)), a concept which is particularly relevant here. 'Adjacency pairs' are consecutive, contingently related utterances produced by two different speakers.[17] Adjacency pairs may be reciprocal (e.g. greeting/greeting) or non-reciprocal (e.g. question/answer). The important point here is that what has been said before constrains the way in which we interpret the response, as in the following example:[18]

Example 21
A: Are you coming to the cinema?
B: I've got an exam tomorrow.

The response is 'heard' as *no* because a 'Yes/No' question predicts *yes* or *no* as an answer — the range of possible interpretations of an indirect pragmatic implication is thereby greatly reduced. On other occasions, however, the possible range of interpretations of an utterance is not heavily constrained either by context or by co-text and then the process of utterance interpretation becomes much more difficult. The following example begins with the speaker, A, making a statement, which was capable of being construed as a request, an observation, a suggestion or invitation, etc. A statement is a 'first pair part' (i.e. the first contribution to a (projected) adjacency pair) which can be followed by a very wide range of 'second pair parts': another statement, a counter-suggestion, acceptance, refusal, agreement, disagreement, etc., or perhaps by nothing at all.

Example 22
This is a reconstruction of a conversation which took place between a friend and me when I was working in the (then Soviet) Ukraine:

A: I'd like to go walking on Saturday if it's fine.
B: It's Lenin's birthday.
A: It's my niece's birthday. And Shakespeare's birthday.

I did not understand the significance of 'Lenin's birthday'[19] and, just as importantly, because the first contribution did not substantially constrain the range of appropriate responses, I had no basis on which to work out whether B was saying that she could/couldn't come, did/didn't want to come, whether she was just making conversation or whether her contribution was a *non sequitur*, a remark prompted, as my own second contribution had been, by remembering the date.

5.4.5 Goals and the interpretation of indirectness

Leech's (1983a: 123) approach to computing indirectness is to 'calculate' the length of the path from the illocutionary act to its illocutionary goal. The path may be a very short or quite complex. For example, suppose S is cold and has the goal of feeling warmer, and says: *Switch on the heater!*

Initial state	Action 1	Intermediate state	Action 2	Final state
S feels cold	S says: *Switch on the heater!*	H understands that S wants the heater on	H switches on heater	S feels warmer

In this case there are 3 stages between the initial state and the final, desired state. If, however, S says: *Cold in here, isn't it?* the path will be longer:

Initial state	Action 1	Intermediate state 1	Intermediate state 2	Action 2	Final state
S feels cold	S says: *Cold in here, isn't it?*	H understands that S is aware that it is cold	H understands that S wants the heater on	H switches on heater	S feels warmer

In this very simplified version there are four stages between the initial state and the final, desired state (obviously, we could give a more sophisticated account of the intermediate states 1 and 2 if we incorporated the type of reasoning proposed by Wilson and Sperber). It may seem perverse to suggest 'combining' Leech's method of 'measuring' indirectness with that of Wilson and Sperber when, as I have already noted, they have diametrically opposed approaches to pragmatics — Leech, like Brown and Levinson, takes a broadly socially-oriented and speaker-oriented approach, whereas Wilson and Sperber take a cognitive and hearer-oriented approach. However, I would argue that the speaker will always bear in mind the interpretive steps the hearer will have to take in order to interpret what is said, and this will be a powerful constraint on the way the speaker formulates his or utterance. Similarly, the hearer, in interpreting what the speaker has said, will necessarily take account of the social (and other) constraints upon him or her.

Leech's focus on the speaker's goal brings me to an important point. There are certainly many occasions when, just as Wilson and Sperber suggest, we work out the speaker's intended meaning by means of a series of deductions made on the basis of what the speaker has said. But there are other occasions when, if we have a good idea of the speaker's goal, we can cut this process short. Ervin-Tripp (1976: 39) cites an exchange which illustrates this point well:[20]

Example 23

A professor telephones room-permits office:

A: Do you have a room for twenty on Monday nights?
B: Just a minute. Yes, I do. Give me your name, department and course number, please.

In this example the 'Yes/No' question is interpreted not as a 'real' question, but as a request to book a room, because B has (correctly) assessed A's goal in asking the question. Often, we are able to assign illocutionary force only when we have worked out **why** the speaker is speaking in a particular way:

Example 24

Each of these questions was put to me (on separate occasions) by a colleague at work:

1.   Have you got a bicycle pump?
2.   Are you going home soon?

In the case of these two examples, I was able to work out what the speaker meant on the basis of the words uttered **plus** an assessment of their respective goals. I had just bought a new bicycle and had been discussing with my colleague the purchase of certain accessories (panniers, etc.). Nevertheless, I guessed that the first speaker's goal was to borrow my bicycle pump (rather than, say, to advise me about buying one or to sell me his) and that the goal of the second speaker goal was to get a lift home (rather than, say, to get me to leave as soon as possible so that he could use my room). In the example which follows, I was completely unable to work out the speaker's goal in asking the question, and therefore to assign pragmatic force to her question:

Example 25

A woman (A) came to my door and, pointing to the car parked outside my house, asked:

A: Is that your car?
B: Why do you want to know?

In chapter 1 I gave this very sentence as an illustration of how many different things the same sentence might mean in different contexts (a complaint, a request for a lift, etc.). The interesting thing here is that I did not seek to find out what the woman meant but **why** she had asked the question. It transpired that she was carrying out a survey on the relative reliability of different makes of car, and mine fitted the bill in terms of age, make and model; as soon as she had explained this, I was able to assign force to her utterance.

From this discussion it should be clear that the term *indirectness* covers a range of phenomena; in some situations it is the illocutionary goal which is unclear, on other occasions (as we shall see in the discussion of **ambivalence** in chapter 7) the speaker's illocutionary goal is perfectly obvious, but the pragmatic force of the utterance is not, as the following example (taken from Leech 1983a: 24) shows:

Example 26
If I were you, I'd leave town straight away.

Here there can be no doubt as to the speaker's illocutionary goal (to get the hearer to leave town). What is unclear is whether the utterance constitutes a piece of advice, a warning, an order or a threat.

There will be times when the illocutionary goal of the speaker is such that it is futile to use too much indirectness — no amount of indirectness can 'soften the blow':

Example 27
The doctor has to inform Leaphorn that his wife had died unexpectedly while undergoing surgery:[21]

'There's no good way to tell you this, Mr. Leaphorn,' the voice had said. 'We lost her. Just now. It was a blood clot. Too much infection. Too much strain. But if it's any consolation, it must have been almost instantaneous.'

5.5 Why use indirectness?

I have spent great deal of time in this book discussing how indirectness is defined, measured, used and interpreted, but we have yet to address the reasons **why** the use of indirectness is so all-pervasive, except to say that people obtain 'some social or communicative advantages' from its use. A variety of reasons has been put forward for the universal use of indirectness, including:

- The desire to make one's language more/less interesting

- To increase the force of one's message

- Competing goals

- Politeness/regard for 'face'.

Some of these factors interrelate, but as far as possible I shall deal with them in order, which also reflects an increasing order of importance. The last dimension, 'politeness', is vastly more important than the other three and for this reason, and because of the very extensive literature on the subject, I have accorded it a chapter of its own.

5.5.1 Interestingness

'Interestingness' is probably the least significant of the reasons given above, but nevertheless its importance should not be underestimated. People may use indirectness because they enjoy having fun with language. For example, I once heard a news item in which a World War II pilot described a Shackleton aircraft as, '20,000 rivets flying in loose formation'. He could have described the aircraft as 'a very poorly constructed machine'. This would have conveyed his proposition perfectly effectively, but would have been extremely dreary, especially for people who, like me, are bored rigid by the subject of military aircraft. Although I had no interest at all in *what* he was saying, I was entertained by the way in which he said it. And think how dull the second chapter of *Sense and sensibility* would have been, if Austen had simply said, 'John was mean and his wife was even meaner' instead of implying this indirectly. Austen's novels are often read for the entertaining way in which they are written, rather than for the plot.

Just occasionally we find examples of people using indirectness (in this case flouting the maxim of Quantity) in order to be **uninteresting, or to deflect interest**. In the extract which follows the speaker is talking about the death of his father. Jerome's father had been killed when a pig fell on his head[22] and every time Jerome relates the story people laugh, and this, not unnaturally, upsets him. He has developed this way of relating the story in order to render an intrinsically entertaining subject so boring that no one could possibly laugh:

Example 28
Sometimes he rehearsed the method of recounting his father's death so as to reduce the comic element to its smallest dimensions ...

'You know Naples and those high tenement buildings? Somebody once told me that the Neapolitan always feels at home in New York just as the man from Turin feels at home in London because the river runs in much the same way in both cities. Where was I? Oh, yes, Naples, of course. You'd be surprised in the poorer quarters what things they keep on the balconies of those sky-scraping tenements — not washing, you know, or bedding, but things like live- stock, chickens or even pigs. Of course, the pigs get no exercise whatever and fatten all the quicker.' He could imagine how his hearer's eyes would have glazed by this time. 'I've no idea, have you, how heavy a pig can be, but these old buildings are all badly in need of repair. A balcony on the fifth floor gave way under one of those pigs. It struck the third floor balcony on its way down and sort of ricochetted into the street. My father was on the way to the Hydrographic Museum when the pig hit him. Coming from that height and that angle it broke his neck.'

5.5.2 Increasing the force of one's message

This point is quite closely related to the previous one — you can increase the 'impact' or effectiveness of your message by employ- ing indirectness. If your hearer has to work at understanding the message, he or she has a greater 'investment' in that message. This is particularly true of jokes, irony and poems as the follow- ing examples illustrate:

Example 29
There is a weekly section in The Guardian *newspaper where readers' questions are answered by other readers. The responses may be serious or humorous:*[23]

Q   Is it really feasible that a chimpanzee with a type-
      writer and an infinite amount of time will be able to

produce the complete works of Shakespeare?

A   Quite probably. After all, he's already produced the
     National Curriculum.

Example 30
*Neil Kinnock (speaking in November 1990) about the state of the
British economy during the Thatcher era:*

'We had problems at the beginning, problems at the end
and an economic miracle in the middle. How does she
explain that?'

The whole of Andrew Marvell's glorious poem 'To his coy
mistress' could be summed up as: 'Let's make love now, we
shan't live for ever!' However, it is unlikely that this would have
quite the same impact as the original version of the poem, even
though my rewording is much simpler and more direct. Here is
a well-known extract:

Example 31
But at my back I always hear
Time's wingèd chariot hurrying near,
And yonder all before us lie
Deserts of vast eternity.
Thy beauty shall no more be found,
Nor, in thy marble vaults, shall sound
My echoing song; then worms shall try
That long-preserved virginity,
And your quaint honour turn to dust,
And into ashes all my lust.

5.5.3 Competing goals

Pyle (cited in Dascal 1983) notes that we often employ indirectness because we have two goals which compete. For example, if
a teacher has to tell a student that the student's work is not up to
standard, the teacher's need/duty to tell the truth may conflict
with the desire not to hurt the student's feelings or discourage
him or her. According to Pyle, the user of an indirect utterance
relies upon his or her interlocutor's ability to detect the problem
— in order to understand what the teacher means, the student
must recognize the conflict of goals. However, the interlocutor
(particularly in cross-cultural situations) may not always be able

to do this, as the following anecdote indicates:[24]

> **Example 32**
>
> '... the authors have heard a Chinese tour-guide in Shang-
> hai telling a tourist that the Yuyuan Garden, one of the
> city's major attractions, had been torn down and that they
> would have to stick to their original plan of a factory visit.
> The garden was intact and still is; the guide resorted to the
> fabrication rather than explain that he would be in trouble
> with the factory management had the expected tour-group
> failed to show up.
>
> '... In such cases, a Westerner might react angrily to what
> he or she perceives as a lie ... A Chinese person would read
> the signal, and would probably drop the matter.'

5.6 Conclusion

So far I have discussed three motives for employing indirectness:
the desire to be interesting, the desire to increase the force of
one's message, and the recognition that the speaker has two (or
more) competing goals — generally a clash between the speaker's
propositional goal and his or her interpersonal goal. These are
genuine underlying motivations governing linguistic choice.
However, an alternative explanation for some of the preceding
examples is that the speaker wishes to avoid the expression of
impolite beliefs — the World War II pilot does not want to say
(explicitly) that the Shackleton was a lousy aircraft (although he
does not mind implying it); Jane Austen does not wish to say that
John Dashwood was incredibly mean (although she does not
shrink from implying this); Andrew Marvell was himself too
bashful to suggest explicitly to his beloved that they leap into bed
(although he is happy to hint at this), etc. In each of examples
29–32 there is an **utterance level** reluctance to be critical,
suggestive or over-explicit. In chapter 6 we shall see that each of
these examples could be explained in terms of an attachment to
politeness at utterance level. It is very important to remember,
however (and this is something widely misunderstood and
misrepresented outside specialist publications on pragmatics),
that in speaking of politeness we are talking of 'what is said' and
not (as in this chapter) of the genuine underlying motivation
which leads the speaker to make those linguistic choices.

Notes

1. As opposed to artificial languages, such as computer programming languages.

2. These points are slightly adapted from Dascal (1983).

3. Reconstructed dialogue.

4. Put forward in Searle (1969: 19).

5. The first three parameters are adapted from Leech (1980 [1977]) and Brown and Levinson (1987 [1978]); 'rights and obligations' is an addition of my own.

6. Tony Hillerman (1993 [1989]) *A thief of time*. Penguin Books, Harmondsworth, p. 134.

7. Advertisement placed by *Which?* in *The Guardian*, 22 August 1994.

8. Joanna Trollope (1992) *The men and the girls*. Black Swan, London, p. 138.

9. Charles Barkley, the 'bad boy' of American basketball, has frequently and publicly commented that he has no intention of acting as a role model for anybody!

10. *The Guardian*, 18 August 1994.

11. ITV News, 17 August 1994.

12. Mike Leigh, *Nuts in May*.

13. John Cleese and Connie Booth (1988) *The complete Fawlty Towers*. Methuen, London.

14. 22 December 1988.

15. For a typology of such contextual clues see Dascal and Weizman (1987).

16. The ideas presented in this 1981 paper, 'On Grice's theory of conversation', are developed more fully in Sperber and Wilson (1985) and more advanced students will want to refer to this more recent version of their work. Beginners, however, will find the earlier version more accessible and concise.

17. For a good, clear overview see Benson and Hughes (1983: 173–82).

18. This is a fabricated example.

19. During the Soviet period, the nearest Saturday to Lenin's birthday (in the year in question it was 23 April) was the occasion of a 'subbotnik', a day devoted to 'voluntarily' clearing up the area around your home, to commemorate the fact that on one occasion Lenin allegedly spent his birthday picking up litter in the Kremlin. Participation in the subbotnik was a much-hated obligation, but very difficult to avoid.

20. Cited in Weizman (1989: 76).

21. Tony Hillerman (1993 [1989]) *A Thief of time*. Penguin, London, p. 16.

22. Graham Greene (1986) A shocking accident. *Collected short stories*. Penguin Books, London, pp. 333–4.

23. R. Epton, Brigg, South Humberside. *The Guardian*, Notes and Questions, 28 October 1991.

24. Richard King and Sandra Schatzky (1991) *Coping with China*. Basil Blackwell, Oxford, pp. 113–14.

CHAPTER 6

Theories of politeness

6.1 Introduction

In the past twenty-five years within pragmatics there has been a great deal of interest in 'politeness', to such an extent that politeness theory could almost be seen as a sub-discipline of pragmatics. Much has been written (comparatively little based on empirical research) and different theories and paradigms have emerged. Inevitably, we find that people are using the same terms in very different ways, are operating with different definitions of 'politeness' and are talking at cross-purposes. In this chapter I shall outline the principal theories of politeness and try to clear up some of the most common misunderstandings.

6.2 Delimiting the concept of politeness

Within the vast literature on politeness which has built up since the late 1970s we find tremendous confusion. The confusion begins with the very term *politeness*, which like *cooperation*, has caused much misunderstanding. Under the heading of *politeness*, people have discussed five separate, though related, sets of phenomena:

- Politeness as a real-world goal
- Deference
- Register
- Politeness as a surface level phenomenon
- Politeness as an illocutionary phenomenon.

6.2.1 Politeness as a real-world goal

Politeness as a real-world goal (i.e. politeness interpreted as a genuine desire to be pleasant to others, or as the underlying motivation for an individual's linguistic behaviour) has no place within pragmatics. We can have no access to speakers' real motivation for speaking as they do, and discussions as to whether one group of people is 'politer' than another (in the sense of genuinely behaving better to other people than do other groups) are ultimately futile. As linguists we have access only to what speakers say and to how their hearers react. We may observe that the Chinese place more emphasis in their talk on the needs of the group rather than those of the individual, but we cannot conclude on the basis of these observations alone that they are genuinely more altruistic than members of other communities.

Deference and register are not primarily pragmatic concepts, but I want to discuss them briefly here for two reasons: politeness (which is of central interest in pragmatics) is frequently confused with deference/register (which are principally sociolinguistic phenomena) and the politeness/deference distinction is a useful illustration of a discussion which will be developed in chapter 7 — the distinction between pragmatics and sociolinguistics.

6.2.2 Deference versus politeness

Deference is frequently equated with politeness, particularly in discussions of Japanese. Deference is connected with politeness, but is a distinct phenomenon; it is the opposite of familiarity. It refers to the respect we show to other people by virtue of their higher status, greater age, etc. Politeness is a more general matter of showing (or rather, of giving the appearance of showing) consideration to others. Both deference and politeness can be manifested through general social behaviour (we can show deference by standing up when a person of superior status enters a room, or show politeness by holding a door open to allow someone else to pass through) as well as by linguistic means.

Deference is built into the grammar of languages such as Korean and Japanese. It is also found in a much reduced form in the grammar of those languages which have a 'T/V system' — languages such as French, German and Russian in which there is a choice of second person pronoun: tu/vous, du/Sie, ты/вы. In French, for example, you *have* to make a choice between the

pronouns *tu* and *vous* in addressing someone; although it is
theoretically possible to avoid the problem by using the pronoun
on, it would be extremely difficult (and would sound very stilted)
to keep this up for long. In other words, speakers of languages
which make the T/V distinction are obliged, because of the
linguistic choices they must make, to signal either respect or
familiarity towards their interlocutor. In the grammar of present-
day English, which, in its standardized form, ceased to make the
T/V distinction (*thou/you*) between three and four hundred years
ago, virtually no deference forms remain. Exceptions are address
forms (*Doctor, Professor,* etc.) and the use of 'honorifics' such as *Sir*
or *Madam* (these are used very rarely in British English, but rather
more frequently in American English) which may be used to
indicate the relative status of the interactants. Conversely, first
names (*Richard, Catherine*) or diminutives of those first names
(*Dick, Kate*) are used to show a friendly, non-deferential relationship. Outside the address system, it is really very difficult to find
markers of deference in present day British English. One
(exceedingly rare) exception that I have found is the following:

Example 1
*A British Member of Parliament, Tim Devlin, was referring to the
Queen's ceremonial speech at the State Opening of Parliament:*[1]

'This year there were substantial references to Europe in
The Gracious Speech.'

As I have indicated, it is very unusual in English to find
deference explicitly grammatically[2] signalled by anything other
than address forms. In languages such as Japanese and Korean,
however, many parts of speech (nouns and adjectives as well as
verbs and pronouns) can be 'unmarked' or marked for deference
(or even super-deference). Indeed, as Matsumoto (1989: 209)
demonstrates, it is impossible in Japanese to avoid marking the
relationship between speaker and hearer. She gives the example
of a simple declarative: *Today is Saturday.* In English, the same
grammatical form[3] could be used regardless of the hearer's social
status. In Japanese the copula (here corresponding to the English
is) would be plain (*da*), 'deferential' (*desu*), or 'super deferential'
(*degozaimasu*) according to the status of the addressee. As Ide
(1989: 229–30) discussing Matsumoto notes, the choice of the
honorific or plain form of the copula is not a matter of individual
choice, it is 'an **obligatory** choice among variants' (my emphasis), reflecting the speaker's 'sense of place or role in a given

situation according to social conventions'.

The reason why I say that deference has little to do with pragmatics is that generally, unless the speaker deliberately wishes to flout the behavioural norms of a given society (and is prepared to accept the consequences[4] of so doing), the speaker has no *choice* as to whether to use the deferent form or not — usage is dictated by sociolinguistic norms (see chapter 7). Thus a soldier has no real choice about addressing a superior officer as *Sir* or *Ma'am* — military discipline dictates the forms used: it is a sociolinguistic norm, with penalties attached to a non-observance of the norm, and does not (necessarily) indicate any real respect or regard for the individual so addressed. My brother recounted the following incident which occurred at the Royal Military Academy, Sandhurst:

Example 2
The speaker was the Academy Sergeant Major (one of the few ranks of non-commissioned officer normally addressed as 'Sir'). He was talking to a newly-arrived group of officer cadets:

'You will address me as "Sir" at all times and I will also address you as "Sir". The difference is that you will mean it!'

If the use of a particular form is **obligatory** in a particular situation, as in example 2, it is of no significance pragmatically; it is only when there is a choice, or when a speaker attempts to bring about change by challenging the current norms, that the use of deferent or non-deferent forms becomes of interest to the pragmaticist. Address forms, the use of T or V forms *(tu versus vous)*, etc., are pragmatically interesting only when a strategic choice is made; for example, when, you suddenly start to address someone by his or her first name or using a T form **with the deliberate aim of changing the social relationship**. Thus, in the Russian opera *Yevgenni Onegin* there is an electrifying moment when Onegin switches mid-sentence from addressing Tatyana as вы to addressing her as ты instead, thereby manifesting the strength of his feeling for her. (This part falls extremely flat in the English language version!)

It is also worth noting that the use of a deferent form does not *in and of itself* convey respect. I overheard the following when, on a school exchange, I was staying with a French family (this was in the late 1960s, when it was exceedingly unusual for children to address their parents using the *vous*-form, but for some reason in this family they did). The speaker manages to express extreme disrespect, while using conventional forms of deference:

Example 3
The speaker was a boy of about sixteen:

Mère, vous me faites chier!

Outside the appropriate sociolinguistic situation, the use of a deference marker can convey the very reverse of respect. In the following extract, the speaker **exploits** the address system, using an inappropriately elaborate and deferential form of address to his wife, in order to imply that she is behaving in an unnecessarily pretentious way:

Example 4
The speaker and his wife have driven a long way and are both very hungry. However, the wife keeps refusing to stop at the diners they pass, because she thinks they look too down-market:[5]

What was the matter with the 'Elite Diner', milady?

Finally, we can demonstrate that politeness and deference are distinct, though related systems, by noting that it is possible to be deferential without being polite, as the following examples illustrate:

Example 5
Brian Wilson, Labour M.P. for Cunninghame North, was addressing Nicholas Soames, Conservative M.P. for Crawley, during the 'poll tax' debate in 1988:[6]

BW: Does the honourable member for Crawley wish to intervene?

NS: No.

BW: The last time I saw a mouth like that it had a hook in it.

The speaker uses an elaborate deference form, while at the same time impolitely implying that Mr Soames looked like a trout.

Example 6
An agricultural student, Ruth Archer, is referring to the estate fore-man, whom she dislikes and mistrusts:[7]

What does old Gaffer Knowles want?

The use of the colloquial form *Gaffer* (meaning *the boss*) as a term of reference (the form used when talking *about* someone) or of address (the form used when talking *to* someone) indicates that the speaker is in a subordinate position, but conveys no politeness whatever (its use in this context conveys contempt).

6.2.3 Register

For the sake of completeness I have also included a brief discussion of register. The term *register* refers to 'systematic variation … in relation to social context' (Lyons 1977: 584) or the way in which 'the language we speak or write varies according to the type of situation' (Halliday 1978: 32).

Certain situations (e.g. very formal meetings) or types of language use (e.g. report-writing versus writing a note to a close friend), as well as certain social relationships, require more formal language use. This 'formality' may manifest itself in English by the choice of formal lexis and forms of address, the avoidance of interruption, etc. (see note 2), while in languages such as Japanese and Korean the formality will be marked additionally by forms such as the Japanese *degozaimasu* discussed in section 6.2.2.

As with deference, register has little to do with politeness and little connection with pragmatics, since we have no real choice about whether or not to use formal language in formal situations (unless we are prepared to risk sanctions, such as social censure). Like deference, register is primarily a sociolinguistic phenomenon: a description of the linguistic forms which generally occur in a particular situation. Choice of register has little to do with the strategic use of language and it only becomes of interest to the pragmaticist if a speaker deliberately uses unexpected forms in order to change the situation (in the same way that we may switch from a V to a T form in order to change a social relationship) or to challenge the status quo. Examples of the former might be if a prospective postgraduate student dropped into a university department for a chat and something which began as an informal, information-seeking event was changed by one of the participants into a formal admission interview. An example of the latter would be if you decided to disrupt a stuffy meeting by using language not normally associated with that particular type of event, such as cracking jokes or making fun of the person chairing the meeting.

6.2.4 Politeness as an utterance level phenomenon

Much early work in the area of politeness focused on utterance level realizations (e.g. the early work of Rintell, Walters, Fraser on cross-cultural pragmatics). Walters (1979a and 1979b) defined his interest as being 'to investigate how much politeness could be squeezed out of speech act strategies alone', and to investigate the perception of politeness by native and non-native speakers of English and Spanish, using a 'standard lexical context' in order to establish a 'hierarchy of politeness', instructing his informants to ignore context as much as possible. In a similar experiment Fraser (1978) asked informants to rate for politeness various forms of request (*would you X?, could you X?, can you X?, do X!*, etc. (where X is some request or imposition)) for which no context was supplied. These experiments, and similar ones conducted across other pairs of languages, allow us to compare the forms available for performing particular speech acts in different languages/cultures. Thus we might find that one language has ten forms available for performing a particular speech act, and that these correspond to just six in another language. English, for example, has an unusually large number of ways of expressing obligation: *You must, you have to, you are to, you've got to, you should,* etc. These studies also found that members of a particular community showed a very high level of agreement as to which linguistic forms were (when taken out of context) most polite, and in general it was found that the more grammatically complex or elaborate the strategy, the more highly it was rated for politeness. Thus (the equivalent in each language of):

I wonder if I might ask you to X?

would be counted (all things being equal) as 'more polite' than:

Please X!

which in turn was ranked as more polite than the unmodified imperative form:

Do X!

Two issues arise from studies of this nature. The first again relates to the pragmatics/sociolinguistics divide: listing the linguistic forms which can be used to perform a speech act in a given language is not pragmatics, any more than, say, listing all the words for 'adult human female' in a given language falls within the realm of pragmatics. These are sociolinguistic phenomena. It only becomes pragmatics when we look at how a particular form in a particular language is used strategically in order to achieve the speaker's goal. 'Doing' pragmatics crucially requires context. This leads to the second issue: as soon as we put a speech act in context, we can see that there is no *necessary* connection between the linguistic form and the perceived politeness of a speech act. There are at least three reasons why this is so. Firstly, consider the following example:

Example 7
A married couple are trying to decide on a restaurant. The husband says:

'You choose.'

In this case we have a direct imperative, but it would normally be seen as perfectly polite. This is because the speech act is what Leech (1983a: 107–8) terms 'costly to the speaker' or (better in this case) 'beneficial to the hearer'. The second reason is well illustrated by the following examples (taken, like the previous one, from a short story by James Thurber).[8] The wife says to her husband:

Example 8
'Will you be kind enough to tell me what time it is?'

[and later]:

'If you'll be kind enough to speed up a little.'

On the face of it (and taken out of context), these forms of request are much more polite than the more normal: *What's the time?* and *Hurry up!* But in the context of an intimate relationship they appear inappropriately indirect. In fact, the couple are getting more and more irritated with one another, and the increasingly elaborate request forms the wife employs testifies to her mounting anger with her husband.

The third reason why it is unsafe to equate surface linguistic form with politeness is that some speech acts seem almost inherently impolite. For example, I can think of no polite way in any language I speak of asking someone to stop picking their nose! Regardless of the elaborateness of the linguistic form, no matter how you hedge it about, it is always going to be offensive. In this regard (i) seems no more polite than (ii):

(i)   I wonder if I might respectfully request you to stop picking your nose?

(ii) Stop picking your nose!

Notice that I am not saying that there is *no* relationship between surface linguistic form and politeness. All things being equal, (i) is more likely to be judged as 'polite' than (ii) or (iii):

(i)   I'm afraid I must ask you to leave.

(ii)   Go away!

(iii) Bugger off!

At the very least, uttering (i) in preference to (iii) is much less likely to leave the speaker open to censure for being rude, itself an important consideration for a person holding some sort of public position (a teacher, say, or a police officer or a civil servant). Whether the utterer of (i) is more motivated by consideration for H than the utterer of (iii), and whether (i) is less hurtful for the hearer than (iii) is debatable. This is why I said in section 6.2.1 that in pragmatics we are not concerned with whether or not speakers are genuinely motivated by a desire to be nice to one another; all we can do is observe what is said and the effect of what is said on the hearer.

In this section we have seen that we cannot assess politeness reliably out of context; it is not the linguistic form alone which renders the speech act polite or impolite, but the linguistic form + the context of utterance + the relationship between the speaker and the hearer.

6.2.5 Politeness as a pragmatic phenomenon

More recent work in politeness theory, notably that of Leech (1980 [1977] and 1983a) and Brown and Levinson (1987 [1978]) has focused on politeness as a pragmatic phenomenon. In these writings politeness is interpreted as a strategy (or series of strategies) employed by a speaker to achieve a variety of goals, such as promoting or maintaining harmonious relations. These strategies may include the strategic use of the conventional politeness strategies discussed in section 6.2.4, but also include a range of other strategies, including many forms of conventional and non-conventional indirectness. Following Fraser (1990) I have grouped the pragmatic approaches to politeness under three headings: the 'conversational-maxim' view (exemplified by Leech) the 'face-management' view (exemplified by Brown and Levinson) and Fraser's own 'conversational-contract' view. I have also added a fourth approach, which I have termed the 'pragmatic scales' view, proposed by Spencer-Oatey (1992), which brings together many of the strengths and avoids some of the weaknesses of the three previous approaches.

6.3 Politeness explained in terms of principles and maxims

Leech (1980 [1977] and 1983a) sees politeness (and the related notion of 'tact') as crucial in explaining 'why people are often so indirect in conveying what they mean' and (1983a: 80) as 'rescuing the Cooperative Principle' in the sense that politeness can satisfactorily explain exceptions to and apparent deviations from the CP. Leech introduces two concepts which are relevant for the present discussion: ambivalence (which will be discussed in greater detail in chapter 7) and pragmatic principles.

6.3.1 Ambivalence and politeness

In section 6.2.4 we observed that it is difficult to put politely into words something which is, by its nature, likely to cause offence to the hearer. This is certainly true when we are dealing with purely surface level (grammatical) encoding of politeness. However, by employing an utterance which is ambivalent (i.e. one which has more than one potential pragmatic force) it is possible to convey messages which the hearer is liable to find disagreeable without causing undue offence. Example 9 illustrates this in relation to a potentially very offensive speech act (requesting people not to steal!). The pragmatic force in each case is ambivalent and it is left to the readers to decide (a) what the precise force of the message is and (b) whether or not it applies to them:

Example 9
Notice in the Junior Common Room, Queens College, Cambridge:

These newspapers are for all the students, not the privi-
leged few who arrive first.

I came across the next example at a very expensive gourmet
restaurant:[9]

Example 10
If you want to enjoy the full flavour of your food and drink
you will, naturally, not smoke during this meal. Moreover,
if you did smoke you would also be impairing the enjoy-
ment of other guests.

In a restaurant of this calibre, the management obviously
thought it inappropriate simply to put up 'No Smoking' signs.
Instead, it is left to the guests to decide for themselves whether
they are being *asked* or *ordered* not to smoke.

6.3.2 Pragmatic principles

In chapter 4 of his *Principles of pragmatics*, Leech introduces the
Politeness Principle (PP) which runs as follows:

Minimize (all things being equal) the expression of impolite
beliefs; Maximize (all things being equal) the expression of
polite beliefs.

Leech sees the PP as being of the same status as Grice's
Cooperative Principle (CP), which it 'rescues' by explaining *why*
speakers do not always observe the Gricean maxims. There is a
good deal of evidence that people **do** respond consciously to
considerations of politeness, for instance, people will often
explicitly 'mark' the fact that they cannot or do not intend to
observe politeness norms, as in the following example:

Example 11
Look, there's no polite way of putting this. Your husband and
I are lovers and he's leaving you for me.[10]

If we reconsider three examples from chapter 3 (examples
12 and 15, which concern flouts of the maxim of Quantity, and
example 18, which concerns the flout of the maxim of Relation

by the vicar's wife), we can see that each of them can be explained rather well by the PP, since in each case the speaker minimizes the expression of impolite beliefs:

Example 12:   I don't like her boyfriend!

Example 15:   You're not coming with us!

Example 18:   I couldn't care less about the role of women in the church!

Notice that Leech is only talking about the **expression** of impolite beliefs — what a person is thinking or implying is a very different matter and it is perfectly clear in each of these examples that the speaker has impolite thoughts or feelings, which she has not hesitated to convey **indirectly**.

Leech (1983a: chapter 6) introduces a number of maxims which, he claims, stand in the same relationship to the PP as Grice's maxims (Quality, Quantity, Relation and Manner) stand to the CP. These maxims are necessary, Leech argues, in order to 'explain the relationship between sense and force in human conversation'. They range from those which have very extensive, but by no means universal applicability, to the somewhat idiosyncratic. The main maxims are: Tact, Generosity, Approbation, Modesty, Agreement and Sympathy (to which are added an assortment of 'sub-maxims'). Like Grice's maxims, Leech's maxims are formulated as imperatives; this, in my view, is unfortunate in both cases, but it does not mean that they are in any sense 'rules for good behaviour'. Rather, Leech claims, they are simply the statements of norms which speakers can be observed to follow. All Leech's maxims need to be interpreted in the light of the pragmatic parameters outlined in chapter 5 (section 5.3). In particular, some care needs to be taken with the interpretation of the term 'other' in each of the maxims. Clearly the maxims will be invoked with more or less strength depending upon whether the 'other' in question is a relative stranger or someone with whom you are on intimate terms. I discuss each of the main maxims briefly below.

6.3.2.1 The Tact maxim
The Tact maxim states: 'Minimize the expression of beliefs which imply cost to other; maximize the expression of beliefs which imply benefit to other'.

One aspect of the Tact maxim relates to the third pragmatic parameter discussed in chapter 5 (section 5.3): size of imposition.

We can use 'minimizers' to reduce the implied cost to the hearer:

> Just pop upstairs and …
> Hang on a second!
> I've got a bit of a problem.

Whether or not the strategy of minimizing the 'expression of cost to other' is perceived as polite or not may be highly culture-specific. One Japanese student whose M.A. thesis I was supervising would regularly send me drafts of her work with a note, such as the following, attached:

Example 12
This is a draft of chapter 4. Please read it and comment on it.

Other students would simply write: *'This is a draft of Chapter 4'* or *'Please could you look at this draft'*. The fact that she spelt out what she wanted done used to infuriate me. (What else did she *imagine* I was going to do with her work? Make paper aeroplanes? Line the parrot's cage?!) I mentioned to a Japanese doctoral student how much it irritated me, and she pointed out that the M.A. student was simply acknowledging how much work she had let me in for and was going on record with the degree of her indebtedness — clearly an eminently reasonable point of view. It would seem that even in the case of 'impositives' minimizing the expression of cost to other is by no means universally polite.

A second aspect of the Tact maxim is that of mitigating the effect of a request by offering optionality. This closely resembles the second of Lakoff's (1973) 'rules of politeness': 'Give options!' Allowing options (or giving the appearance of allowing options) is absolutely central to Western notions of politeness, but again, as Spencer-Oatey (1992: 17) notes,[11] has little place in the Chinese conception of politeness. Just as a polite Chinese host will choose your dishes for you in a restaurant without consulting you (and will often go so far as to place the choicest pieces directly onto your plate), so the linguistic expression of optionality in, say, inviting someone to one's home, is not seen as polite.

A third component of the Tact maxim is the cost/benefit scale: if something is perceived as being to the hearer's benefit, X can be expressed politely without employing indirectness: *Have a chocolate!* However, if X is seen as being 'costly' to the hearer, greater indirectness may be required: *Could I have one of your sandwiches?* Here again there is an obvious connection with the 'size of imposition' dimension.

6.3.2.2 The Generosity maxim

Leech's Generosity maxim states: 'Minimize the expression of benefit to self; maximize the expression of cost to self.' I think this formulation reads very oddly, and that it would be better to say: 'Minimize the expression of cost to other; maximize the expression of benefit to other.' The Generosity maxim explains why it is fine to say: *You must come and have dinner with us*, while the proposition that we will come and have dinner with you requires (generally speaking) to be expressed indirectly; *Help yourself!* (a direct, unmodified imperative) is (generally speaking) perfectly polite while the proposition that you will help yourself may require a degree of indirectness.

As Leech indicates, languages/cultures vary in the degree to which you are expected to apply this maxim — underapplying it will make the speaker appear mean (*Have a peanut!*), overapplying it will seem sarcastic, as the following examples[12] illustrate:

> **Example 13**
> *Basil Fawlty to his wife:*[13]
>
> Have another vat of wine, dear.

> **Example 14**
> *Basil's wife is in hospital:*
>
> You just lie there with your feet up and I'll go and carry you up another hundredweight of lime creams ...

Leech also points out that some cultures attach much more importance to the Generosity maxim than do others (he suggests that it is particularly important in Mediterranean cultures), but remember that we are only dealing with the importance attached to the **linguistic expression** of generosity — there is no suggestion that members of one culture really **are** more generous than members of another.

6.3.2.3 The Approbation maxim

The Approbation maxim states: 'Minimize the expression of beliefs which express dispraise of other; maximize the expression of beliefs which express approval of other.' The operation of this maxim is fairly obvious: all things being equal we prefer to praise others and if we cannot do so, to sidestep the issue, to give some sort of minimal response (*Well ...*) or to remain silent. Once again, societies (and sub-cultures, such as universities, within those societies) will vary greatly in the degree to which criticism is acceptable. And in any society there will be times when adverse criticism is expressed very strongly, and some activity types (e.g. in the British House of Commons) when gratuitously vicious and destructive criticism is the norm. Thus it is normal to say: *I enjoyed your lecture*, while if you did not enjoy it, you would either keep quiet about it or convey the fact more indirectly.

As Leech points out, the 'other' may not be the person directly addressed, but someone or something dear to him or her. Thus in most societies it is as unacceptable to say: *Did you do these ghastly daubings?* as it would be to ask: *Are these talentless children yours?*

Often in pragmatics (and in linguistics in general) we only become aware of the fact that a norm or regularity exists when someone (often an immature member of, or an outsider to, a particular group) fails to observe the norm.

6.3.2.4   The Modesty maxim

The Modesty maxim states: 'Minimize the expression of praise of self; maximize the expression of dispraise of self'. This is another maxim which varies enormously in its application from culture to culture. Leech (1983a: 137) notes that in Japan the operation of the Modesty maxim may, for example, lead someone to reject a compliment which had been paid to them:

> [In Japan] the Modesty Maxim is more powerful than it is
> as a rule in English-speaking societies, where it would be
> customarily more polite to accept a compliment 'graciously'
> (e.g. by thanking the speaker for it) rather than to go on
> denying it. Here English-speakers would be inclined to
> find some compromise between violating the Modesty
> Maxim and violating the Agreement Maxim.

The following example is a fairly typical example of the way in which the Modesty maxim operates in British English.[14] It is worth noting that speaker B consistently invokes the Approbation maxim, while speaker A is invoking the Modesty maxim:

Example 15
A and B were giving a series of lectures in a foreign country where decent coffee was an uncertain commodity. At the airport A had bought a good supply of ground coffee and a gadget for percolating it. She makes a first attempt at using it:

A: This isn't bad is it?
B: The coffee? It's very good.

A few hours later she makes some more:

B: This coffee's very good.
A: Not bad, is it?

Throughout this discussion I have emphasized that with all these maxims we are discussing the **linguistic expression** of certain values; there is no suggestion that any one group actually **is** more modest than another. But inevitably, there are individuals within any culture who are genuinely modest or (as in the following example) immodest:

Example 16
The person referred to is Jeanette Winterson, author of a highly acclaimed semi-autobiographical first novel.[15] She has since written four more novels, each achieving ever-diminishing popular success. She was interviewed after her most recent book[16] had been panned by the critics:[17]

When asked to nominate her favourite book of the year, she nominated her own.

Example 17
Another critic,[18] writing about the same event, describes Winterson as 'an author quite drunk with self-congratulation' and comments that her exaggerated praise of her own work shows:

… a gutsy defiance, a talent to offend against good taste and modesty.

I must admit that when I first read Winterson's lavish praise of her own writing, I assumed that she had really been joking and that she had been misrepresented by a biased, anti-feminist press. However, during a radio interview[19] she made it clear that what she said had been very much in earnest. I include this example of the non-observance of the Modesty maxim because the reaction to the interview (which had been widely reported throughout the

British press) was so startling. Pages were devoted to decrying Winterson's hubris and lack of modesty, a fact which neatly underlines the point I tried to make in relation to the Approbation maxim — that we become aware of the fact that a norm or regularity exists only when someone so spectacularly fails to observe it! It is important in pragmatics (perhaps in linguistics in general) to take careful note of incidents such as this one which jar or cause embarrassment or (mock) outrage — they will often point up the existence of a particular norm in a given society.

6.3.2.5 The Agreement maxim

The Agreement maxim runs as follows: 'Minimize the expression of disagreement between self and other; maximize the expression of agreement between self and other.' As with all the other maxims, the usual caveats apply concerning the need to take account of the relationship between speaker and hearer and of the nature of the interaction in which they are involved. Remember, too, that it is not being claimed that people avoid disagreeing with one another. We simply observe that they are much more direct in expressing their agreement, than disagreement. Time and again you will hear someone who holds a diametrically opposed view to the one just expressed begin a counter-argument by saying: *Yes, but ...* And compare the following:

Example 18
A: ... I don't want my daughter to do CSE, I want her to do 'O' level.
B: Yes, but Mr Sharma, I thought we resolved this on your last visit.

Example 19
A: Nehemulla is ideally suited to the class she's in and this class will do CSE in two years' time.
B: No, my dear, no, no, it's wrong!

These two examples are both taken from the film *Cross Talk*. Speaker B is Mrs Green, the deputy headteacher of a school (a British woman), speaker A is Mr Sharma, the Indian-born father of one of the pupils attending her school. They are involved in a major disagreement concerning the courses Mr Sharma's daughter will take the following year. Although Mrs Green disagrees strongly with Mr Sharma, she nevertheless observes the 'Agreement maxim' to a high degree (remember, we are here considering only what occurs at utterance level). Mr Sharma speaks excellent English, but many of his contributions are characterized by an absence of indirectness and, more specifically, a failure (refusal?) to observe the Agreement maxim.

6.3.2.6   The Pollyanna Principle

I shall finish with an example of what is, in my view, the least generalizable of Leech's maxims, 'The Pollyanna Principle' (1983a: 147). Pollyanna was the eponymous heroine of Eleanor H. Porter's novel, an appallingly saccharine child who always looked on the bright side of life! And this is what observance of the 'Pollyanna Principle' leads us to do — to put the best possible gloss on what we have to say. In its least contentious form, this may refer only to the use of 'minimizers' such as *a bit* ('This essay's a bit short', when in fact it is much too short), but this is a strategy which is already adequately dealt with under the heading of 'reducing the size of imposition' (see chapter 5, section 5.3.5). Other aspects of it simply relate to relexicalization (see chapter 3, section 3.8.1), replacing an unpleasant term (e.g. *body-snatcher*) with a supposedly less unpleasant one (*resurrection-ist*). However, we can find instances of the 'Pollyanna Principle' in operation which do not seem to be explained by other maxims or principles. Shen Jiaxuan (1994) notes that in Chinese (as in English) there is a bias towards the positive in assigning utterance meaning. Thus, in English we find that 'Good luck!' means 'I wish you good luck', whereas 'Bad luck!' is an expression of commiseration (it does not wish the hearer bad luck!). So in Chinese you + Noun expressions (which translates as 'has + N') are all biased towards a positive meaning: you diwei (literally 'has status') means 'has high status'; you shuiping (literally 'has level') means 'has a high level', and so on. In interpersonal pragmatics, too, we can find examples of the Pollyanna Principle in operation (although since it has taken me so many years to find these few examples we must assume that the Pollyanna Principle is not widely observed by individual speakers):

Example 20
The speaker had just 'lost' two hours' work on the word-processor:[20]

'Ah well, I'll probably write it better second time around.'

Example 21
The two speakers were discussing the bad impression which visitors would gain because of the appalling weather on a University Open Day:[21]

A: They're not exactly seeing the place at its best!
B: Well, at least it's not snowing.

Example 22
A managing director has to tell one of his managers that he has not been given the promotion he had hoped for:

'You're too valuable where you are. If we were to offer you the job we would lose the most valuable marketing manager we ever had.'

In my final example the speaker out-Pollyannas Pollyanna, by finding something positive to say about a rotten egg (but I had to look back 100 years to find it!):

Example 23
This is the famous 'Curate's Egg' joke, first published in the humorous magazine, <u>Punch</u>, in 1895. A young curate is having breakfast with his Bishop. Bishop to curate:

I'm afraid you've got a bad egg, Mr Jones!

Oh no, my Lord, I assure you! Parts of it are excellent!

6.3.3 Problems with the Leech's approach

There is a major flaw in Leech's approach to politeness as presently formulated, which has been discussed by a number of people (see, for example, Dillon *et al.* 1985, Thomas 1986, Brown and Levinson 1987, Fraser 1990): there appears to be no motivated way of restricting the number of maxims. In theory it would be possible to produce a new maxim to explain every tiny perceived regularity in language use (I have already indicated, for example, the very limited applicability of the 'Pollyanna Principle'). This makes the theory at best inelegant, at worst virtually unfalsifiable.

I have nevertheless spent a considerable time explaining and exemplifying Leech's approach because, for all its problems, it allows us, better than any of the other approaches discussed here, to make specific cross-cultural comparisons and (more importantly) to **explain** cross-cultural differences in the perception of politeness and the use of politeness strategies. The inelegance of Leech's approach could perhaps be overcome if, instead of being viewed as maxims *à la* Grice, Leech's 'maxims' were seen as a series of social-psychological constraints influencing, to a greater or lesser degree, the choices made within the pragmatic parameters. Some of these constraints may apply (in differing degrees) universally (the Politeness Principle itself); others might be entirely culture-specific (certain taboos); others still (Pollyanna?) might be totally idiosyncratic. Viewed in this way, it is entirely reasonable that we should have a list which is open-ended, but in which the different factors influencing linguistic behaviour could be ranked in terms of their relative importance in different cultures, or in different activity types.

6.4 Politeness and the management of face

The most influential theory of politeness was put forward by Brown and Levinson (1978 and revised in 1987). Central to Brown and Levinson's theory of politeness is the concept of '**face**', as proposed by Goffman (1967). The term 'face' in the sense of 'reputation' or 'good name' seems to have been first used in English in 1876 as a translation of the Chinese term 'diū liǎn' in the phrase 'Arrangements by which China has lost face'.[22] Since then it has been used widely in phrases such as 'losing face', 'saving face', as in the following example from James Galsworthy:[23]

> **Example 24**
> 'They've got to save face. Saving face is the strongest motive in the world.'

Goffman himself (1967: 5) defined face as:

> ... the positive social value a person effectively claims for himself by the line others assume he has taken during a particular contact. Face is an image of self delineated in terms of approved social attributes — albeit an image that others may share, as when a person makes a good showing for his profession or religion by making a good showing for himself.

Within politeness theory 'face' is best understood as every individual's feeling of self-worth or self-image; this image can be damaged, maintained or enhanced through interaction with others. Face has two aspects — 'positive' and 'negative'. An individual's positive face is reflected in his or her desire to be liked, approved of, respected and appreciated by others. An individual's negative face is reflected in the desire not to be impeded or put upon, to have the freedom to act as one chooses.

6.4.1 Face-threatening acts

According to Brown and Levinson, certain illocutionary acts are liable to damage or threaten another person's face; such acts are known as 'face-threatening acts' (FTAs). An illocutionary act has the potential to damage the hearer's positive face (by, for example, insulting H or expressing disapproval of something which H holds dear), or H's negative face (an order, for example, will impinge upon H's freedom of action); or the illocutionary act may potentially damage the speaker's own positive face (if S has to admit to having botched a job, for example) or S's negative face (if S is cornered into making an offer of help). In order to reduce the possibility of damage to H's face or to the speaker's own face, he or she may adopt certain strategies. The choice of strategy will be made on the basis of the speaker's assessment of the size of the FTA. The speaker can calculate the size of the FTA on the basis of the parameters of power (P), distance (D) and rating of imposition (R). These combined values determine the overall 'weightiness' of the FTA which in turn influences the strategy used.

6.4.1.1 Superstrategies for performing face-threatening acts

According to Brown and Levinson, the first decision to be made is whether to perform the FTA or not. If the speaker does decide to perform the FTA, there are four possibilities: three sets of 'on-record' superstrategies (perform the FTA on-record without redressive action (bald-on-record), perform the FTA on-record using positive politeness, perform the FTA on-record using negative politeness) and one set of 'off-record' strategies. If the speaker decides that the degree of face threat is too great, he or she may decide to avoid the FTA altogether (in other words, to say nothing). I shall discuss each set of superstrategies in turn.

6.4.1.2   Performing an FTA without any redress (bald-on-record)

There are occasions when external factors constrain an individual to speak very directly (and in full conformity with the Gricean maxims), for example, if there is an emergency of some sort, or where there is a major time constraint (making an international telephone call) or where there is some form of channel limitation (e.g. speaking on a field telephone). A situation which combines all these external constraints would be making a 'May Day' call from a foundering ship; this would certainly demand speaking with maximum efficiency. In emergencies or in highly task-oriented situations, such as teaching someone to drive, we find that the speaker is likely to focus on the propositional content of the message, and pay little attention to the interpersonal aspect of what is said:

Example 25
The speaker knows that a bomb has been planted in the stands at his racecourse. He thinks his young nephew is hiding in the stands:[24]

... Toby, get off the stands. The stands are not safe. Toby, for Christ's sake do what I say. This is not a game. Come on, you little bugger ... for once in your life, be told.

If the speaker decides that the overall 'weightiness' of the FTA is very small (e.g. you are making a trivial request of someone you know well and who has no power over you) the request may be made 'bald-on-record'. I have already offered such an example, of my mother saying: 'Shut the window, Jen.' The same is true when the face-threatening act is perceived as being in the hearer's interest: 'Have a chocolate.'

Other situations in which no attempt is made to mitigate the FTA, regardless of the rating of the imposition, are to be found where the power differential is great. In such cases the powerful participant will often employ no indirectness at all:

Example 26
The speaker is a senior rating at a naval detention centre. He is addressing a prisoner of lower rank:

'You are to stand to attention in the centre of your room every time the door is opened. You are to obey all orders given to you by any member of the remand wing staff at all

times. You are not to engage any member of the remand
wing staff in casual conversation.'

But many of the most striking examples of bald-on-record
utterances fall into none of the categories mentioned by Brown
and Levinson.[25] Far from employing a bald-on-record strategy
because the speaker estimates that the degree of face threat is
small (as politeness theory appears to predict), in each of the
examples which follow, the speaker takes no redressive action
because he has deliberately chosen to be maximally offensive:

Example 27
Bob Champion, champion jockey, referring to women jockeys:

'I'm dead against them! They're a mistake and get in the
way. Women are not strong enough or big enough.'

Example 28
*Mr Tam Dalyell, M.P., in the British House of Commons (refer-
ring to the then Prime Minister, Margaret Thatcher):*[26]

'I say that she is a bounder, a liar, a deceiver, a crook.'

Example 29
*Australian Judge in the court case brought by the British Govern-
ment to try to prevent the publication of the memoirs of Peter
Wright, an ex-member of MI5. The judge is referring to the evi-
dence given by the then British Cabinet Secretary, Sir Robert
Armstrong:*[27]

'His evidence is palpably false and utter humbug.'

6.4.1.3 Performing an FTA with redress (positive politeness)

Within Brown and Levinson's theory, when you speak to
someone you may orient yourself towards that individual's
positive face, and employ positive politeness (which appeals to
H's desire to be liked and approved of). Brown and Levinson
(1987 [1978]: 101-29) list fifteen positive politeness strategies,
giving copious illustrations from many different languages.
Examples in English are readily observable in almost any informal
setting:

Example 30

Male first-year student calling to female-first year student (whom he didn't know) in their college bar during 'Freshers' Week':

Hey, blondie, what are you studying, then? French and Italian? Join the club!

The young man employed no fewer than three of Brown and Levinson's positive politeness strategies: 'use in-group identity markers' (*blondie*), 'express interest in H' (asking her what she is studying), 'claim common ground' (*Join the club!*).

Unsurprisingly, perhaps, a number of Brown and Levinson's positive politeness strategies find close parallels in Leech's politeness principles: 'seek agreement', 'avoid disagreement', 'be optimistic', 'give sympathy'.

6.4.1.4 Performing an FTA with redress (negative politeness)

Negative politeness is oriented towards a hearer's negative face, which appeals to the hearer's desire not to be impeded or put upon, to be left free to act as they choose. Negative politeness manifests itself in the use of conventional politeness markers, deference markers, minimizing imposition, etc. Brown and Levinson list ten negative politeness strategies and, once again, examples in English are easy to find in more formal settings. The following brief note (absolutely authentic!), includes an astonishing seven negative politeness strategies (eight if the salutation is counted as strategy 5 (give deference)):

Example 31

This is an extract from a note that was sent to me by an academic from another university. She was visiting Lancaster for a conference and we had arranged to meet on Friday, but unfortunately I forgot our appointment:[28]

Dear Jenny Thomas,

I'm sorry I missed you today. I wanted to discuss with you
…

I know it is a terrible imposition, but if you had any time, Sat. p.m. we could perhaps meet in Lancaster for a coffee? I'd be very grateful.

Best wishes,
[Name deleted]

We could … meet is an example of strategy 1 ('be convention-ally indirect'); *perhaps* is an example of strategy 2 ('hedge'); *if you had any time* is an example of strategy 4 ('minimize imposition'); *I know it's a terrible imposition* and *I'm sorry I missed you* (in fact, it was I who missed her!) are examples of strategy 6 ('admit the impingement' and 'beg forgiveness'). Strategy 7 ('point of view distancing') is evident in *I wanted to …*, where the tense is switched from present to past, so that the writer distanced herself from the act. And, finally, *I'd be very grateful* is an example of strategy 10 ('go on record as incurring a debt').

Many warning notices which have a wide readership employ negative politeness. The following notice appeared on the screen of everyone logging onto our university mainframe during December 1994. Since it could have been read by anyone from first-year undergraduate to the Vice-Chancellor, it could not be too rude, and so strategy 7 ('impersonalize S and H') was invoked:

Example 32
It is necessary to request senders of 'junk' e-mail, e.g.
'chain' letters, to desist. It's a nuisance, against the Rules,
and invites disciplinary action.

And not only human beings, but even cartoon characters use negative politeness! In the following example Daffy Duck employs strategy 8 ('state FTA as a general rule') to get Silvester the cat to part with some of his food:

Example 33
'Friends always share!'

6.4.1.5 Performing an FTA using off-record politeness
Brown and Levinson list a further fifteen strategies for perform-ing off-record politeness. These include: 'give hints', 'use meta-phors', 'be ambiguous or vague'. Here are just three examples, the first of strategy 1 (hinting), the second of strategy 9, involving a widely-invoked Japanese metaphor; the final example is of strategy 15 ('be incomplete', 'use ellipsis'), which is one of the most frequently-encountered off-record politeness strategies:

Example 34
One student to another:

That isn't a creme egg I can see you eating, is it?

Example 35
A Japanese student who lived outside the capital had taken a University entrance examination in Tokyo. One of her class-mates sent her the following telegram, to inform her that she had not passed:

サクラ チル
sakura chiru
[The cherry blossom has fallen].

Example 36
The following is an extract from a novel in which Hosteen Pinto, a native American, has been accused of murder. Professor Bourbebonette is an anthropologist who has worked with him in the past. She believes him to be innocent and thinks the non-Indian FBI officers have not investigated the case properly. In this extract she is trying to persuade a Police Lieutenant (himself a Navajo), to take an interest in the case:[29]

'She [Pinto's attorney] didn't know much ... she told us the Federal Public Defender's office had two investigators who might be helpful. But ...'

Professor Bourbebonette let the sentence trail off, intending to let the scepticism in her tone finish it.

Professor Bourbebonette is reluctant to criticize one police officer in front of another. She tries to avoid performing the FTA by not completing her sentence, but she nevertheless expects the lieutenant to understand what she means. The lieutenant, however, forces her to go 'on-record' and she goes on to say:

'But I got the impression that she didn't think they'd be very helpful.'

6.4.1.6 Do not perform FTA
Brown and Levinson's final strategy 'Do not perform FTA', appears to be self-explanatory: there are times when something is potentially so face-threatening, that you don't say it. Brown and Levinson do not discuss this strategy (there's not a lot to say about saying nothing!), but Tanaka (1993) discusses two sorts of

'saying nothing' (which, following Bonikowska (1988), she terms the 'opting out choice' or OOC). There are times when the speaker decides to say nothing and genuinely wishes to let the matter drop; there are other occasions when an individual decides to say nothing (decides not to complain, for example) but still wishes to achieve the effect which the speech act would have achieved had it been uttered. Tanaka (1993: 50–1) terms these two strategies OOC-genuine and OOC-strategic:

OOC-genuine: S does not perform a speech act, and genuinely intends to let the matter remain closed.

S/he does not intend to achieve the perlocutionary effect.

OOC-strategic: S does not perform a speech act, but expects A to infer her/his wish to achieve the perlocutionary effect.

There is a third situation — where there is such a strong expectation that something will be said, that saying nothing is in itself a massive FTA (for example, failing to express condolences to someone on the death of a loved one). The following example, taken from the autobiography[30] of Sir Kenneth Dover (a former President of the British Academy and Master of Corpus Christi, Oxford) relates one such incident, which reflects little credit on himself:

Example 37
Aston was a senior research fellow at Corpus Christi. He was subject to bouts of drinking and severe depression; he could be difficult to work with and was something of an embarrassment to the College. At a meeting between President and Fellow, Aston said to Dover:

'You're trying to push me out of the College!'

Dover commented:

' … this was so obviously true that I didn't say anything.'

A few days later Aston killed himself.

6.4.2 Criticisms of Brown and Levinson

Brown and Levinson's work has been extraordinarily influential and very widely discussed. It is not surprising, therefore, that a number of criticisms have been made of their model of politeness.

The description of the FTA implies that an act is threatening to the face of either the speaker or the hearer; in fact many acts can be seen to threaten the face of both S and H simultaneously. An *apology*, for example, threatens the speaker's face in an obvious way, but it can also be the source of considerable embarrassment to the hearer.

Brown and Levinson claim that positive and negative politeness are mutually exclusive. In practice, a single utterance can be oriented to both positive and negative face simultaneously:

Example 38
Woman addressing importunate man:[31]

Do me a favour — piss off!

Brown and Levinson's model appears to predict that the greater the degree of face-threat, the greater will be the degree of indirectness. But many counter-examples are readily available. In addition to the examples of the type of bald-on-record utterances I offered in examples 27, 28 and 29, we find very different norms of directness in operation within long-term relationships and within different sub-groups.

Brown and Levinson argue that some speech acts are inherently face-threatening (cf. Leech, who claims that some speech acts are inherently polite). From these two observations it might be concluded that some utterances pose no face-threat at all. Dascal (1977: 315) argues, rightly in my view, that merely speaking to someone sets up what he terms a 'conversational demand' (cf. also Nofsinger (1975)): simply by speaking we trespass on another person's space. Saying anything at all (or even saying nothing!) is potentially face-threatening.

6.5 Politeness viewed as a conversational contract

According to Fraser (1990), people are constrained in interaction by what he calls a 'conversational contract' (CC) — the understanding which people bring to an interaction of the norms obtaining within that interaction and of their rights and obligations within it. On the face of it, Fraser takes a more sociolinguistic (deterministic) approach to politeness than do Leech or Brown and Levinson — people employ the degree of politeness required by the event or situation in which they find themselves:

> ... being polite constitutes operating within the ... terms of the CC.

However, Fraser (1990: 232) is careful to point out that norms of politeness are:

> ... renegotiable in light of the participants' perception and/or acknowledgements of factors such as the status, the power, and the role of each speaker, and the nature of the circumstances.

Fraser's model of politeness is very sketchy compared with those of Leech and Brown and Levinson and it is difficult to judge how it might operate in practice. His inclusion of the 'rights and obligations' dimension is welcome, and the approach fits in well with the notion of 'activity types' (see chapter 7).

6.6 Politeness measured along pragmatic scales

Spencer-Oatey (1992: 30–3) argues that the way Brown and Levinson (1987 [1978]) and Leech (1983a) formulated their theories of politeness left them open to being criticized on the grounds that they are culturally biased. For example (as I noted in section 6.3.2.1), 'autonomy' is highly valued in Western society, but not always within Oriental cultures. In order to overcome the problems of cultural-specificity, Spencer-Oatey proposes sets of dimensions. She suggests that all the research on politeness can be summarized in terms of these three sets of dimensions: individuals will select the point on the scale according to their cultural values and the situation within which they are operating:

> [Despite their different approaches] these various researchers have one thing in common: they all assume that face needs lie universally at set points on each of the relevant dimensions ... However, I contend that in different cir-

cumstances, different options may be favoured, and that factors such as type of speech act (Leech) and cultural variation (Wierzbicka) will influence which point on the dimension is preferred.

Spencer-Oatey's scales are as follows (1992: 30):

1.	Need for Consideration:	autonomy	–	imposition
2.	Need to be Valued:	approbation	–	criticism
		interest/ concern	–	disinterest
3.	Need for Relational Identity:	inclusion	–	exclusion
		equality	–	superordination/ subordination

6.7 Conclusion

Within pragmatics, most people have been careful to define 'politeness' as a pragmatic/communicative phenomenon and not to equate it with any moral or psychological disposition towards being nice to one's interlocutor. Green (1989: 147) expresses this particularly well:

> ... the speaker is really only going through the motions of offering options or showing respect for the addressee's feelings. The offer may be a facade, the options nonviable, and the respect a sham. It is the fact that an effort was made to go through the motions at all that makes the act an act of politeness.

Outside pragmatics, however, this specialized conception of politeness is misinterpreted with tiresome frequency: pragmaticists are accused of viewing the world through rose-coloured glasses, of having a vision of society where everyone is nice and kind to everyone else! The very term 'politeness', with its widespread use in everyday interaction, encourages this misinterpretation and for that reason is, in my view, unfortunate (although, like the equally misused specialized definition of 'co-operation' in chapter 3, it is so deeply entrenched within pragmatics that we are probably stuck with it for ever!). All that is really being claimed is that people employ certain strategies (including the 50+ strategies described by Leech, Brown and Levinson, and others) for reasons of expediency — experience has taught us that particular strategies are likely to succeed in given circumstances, so we use them. I would prefer terminology which does not give even the appearance of committing the analyst to any view of the psychological disposition of the speaker, but instead relates pragmatic choice to discourse goals. Such an approach was proposed by Pyle (1975) (cited in Dascal 1983: 161), who argues that people employ indirectness when their communicative goals conflict: for example, when their desire to avoid hurting someone's feelings conflicts with their obligation to tell the truth:

> ... being indirect is a mechanism for dealing with conflict-ing intentions and desires. The general form of the conflict is that the speaker wants to convey X for some reason and he does not want to convey X for other reasons. By being indirect he can convey X in one sense but not in another.

Consider the following examples:

Example 39
This notice was displayed in a four-star London hotel:

Dear Guest, We have found it necessary to introduce an anti-theft alarm system on our colour televisions. We would therefore ask you <u>not</u> to disconnect this set. Thank you for your cooperation.

Example 40
The following interview was reported by Ann Cadwalida:[32]

Asked if Libya had supplied weapons to the IRA, Colonel Gadaffi did not reply directly: I am obliged to support the Irish cause, a liberation cause, a just cause.

In example 39 the hotel authorities clearly want to convey the message 'Don't steal the television!' but (for fear of offending their law-abiding guests) are reluctant to express this proposition directly. Their choice of wording could be explained convin-cingly either within politeness theory or as prompted by a clash of goals. The indirectness in example 40, however, is less readily explained by 'politeness' (in either its everyday or its specialist sense), but seems a classic case of a 'clash of goals'. Colonel Gadaffi wanted to convey the fact that he has supplied weapons to the IRA, without going on-record with that fact (he might perhaps need to deny it in the future). Competing goals seems to offer a more general explanatory framework.

Notes

1. 7 November 1990 ('the Queen's Speech' is a speech written by the Government and read by the Queen at the ceremonial opening of a new parliamentary session).

2. Of course, English-speakers signal deference at many other linguistic levels: phonetic (they will probably be extra careful with their pronunciation, particularly avoiding socially stigmatized usage, such as dropping initial /h/ and medial or final /t/) semantic (choice of more formal lexis), pragmatic (greater use of indirectness), discoursal (allowing the socially superior participant to initiate and terminate talk, to complete their contribution without being interrupted, etc.).

3. Obviously, the intonation might very well vary according to the social status of the hearer.

4. The consequences could range from disciplinary action (e.g. in the military, in law courts or schools) to social censure.

5. James Thurber (1963) A couple of hamburgers. *Vintage Thurber*. Hamilton, London, p. 103.

6. House of Commons, 28 March 1988.

7. *The Archers*. BBC Radio 4, 11 November 1990.

8. James Thurber (1963) A couple of hamburgers. *Vintage Thurber*, Hamilton, London, p. 103.

9. The Miller Howe, Cumbria, 31 December 1990.

10. ITV play *The men's room*, 1991.

11. Spencer-Oatey notes that Wierzbicka (1991) and LoCastro (1990) make similar points with respect to Polish and Japanese cultures respectively.

12. Both taken from John Cleese and Connie Booth (1988) *The complete Fawlty Towers*. Methuen, London.

13. John Cleese and Connie Booth (1988) *The complete Fawlty Towers*. Methuen, London.

14. I take up the question of the interaction between the different Maxims and the differential value attached to them in different cultures in *The dynamics of discourse*.

15. Jeanette Winterson (1985) *Oranges are not the only fruit*. Vintage, London.

16. Jeanette Winterson (1994) *Art and Lies*. Cape, London.

17. This particular report was taken from the *Daily Mail*, 17th July 1994, but the remarks were very widely reported.

18. Andrew O'Hagan, *London Review of Books*.

19. *Desert Island Discs,* BBC Radio 4, 21 October 1994.

20. This appears to be a 'genuine', rather than merely surface-level, observation of the Pollyanna Principle.

21. Lancaster, 25 January 1995.

22. R. Hart (1901 [1876]) *Those from the land of Sinim*.

23. James Galsworthy (1928) *Swan song*.

24. Dick Francis (1993) *Decider*. Michael Joseph, London, p. 80.

25. Although the very fact that these three examples are so striking and memorable suggests that they are deviations from the expected norms, which in turn supports Brown and Levinson's argument.

26. 29 October 1986. Note the interesting use of the metalinguistic performative 'I say', which makes Mr Dalyell's utterance unfalsifiable!

27. Widely reported, 29 October 1986.

28. 17 February 1994.

29. Tony Hillerman (1993 [1991]) *Coyote Waits*. Penguin, London, p. 17.

30. Kenneth Dover (1994) *Marginal comment: a memoir.* Duckworth, London.

31. *The older woman.* BBC Radio 4, December 1994.

32. RTE, 29 October 1986.

CHAPTER 7

The construction of meaning

7.1 Introduction

There seems to be an unchallenged assumption within pragmatics that a methodology developed in one area of linguistics is
appropriate for another — the unspoken conviction that formal
approaches are always best and that what may be a good approach
to grammar is also a good approach to pragmatics. But pragmatics
is crucially different from grammar (within which I include
phonology, morphology, syntax, semantics, etc.), in a number of
ways. Pragmatics, as we saw in chapter 4, makes different sorts of
generalizations (principles or maxims) from those made in other
areas (which invoke rules). Pragmatics, as we saw in chapters 5
and 6, is **motivated**: people have reasons for speaking as they do,
for choosing one grammatical form rather than another, for
preferring one lexical item over another, for employing indirectness and politeness. Pragmatics relies on different forms of
evidence from those used in grammar. Pragmatics is **dynamic**:
the way in which people use language is not solely a reflection of
sets of social and contextual variables — people can be seen to use
language in order to bring about change. Pragmatics is not about
meaning; it is about **making meaning**, about meaning potential,
showing how people negotiate meaning in interaction.

It is therefore unfortunate to see in the work of many
linguists who claim to be 'doing pragmatics' the uncritical
adoption of rule-governed approaches to the description of
pragmatic phenomena (such as speech acts), of static notions of
context and of role relationships and a view of meaning as the
'property' of the speaker, as given rather than negotiated. In this
chapter I shall argue that it is time for pragmatics to come of age,
to examine its aims, claims and methodologies and not to take
over unthinkingly a descriptive apparatus developed for another

discipline and a different purpose.

Two questions are often asked about pragmatics: the first — is pragmatics part of linguistics? and the second (and more frequently asked) – how does pragmatics differ from socio-linguistics? The two questions are connected and I shall take them in order.

7.2 How does pragmatics fit into linguistics?

Pragmatics is a level of linguistic description like phonology, syntax, semantics and discourse analysis. Like the other levels, it has its own theories, methodologies and underlying assumptions. It has its own foci of interest, which may change over time, come to the fore or fade away completely (for example, at present politeness still commands a disproportionate amount of space in pragmatics journals while no one seems to be much interested in pragmatic presupposition any more!). As we have seen in this book, pragmatics is concerned with issues not addressed within other areas of linguistics, such as the assignment of meaning in context — utterance meaning and pragmatic force — speech acts, implicature, indirectness and the negotiation of meaning between speaker and hearer.

Pragmatics is a separate level of description, but there are also pragmatic aspects to other levels of linguistic description. This may seem confusing, but in this pragmatics is no different from other areas of linguistics. For example, there are very obvious phonological aspects to morphology (the appearance of *im-* or *em-* instead of *in-* or *en-* before bilabial plosives — *im*possible, *em*bedded) and a phonetician may have things to say about discourse analysis (cf. Local *et al.* 1985) or the pragmatics of intonation (see Wichmann 1991). In the same way the prag-maticist will have things to say about choices made within phonetics, syntax, semantics and discourse. For example, Trudgill (1972 and 1974) has reported on 'h'-dropping among working-class males in Norwich. There are times when the pronunciation can be explained not in terms of sociolinguistic variables (age, gender, social setting) but by pragmatic factors — the desire of one particular male on one particular occasion to distance himself from or align himself with another person by consciously choosing not to pronounce /h/. Similarly there are often prag-matic reasons for grammatical choice: a professor from another department once overheard me talking to a new member of staff in my own department about a course which the newcomer had originally been scheduled to teach, but which I had agreed to take over in his stead. The professor remarked: 'Only someone from linguistics could say "Me and Geoff will be teaching the course together!" '. What he failed to realize (being a literary type!) was that this use of the stigmatized 'Me and Geoff' instead of 'Geoff and I' was a deliberate choice on my part, designed to reduce the social distance between the new colleague and me.

7.3 Pragmatics versus sociolinguistics

If it is clear where pragmatics fits in as a level of linguistic description, it is not always clear where it differs from sociolinguistics, particularly what Gumperz (1982) terms 'interactional sociolinguistics'. There are certainly areas of overlap, but roughly we could say that sociolinguistics is mainly concerned with the systematic linguistic correlates of relatively *fixed* and *stable* social variables (such as region of origin, social class, ethnicity, sex, age, etc.) on the way an individual speaks. Pragmatics, on the other hand, is mainly concerned with describing the linguistic correlates of relatively *changeable* features of that same individual (such as relative status, social role) and the way in which the speaker exploits his/her (socio)linguistic repertoire in order to achieve a particular goal.

Sociolinguistics is static, offering a 'snapshot' of the language of a particular community at a particular moment in time. Pragmatics is dynamic, describing what a speaker from that community does with those resources, how he or she uses them to change the way things are or in order to maintain the status quo. Pragmatics is parasitic upon sociolinguistics, taking the sociolinguistic description of an individual's repertoire as the point of departure: sociolinguistics tells us what linguistic resources the individual has, pragmatics tells us what he or she does with it. Let us see how this works out in practice:

The two extracts which follow were recorded when my father (F) and mother (M) were visiting my house. It was my birthday and I had only just moved into this house. The first discussion relates to a dining table which I had bought second-hand, stripped down and restored. The second discussion concerns a tapestry (a copy of the mediaeval tapestry 'La Dame à la Licorne') which my mother had made me for my birthday (the symbol '/' indicates an interruption):

Example 1

F: Our Jen done that.
M: How many coats did you put on it, Jen?
J: How many what?
M: Coats.
J: Oh, quite a lot.
F: And 'ow about the waistcoats and socks?
M: Oh, she didn't bother with those.
F: She'm lazy.

Example 2

J: What's that supposed to be in the corner?
M: I think it's meant I've decided it's meant to be a squir-
rel.
J: Hmm
M: But it's erm whoever designed it was a little out of/
F: /it could be a beetle!

Sociolinguists listening to (or even reading) example 1 could tell a lot about the speakers. For instance, they could tell that F was from the working class and was not highly educated (use of *done* instead of *did*, and *òw* instead of *how*). They could tell that he was elderly (the use of the lexical item *waistcoat* and, more particularly, the fact that he used the very old-fashioned pronunciation of /weskɪt/ and that he came from the West Country (use of the regional form *she'm*).

A pragmaticist would note the use of the intimate address and reference forms (*Jen* and *Our Jen*) and that in both extracts F uses linguistic strategies to disrupt a serious conversation and turn it into a joke, first with the play on the ambiguity of the word *coat* (*layer of varnish* and *item of clothing*) and secondly by suggesting that the slightly distorted squirrel his wife had stitched might be a beetle.

7.3.1 Overlap between pragmatics and sociolinguistics

There are certain areas where pragmatics and sociolinguistics appear to overlap. Again, this is no different from the apparent overlap between, say, phonology and sociolinguistics: seminal studies by sociolinguists such as Labov (1966), Milroy (1980) and Trudgill (1972, 1974) have all taken as their main object the sound system of the community they were investigating. Knowles (1978) undertook an investigation into the nature of phonological variables in Scouse. Although the focus of the sociolinguistic and phonological studies appear to be the same, the purposes were different. The sociolinguists were not primarily interested in the theoretical niceties of phonological theory, but in establishing as full a description as possible of a particular variety of a language, both for itself and for the insight such a description gave to sociolinguistic theory. The phonologist, by contrast, undertook the description for the insights it gave into phonological theory.

Today most sociolinguists undertaking a description of a particular variety of English will include a description of phonological, syntactic and lexical features of that variety (see, for example, Sebba 1993). For some reason, few have anything to say about the pragmatic and discourse norms of a particular community (although Scollon and Scollon (1983) do include in their description of the English of Athebaskans in Canada, a discussion of face considerations, the Athebaskans' use of indirectness and of their turn-taking norms). On those (few) occasions when sociolinguists do discuss the forms of indirectness or the speech act repertoire of a particular language variety, they are doing so in order to establish a comprehensive description. The pragmaticist does it in order to contribute to pragmatic theory (cf. Ochs (1976), on the (non)-observance of the conversational maxims among the Malagasy). Similarly, there are both sociolinguistic and pragmatic[1] dimensions to code-switching and code-mixing. A sociolinguistic study might focus on how factors such as the setting, the nature of the speech event in which speakers are participating, the age or social status of the participants influence choice of code (see Milroy and Milroy 1990: 506–9). A pragmatic study would focus primarily on the way in which code-switching is used in order to increase or decrease social distance, or to reinforce shared norms (see, for example, Scotton 1983 and 1988, Burt 1990, 1992, 1994).

In short, it makes as much (or as little) sense to say that sociolinguistics is the same as pragmatics as it does to say that phonetics and sociolinguistics are the same.

7.4 Activity types versus speech events

Sociolinguistics and pragmatics are both centrally concerned with the effect of context on language: the sociolinguist is primarily interested in the **systematic** linguistic correlates of social and contextual variables. Within sociolinguistics the most fully-developed and best known framework for describing context is the one proposed by Hymes (1962) in his seminal article 'The ethnography of speaking'. With his SPEAKING mnemonic he offers a comprehensive checklist for the description of what he terms '**speech events**'. These are summarized below:

Situation
: This can be a physical setting (e.g. classroom) or an abstract setting (e.g. a committee meeting, a graduation ceremony).

Participants
: Speaker, hearer, audience, etc.

Ends
: Some speech events have conventional outcomes (e.g. 'diagnosis', 'verdict'). Can also include individual goals.

Act sequences
: Message form, message content.

Key
: Tone, manner or spirit of act (e.g. serious, ironic).

Instrumentalities
: Channel or mode (is the language spoken, written, etc.?).
Forms of speech (which dialect, accent or other variety does the speaker employ?).

Norms
: Norms of interpretation.
Norms of interaction.

Genre
: Categories such as joke, lecture, advertisement.

This same framework is often used by pragmaticists for describing context, but it is not obvious that it is the most appropriate one. Hymes, it should be noted, was primarily interested in describing rather formal, often highly ritualized events, such as weddings, funerals, welcoming ceremonies (see Hymes 1962 or, for a clear and simple overview, Saville-Troike 1982). It is not necessarily the case that less formal, rigid or predictable events, such as 'a university admissions interview', 'a visit to the doctor's', 'a dressing down by the headmaster' are well-handled within this framework and casual conversations certainly are not.

Hymes's framework does an excellent job of revealing to us the taken-for-granted aspects of interactions, but the most interesting features can be obscured by a welter of (frequently incidental) detail. Moreover it does not enable us (nor was it so designed) to explain why it is that one person performs very differently from another in the 'same' linguistic situation (for example, why one student emerges from an interview having succeeded in gaining a university place, while another does not; why one person succeeds in talking his or her way into a private function, while another does not). Hymes's framework leaves no room for the individual's contribution, for showing how one speaker successfully exploits a situation to achieve his or her goals, while the other fails dismally.

So although pragmaticists might want to use a framework such as Hymes's as a point of departure, we cannot leave it there. A possible way forward is suggested by Levinson's notion of **activity type**. Taking his approach and terminology from prototype theory, Levinson (1979: 368) defines an activity type as:

> … a fuzzy category whose focal members are goal-defined,
> socially constituted, bounded, events with *constraints* on
> participants, setting, and so on, but above all on the kinds of
> allowable contributions. Paradigm examples would be
> teaching, a job interview, a jural interrogation, a football
> game, a task in a workshop, a dinner party and so on.

It is surprising how few pragmaticists have adopted this, in my view, very promising framework. Hymes's framework for describing a speech event has many points in common with Levinson's activity type, but there is an important difference in emphasis (precisely reflecting the different approaches of the sociolinguist and the pragmaticist to the description of linguistic interaction). Put very simply, Hymes sees context as constraining the way the individual speaks; Levinson sees the individual's use of language as shaping the 'event'. The sociolinguist tries to show how features of context **systematically** constrain language use. The pragmaticist tries to show how speakers use language in order to change the situation they find themselves in. Now some events (and this is particularly true of the type of ritualistic events which most concerned Hymes) clearly give little or no room for manoeuvre; to give a very extreme example, the coronation of a British monarch gives virtually no opportunity for the individual participant to change anything — every word is scripted, every gesture rehearsed, each burst of 'spontaneous applause' elaborately choreographed.[2] At the other extreme, some situations can be completely transformed by a particular use of language — a particularly dramatic example of this is the way in which a single courageous heckler began the process which turned President Ceauşescu's rally for the Communist Party faithful into a ferocious anti-government protest.[3] Less sensationally, tense situations can be defused by a particular speaker's contribution; a skilful speaker can use language in a multitude of ways in order to turn the tables on an opponent.

Clearly most situations lie between the totally pre-scripted and the totally unscripted and a good description of context could usefully take as its point of departure the sociolinguist's description of givens (in this and many other regards pragmatics can be seen to be parasitic upon sociolinguistics), but it would not stop there. The pragmaticist will go on to explore how individuals, given the situation in which they find themselves and the linguistic means at their disposal, use their linguistic resources to try to achieve their goals. So how do we describe an activity type? An activity type description could include a statement of:

- **The goals of the participants**: notice that we are talking about the goals of the individuals, rather than the goals of the event (as in Hymes's model). The goals of one participant may be different from those of another. For example, the goal of a trial is to come up with a fair verdict, but the goals of the prosecution lawyer (to get a verdict of 'guilty') are diametrically opposed to those of the defence lawyer and the defendant. An individual's goals may change during the course of the interaction.

- **Allowable contributions**: some interactions are characterized by social or legal constraints on what participants may say. For example, in courts of law the prosecution is not allowed to refer to a defendant's previous convictions; in the British House of Commons members may not use certain abusive terms; at academic conferences you are not supposed to make *ad hominem* comments. What is pragmatically interesting is the way in which people will work round these restrictions. Coulthard (1989), for example, relates how one prosecution lawyer was able to indicate that the defendant had previous convictions by referring to the circumstances in which the defendant had injured his foot (it had been broken during a burglary); Churchill (prohibited from calling an opponent a 'liar'), famously came up with the phrase 'guilty of a terminological inexactitude'.[4]

- **The degree to which Gricean maxims are adhered to or are suspended**. The expectation of the way in which the maxims will be observed varies considerably from culture to culture and from activity type to activity type. In some activity types (e.g. in Parliament, in media interviews with politicians, or in the law courts), there is a very low expectation that what is said (or implied) will be the whole truth; in other activity types (such as going to Confession) the expectation that the speaker will tell the whole truth without prevarication is extremely high (see chapter 3). Some inferences can only be drawn in relation to the activity type. For example, the actor Nigel Hawthorne, talking about unsuccessful plays he had been in before he became famous,[5] said: 'Friends would come backstage and talk about the weather.' The irrelevance of the friends' comments can only be judged in relation to an activity type in which there was a powerful expectation that they would congratulate Hawthorne on the excellence of his performance.

- **The degree to which interpersonal maxims are adhered to or are suspended**. As with the Gricean maxims, the expectation of the way in which interpersonal maxims (see chapter 6) will be observed varies from culture to culture and from activity type to activity type. Thus (as we have seen) the Modesty maxim is more highly valued in Japan than in Britain, but within Britain it would be more highly valued in some activity types than in others. For example, at an awards ceremony, the person receiving an award (an actor, say) would be expected to minimize his or her own achievements and give credit to the director, producer, fellow actors, and so on; at a job interview, by contrast, the interviewee would try to maximize his or her achievements, while striving not to appear *too* big-headed.

- **Turn-taking and topic control**: to what degree can an individual exploit turn-taking norms in order to control an interaction, establish his or her own agenda, etc.?

- **The manipulation of pragmatic parameters**: to what

degree can an interactant use language in order to increase
or decrease social distance (e.g. by the use of intimate or
formal address terms), power, rights and obligations and
size of imposition? To what extent (e.g. by the strategic use
of different registers) can the individual increase or decrease
the formality of the situation (see chapter 5)?

The two examples which follow are both taken from the
same 'speech event' — a PhD supervision. Speaker A is a male
academic, speaker B a female research student. They have known
each other for several years and are good friends. The interaction
took place in A's office and the two examples occurred within a
few minutes of one another. The symbol / is used to indicate
overlapping speech, italics are used to indicate an interpolation
(generally a backchannel) by the other speaker:

Example 3

A: That's right. But then, there's a difference between
that and what your um *[mm]* ultimate sort of social
[mm] if you like purpose *[mm]* or objective *[mm mm]*
is in the encounter *[mm]*. Okay? Now, would there
be ... would there be a further subdivision ... I mean
that's a question, would there be a further subdivision between, as it were tactical goal-sharing and
long-term goal-sharing and would the tactical goal-
sharing be equivalent to what you're calling 'observance of the conventions of the language game' or
not? Because it did seem to me when I was reading
this that I could see the difference you were drawing
between linguistic cooperation and goal-sharing but I
wondered whether there wasn't a further sub-divi-
sion within goal-sharing between the tactical and the
strategic?

B: Okay well/

A: /and that the 'tactical' might be ... might be in
harmony with 'observance of the conventions of the
language game' *[mm]* but might not, actually.

B: Well um er um what I was trying to get at here was
why so many otherwise intelligent people have completely and utterly rejected Grice *[mm hmm]* and they
have *[sure]* and it seems to me that why they've done
it is because they do not see man as a fundamentally
cooperative animal *[that's right]*. Now ...

Example 4

A: Oh, 'e's back is 'e? From Columbia?

B: Mm and I snapped off his fl... you know how I fidget when I'm nervous and there was this 'orrible looking thing and I thought it was a a a spider on the end of a cobweb and I snapped it off and apparently he'd been nurturing it in his breast for about two years.

A. What was it?

B: I don't know. Some silly plant but he was obviously/

A: /our plants got nicked.

B: Really?

A: In the last week yeah we've had all our plants knock-ed off.

B: What where from?

A: Here.

B: Really?

A: Must've been stolen from here and the Institute and the Literature Department.

B: How strange. Oh and a bird shat on my head and then/

A: /I thought that was good luck!

B: Yes. You wouldn't've if it had happened to you. And and I thought all that remains is for me drawers to fall down and my happiness is complete. Well the lecture went very well indeed and er there was him there was a man called somebody or other Charles or Charles somebody.

A: Charl ... No. I don't know him.

B: And he said he's got a good friend in Finland and apparently she heard this lecture I gave over there. She's doing her bloody PhD on it.

A: Is she?

B: Yeah. On pragmatic failure.

A: Oh well, I mean, it's a ... it's quite a likely phenome-non I would have thought.

B: Anyway

A: Anyway, it went all right?

The point I am concerned to make here is that a sociolin-guistic (Hymesian) description of context would not explain the differences between the two examples. The physical setting (the supervisor's office), the participants, etc., all remain constant. An 'activity type' approach would show that what is different is the participants' use of language. From within their respective (socio)linguistic resources each speaker has drawn upon a range of pragmatic strategies to change the nature of the activity in which each is involved. At every level of linguistics, we can observe deliberate choices which, in example 4, have the effect of systematically reducing the social distance between A and B, emphasizing common ground and shared values.

Although both speakers clearly *can* pronounce /h/ and both do so all the time in example 3 (harmony, here, have), both 'drop their h's' and used stigmatized forms in example 4: *'e's back is 'e* and *'orrible looking thing*. At the level of syntax, we see that the grammatical structure of example 3 is more formal (e.g. use of *do not* instead of *don't*, compared with the informal *wouldn't've* in example 4) and more complex (compare the number of subordinate clauses which occur in A's first contribution in example 3 with the simple coordination which occurs in B's first contribution in example 4). The vocabulary in example 3 is formal and technical; example 4 has a plethora of informal, slang and taboo terms (*drawers, nicked, knocked off, shat, bloody*). Example 3 has a number of polite hedges to mitigate face-threat (*I wondered ...*, *it did seem to me ...*), metapragmatic comment (*I mean that's a question*) which are in contrast to the direct contradiction which occurs in example 4 (*You wouldn't've if it had happened to you*). The turn-taking and topic control in the two extracts are strikingly different: in example 3, A controls both; in example 4, the turns are very evenly distributed and both participants have their own topic (B wants to talk about the lecture she had just given at Aston University, A wants to talk about the theft) which each develops successfully, although in the end B's topic is jointly developed by both speakers.

In short, what we see in examples 3 and 4 is language which is not simply a reflexion of the physical or social context, or of the role relationship between the two speakers, but language used in order to establish and then change the nature of the relationship between A and B and the nature of the activity type in which they are participating.

In this section I have tried to show that context cannot be seen only as a 'given', as something imposed from outside. The participants, by their use of language, also contribute to making and changing their context. In the next section I shall try to make a similar point: namely that meaning is not something which exists independently of the participants. Pragmatic meaning is something which is constructed between S and H.

7.5 The construction of meaning

7.5.1 Pragmatic ambivalence

The concept of **ambivalence** is particularly important in taking forward the view of pragmatics as 'meaning in interaction' in which both speaker and hearer have a part to play. The phenomenon was first described by Leech (1977) and Brown and Levinson (1987 [1978]). It was noted that the intended force of an utterance such as: *Is that the 'phone?* may be quite deliberately indeterminate — it might be either a *straight question* or a *request* to the hearer to answer the telephone. Where the relative rights and obligations of participants, or the role relationships between them, are unclear (as they frequently are), it may be in the interests of both participants that the force of the utterance should be negotiable. By using an ambivalent utterance instead of making a direct request, the speaker reduces the risk of a confrontation or of receiving an embarrassing refusal, since the hearer is at liberty either to respond to the *straight question* by saying: *Yes, it is*, or, alternatively, to interpret the utterance as a *request* and to comply. Leech (1977: 99) describes ambivalence as follows:

> ... the rhetoric of speech acts often encourages ambivalence:
>
> 'Would you like to come in and sit down?'
>
> depending on the situation could be an invitation, a request or a directive. Or, more important, it could be deliberately poised on the uncertain boundary between all three. It is often in the speaker's interest, and in the interests of politeness, to allow the precise force of speech acts to remain unclear.

Ambivalence, then, occurs when the speaker does not make clear precisely which of a range of related illocutionary values is intended, as in the two examples which follow:

Example 5
A: Next door's dog's in our garden.
B: I must have left the gate open.

Example 6
Restaurant customer to waiter:

We ordered some beer.

In example 5, *I must have left the gate open*, could be situated anywhere along the cline of meaning from *statement of fact* → *reluctant admission* → *apology*. The meaning of the customer's utterance in example 6 could range along the continuum of meaning from *reminder* → *complaint*. It is for the hearer to decide how to interpret the force and also how to react, although ambivalence (as I discussed in 5.4.5) is rather different from other forms of indirectness, in that while the speaker's illocutionary **force** is unclear (is it an *invitation* or an *order*; a *reminder* or a *complaint*?) the illocutionary **goal** is perfectly clear (in Leech's example, to get the hearer to sit down, in example 6 to get the waiter to bring some beer).

7.5.2 The collaborative nature of speech acts

In chapter 1, I noted that certain performatives (*betting, bequeathing*) are *necessarily* collaborative in nature (the collaboration of the hearer is necessary in order for the speech act to 'succeed'). In fact, we find that almost all speech acts are collaborative, at least to a degree. Exceptions to this generalization are performatives such as *I sentence you …* (it is irrelevant whether the defendant goes along with the judge or not — the sentence is still imposed) and possibly performatives such as *I order you*, uttered in unequal situations in institutional settings (in the military, say) — I say 'possibly' because it is not obvious that the latter category of performative invariably succeeds, irrespective of the hearer's reaction. For example, a rather silly legal case was widely reported in England,[6] concerning a woman who had been annoyed over a long period by her neighbours' young son, who constantly hit his ball into her garden. Driven to distraction by the damage inflicted on her plants when he retrieved it, she took the ball and refused to give it back. The neighbours called the police, who arrested the woman and locked her up! Asked why they had taken such drastic action over such a trivial matter, the police claimed that they had been forced to arrest her 'because she refused to accept an official caution'. What is important here is that it is not sufficient for a police officer to pronounce some legally-prescribed formula; for the caution to 'work' the other person must accept it.

Leaving aside the very limited range of special circumstances (often associated with legal or religious events), it is almost always the case that the hearer has a contribution to make in determining the successfulness (or otherwise) of a speech act. Consider these two very ordinary examples:

Example 7
The following is an extract from The Archers.[7] *Steve had just succeeded in repairing the bailer (which was not his job):*

Steve: I think that's fixed it.
Debbie: If it holds, I'll buy you a pint.
Steve: You're on!

Example 8
*Commander Dalgliesh and Inspector Kate Miskin of Scotland Yard
are interviewing the literary agent of a murder victim:*[8]

Dalgliesh said, 'Violent death destroys privacy, I'm afraid.
Did she commonly raise hell?'

As if she hadn't heard him, Mrs Pitt-Cowley said: 'Do you
know what I'd really like now? What I really need is a good,
strong, black coffee. There's no chance of any, I suppose?'

It was Kate she looked at, and Kate who replied. 'There's a
jar of coffee grains in the kitchen and a carton of milk in
the fridge unopened. Strictly speaking I suppose we should
get the bank's permission, but I doubt whether anyone
would object.'

When Kate made no immediate move towards the kitchen,
Velma gave her a long speculative stare, as if assessing the
possible nuisance value of a new typist. Then, with a shrug
and a flurry of fingers, she decided on prudence.

'Better not, I suppose …'

In example 7, Debbie's *offer* only 'succeeds' when Steve
takes it up. Similarly, in example 8 Mrs Pitt-Cowley's *request* fails
when Kate chooses not to understand her. I once heard a speaker
from Relate (the Marriage Guidance Service) observe that after
a quarrel between husband and wife, one party will often make
a tentative effort to make things up by saying: *I'm making a cup of
tea.* According to the Relate speaker: 'They never make a direct
offer for fear of a snub, but it becomes an offer if the other one
takes it as such.'

7.5.3 The negotiability of force

There is another reason for moving away from the view that illocutionary force comes neatly packaged from the mouth of the speaker and towards a theory of pragmatics in which the hearer is seen as playing at least *some* part in assigning pragmatic value to the speaker's words. I shall begin with a very simple illustration of what I mean. In the two examples which follow the speaker utters the words *Tea or coffee?* In each case the speaker puts the same simple question, but let us see what the hearer contributes to the meaning:

Example 9
At breakfast in a hotel during a staff conference. The tea and coffee pots are on the table beside David:

David: Tea or coffee?
Jenny: Coffee, please.

Example 10
Same setting as in the previous example:

David: Tea or coffee?
Francis: Yes, please.
David: Coffee?
Francis: Thank you.

In example 9, I chose to interpret the utterance as an *offer* to provide me with whichever drink I chose. In example 10, the addressee chose to interpret the utterance as a *question* about whether he wanted a drink at all. The point I want to make is that David's initial utterance had the **potential** to be either an offer or a question. It **became** an offer or a question when the other interactant made it so. The next example makes the same point in a more obvious manner. In November 1990 *The Sun* newspaper[9] was celebrating its 21st year of publication and had asked several political leaders to make some comment. The following was Neil Kinnock's contribution on the occasion:

Example 11
It's certainly in a class of its own.

The Labour leader deliberately left it up to the reader to contribute part of the meaning and to decide whether the 'class' in question was high or low!

Example 12

*The following conversation took place on a walk in the mountains.
On these occasions (for reasons of weight and safety) people carry
their own food and do not usually share:*

A: Do you want a Tracker?
B: Well, I've got a banana.

B skilfully formulates a response with an unusually wide
range of potential meanings: yes, no, an offer to swap or an offer
to share. It is for A to decide what meaning to assign. In my final
example in this section, the men deliberately 'misunderstand' and
assign to the women's utterances literal interpretations which are
possible, but clearly unintended. The extracts are taken from a
radio adaptation by Tom Stoppard of Jerome K. Jerome's famous
novel, *Three men in a boat*. The radio version differed in parts in
very Stoppardian ways from the original and the extract I have
chosen is a case in point. The male speakers are on a boating
holiday on the Thames and are exploring some of the river's little
backwaters (I wasn't sure which of the men was speaking in these
bits). The female speakers live in properties adjoining these
backwaters and, to the boaters' annoyance, consider them to be
their own private waters (they are not, and never were, privately
owned):

Example 13

Woman 1: Excuse me, where do you think you're going?
Man 1:   We *think* we're going to Wargrave to view the
          famous memorial to Sara Hill, who ...
Woman 2: Here, can you read what that notice says?
Man 1:   Certainly, anything to oblige. Um, 'Private,
          keep out!'
Man 2:   And that one says 'No boating'!
Man 1:·   I must say, these notices are disgracefully in-
          accurate.
Man 2:   Untruthful to a fault!
Woman 2: And don't come back!

7.5.4 Preparing the ground for a speech act

One criticism often levelled at pragmatics (see, for example,
Fairclough 1989: 10) is that it restricts itself to single, isolated

(and sometimes invented) utterances. While this observation was certainly true of the work of Austin, Grice and Searle, the briefest glimpse at specialist publications such as the *Journal of Pragmatics*, *Pragmatics*, *Cognitive Pragmatics* or at the many monographs and doctoral theses being produced in different areas of pragmatics show that this criticism has not been valid for fifteen years and more. Every year extensive pragmatic studies appear, based on many hours (sometimes hundreds of hours) of naturally-occurring spoken data or on vast corpora of written texts.[10] Where Fairclough's criticism can apply is not to pragmatics as a discipline but to introductory textbooks on pragmatics.[11]

There are several reasons why it is important to take account of the discourse within which a particular utterance is situated; the one which is relevant to the present discussion is that speakers often 'build up to' the performance of a particular speech act, as the following (reconstructed) example shows:

Example 14
Speaker A is a university secretary, speaker B a lecturer in the same department. B was officially on study leave and not required either to come into the university or to undertake any administrative work:

A1: Are you going to be in on Monday?
B1: Why?
A2: I need someone to look at our entry in the *UCAS Handbook.*
B2: I'll be in for a couple of hours first thing.
A3: Will you be able to check it for me then?
B3: O.K.

A's first and second utterances serve to prepare the ground for making the request: the first trying to make sure that B will not have to put herself out unduly by having to make a special trip into the university, the second indicating that the task required is both pressing and important. If we were to judge utterance A3 in isolation, the request might be thought to be somewhat lacking in politeness (given that the task is not B's responsibility and could cause inconvenience), but taken in the context of the preceding utterances it seems reasonable enough.

Of course, the build up to the performance of a particular speech act may be considerably longer than in the example given: it may even stretch over several days. As I noted in chapter 5, the process of building up to the performance of a speech act may also give the speaker the opportunity of 'manipulating' certain factors (for example, the imposition in example 14 would have been greater if B had *not* intended to go into the university on Monday).

In my final example[12] the force of A's first utterance is sufficiently ambivalent for B to pretend to have misunderstood. Nevertheless, from utterance A2 onwards it is clear that one force and one force only was intended (A wanted B to move); in utterance A3, A removes all possibility for misunderstanding.

Example 15

A is trying to watch television. His daughter, B, is reading on the settee:

A1:   Do you want to change places?
B1:   I'm O.K.
A2:   I can't see the television.
B2:   Can't you?
A3:   Get off the settee!

This example also illustrates the importance of dealing only in situated discourse. The extreme directness of A's final utterance is only explicable in the context of his two previous attempts to get his daughter to move.

7.5.5 Successive utterances in situated discourse

A second reason why it is important to take account of the situation of the utterance in the discourse is that the pragmatic force of successive utterances can have a cumulative effect. Consider the following example:

Example 16

The following letter was read out in the 'Listeners' Letters' slot during the early evening news.[13] It was written in response to a letter complaining about the introduction of peace studies in some London schools:

The listener who registered alarm at her child's talking about peace studies at school was right to do so. In contrast, the army regularly visits our school, describing with slides and films the very latest ways of killing people. An understanding of the benefit to society of nuclear weapons and other means of mass destruction is clearly well worth passing on to our children.

After hearing the first sentence, I was not sure which side of the debate the woman was on: was the first sentence intended to be ironical or serious? However, the cumulative effect of the three sentences left no doubt that the correspondent was being ironical and disagreed strongly with the writer of the original letter. It is often the case that the interpretation of utterances later in the discourse is influenced by the force the hearer has assigned to earlier utterances. In the next extract, for example, it is not clear whether Sybil's first utterance is a flout of the maxim of Relation or whether she has really not heard Basil. After her second utterance, however, it is obvious that she is deliberately ignoring what he says:

Example 17
In this example, Sybil is in hospital awaiting an operation for an in-growing toenail. Her husband, Basil, is hovering about:

Basil: So you're sure you'll be all right?
Sybil: What, Basil?
Basil: I said you're sure you'll be all right?
Sybil: Will you get me my bed jacket?

The importance of considering the cumulative effect of successive utterances is illustrated at greater length by Leech (1983b) in his discussion of 'The celebrated letter' sent by Dr Johnson to the Earl of Chesterfield.

7.5.6 Discoursal ambivalence

An utterance can be shown to be ambivalent, not only in terms of its illocutionary force, but also in relation to its discoursal function. Let us look again at example 14. A discourse analyst looking at this exchange would have classified A's second contribution: *I need someone to look at our entry ...* as a *pre-request*, but this (as Levinson 1979 observes) is a *post hoc* classification by the analyst: in pragmatics we want to know what the **participants** understood to be going on at this point.

On hearing A2, B almost certainly understands what A wanted done and *could* have agreed there and then to do the checking; utterance A3 would then have become unnecessary. If the interaction had finished at A2, a discourse analyst would have classified A2 as a *request*. At the moment of uttering A2, however, A could not have known how B would respond; at the moment of hearing A2, B could not know whether A intended to stop there or go on to make the request explicit (suppose at this point the lecturer had started to show reluctance, to complain that she was on sabbatical, etc., the secretary would have had the option of aborting the direct request). The point I am trying to make is that, at the moment of utterance, neither A nor B could know whether A2 would function as a *request* or as a *pre-request*: the secretary's utterance had the **potential** to function as either.

7.5.7 Dynamic pragmatics

Notice that assigning meaning is an active (dynamic) procedure. Meaning is not given, but is constructed (at least in part) by the hearer; it is a process of hypothesis-formation and testing, of making meaning on the basis of likelihood and probability. Of course, this process may let us down and we may be forced to revise our initial hypothesis, as in the following example:

Example 18
Detective Chief Inspector Morse is renowned for his fondness for the bottle and for a disinclination to pay for his own drinks. Lewis is his detective sergeant:[14]

Morse had resisted several pubs which, *en route*, had paraded their credentials — at Lutterworth, Rugby, Banbury. But, as Lewis knew, the time of drinking, and thinking, was surely soon at hand.

In North Oxford, Morse had asked to be dropped off briefly at his flat: 'I ought to call in at the bank, Lewis.' And this news had further cheered Lewis, since (on half the salary) it was invariably *he* who bought about three-quarters of the drinks consumed between the pair of them. Only temporarily cheered, however, since he had wholly misunderstood the mission: five minutes later it was he himself who was pushing a variety of old soldiers through their appropriate holes (White, Green, Brown) in the Summertown Bottle Bank.

In those cases where hearers cannot ask for more context, they will often *construct* a context and from that derive a meaning for an ambiguous word or an ambivalent utterance. Even though the hearer may be conscious of having constructed a rather improbable scenario, rather than accept a 'vacuum of meaning' (Leech 1981: 7) he or she will hold on to that interpretation (will 'deem' it to be correct[15]) until more evidence is forthcoming. The following extract, taken from the diaries of the British writer Alan Bennett[16], illustrates this point well:

> **Example 19**
> Supper at Warwick and Susan's. We have fish and chips, which W. and I fetch from the shop in Settle market-place. Some local boys come in and there is a bit of chat between them and the fish-fryer about whether the kestrel under the counter is for sale. W. takes no notice of this, to me, slightly surprising conversation, and when the youths have gone I edge round to see if I can get a glimpse of this bird, wondering what a cage is doing under the counter and if such conditions amount to cruelty. I see nothing, and only when I mention it to W. does he explain Kestrel is now a lager. I imagine the future is going to contain an increasing number of incidents like this, culminating with a man in a white coat saying to one kindly, 'And now can you tell me the name of the Prime Minister?'

7.6 What counts as evidence in pragmatics?

For many of the issues that I have raised in this book, evidence for the claims I have made is available (as in other areas of linguistics) in the language produced: pronoun choice, choice of address forms, use of indirectness — all can be observed in the text itself. But for other areas of major importance in pragmatics (motivation, indeterminacy of meaning and of pragmatic force, the interpretation of utterances, the existence of mechanisms for informal reasoning (Gricean maxims) and of interpersonal maxims) no such direct textual evidence is available. So how can the claims for the existence of such phenomena be justified? One answer is that in pragmatics (as in other areas of linguistics) we appeal to the intuitions of the analyst or to retrospection on the part of participants in interaction, but these sources of evidence (while not counter-intuitive) are necessarily subjective. Throughout this book I have had recourse to additional sources of evidence; these sources of evidence are closely interrelated and difficult to distinguish entirely from one another, but they can be summarized as follows:

- The perlocutionary effect of an utterance on the hearer

- Explicit commentary by the speaker

- Explicit commentary by someone other than the speaker

- Subsequent discourse.

7.6.1 Perlocutionary effect

The first source of evidence is the perlocutionary effect (linguistic or non-linguistic) of a particular utterance on the hearer. For example, if A says: 'It's hot in here' and B opens the window, and A smiles in gratitude, we have a *prima facie* case for saying that B interpreted A's utterance as a plea/request/order for more ventilation and that A intended that someone, possibly B, should so interpret it.

On page 57 (in relation to example 5) we saw the per-locutionary effect on the actress Kathleen Turner of the slur conveyed by the conventional implicature of the word *but* in '… the main character was thirty-seven, but still attractive': she was so angry that she wrote to the film company straight away to complain. I have also alluded several times (in section 6.3.2.3 on page 163, for example) to the perlocutionary effect of the violation of pragmatic norms by non-members or immature members of a community. For example, I was once having lunch in a rather smart restaurant. A young couple were eating at the next table, while their two young children (aged about 2 and 3) played on the lawn just outside the french windows. Suddenly the little boy started to howl and his sister came running in. Asked why her brother was crying, she replied, 'Sammy shat himself'. Her father leaned across and slapped her hard — he appeared to be so outraged by the child's public infringement of politeness norms, that he ignored the fact that she was presumably using the only form of words she knew to express what had happened.

7.6.2 Explicit commentary by speaker

A second source of evidence is sometimes available in the discourse itself; for instance, on page 19 (example 22), I quoted Barry Manilow discussing his inability to interpret Bob Dylan's words. Explicit commentary may also appear in the form of metapragmatic or metadiscoursal comments made by the speaker, or in the form of 'repair' strategies. These might include comments such as 'I wasn't asking you, I was telling you', where the speaker makes explicit the intended pragmatic force of an utterance, as in the following example:

Example 20
Samuel Pepys had written to his patron, the Earl of Sandwich, warning the Earl that his liaison with Betty Becke was giving rise to considerable scandal and that his absence from court had been remarked on. Pepys was afraid that the Earl had taken offence at his letter and might withdraw his patronage. He later tried to explain himself to the Earl:[17]

I entended it not a reproach, but a matter of information.

I have also drawn attention to a number of examples of explicit reference on the part of speakers to the felicity conditions governing utterances (on page 40, in example 9, Mr Speaker Weatherill refers to the power associated with his social role, 'I have no alternative but to exercise the power invested in me ...'). Wilson (1992: 115) gives a similar example from St Paul's Epistle to Philemon: 'Therefore, although I have much authority in Christ to order you to do this, because of my friendship, rather I beg you.'

We have also seen many instances of a speaker's making specific reference to the observance or non-observance of the maxims (on page 75, in examples 23, 24 and 25 we find instances of speakers expressly opting out of a maxim) or to pragmatic parameters such as power, rights and obligations, etc. (for example, on page 127, in example 8, Kate makes explicit reference to her power over her daughter) or to the observance or non-observance of interpersonal maxims (e.g. on page 159 in example 11, the speaker explicitly marks her imminent flouting of politeness norms).

7.6.3 Explicit commentary by others

A third source of evidence to which I have sometimes appealed (which is different from relying on other people's intuitions only in that the commentary comes unprompted) are the meta-linguistic or metapragmatic comments made by others. For instance, on page 3 (example 1) the hearer comments on the ambiguity of 'What's wrong with the cat?' In section 6.3.2.4 (on page 164) I reproduced criticisms made by various commentators on the writer Jeannette Winterson's blatant failure to observe the Modesty maxim.

Authors will often comment on the intended pragmatic force of a character's words, as in the following example:

Example 21

The speaker was a caddie, who had been promised a reward if the competitor for whom he was caddying won the golf tournament:[18]

'It's nae for the guinea I've come', said McTavish <u>by way of gentle reminder</u>.

7.6.4 Co-text (subsequent discourse)

Other, less explicit, sorts of repair which reveal the intended pragmatic force of a pragmatically ambiguous utterance, take the form of increasing directness. Thus, if a speaker said 'Are you comfortable in that chair?', followed by: 'I can't see the television', followed by 'Would you mind changing places?' and finally 'Move!', we would have some evidence for assuming that the initial utterance had been intended as a request to the addressee to move. In the example which follows, Kate's first utterance is (for reasons of politeness) ambivalent, but notice the way in which, when Lady Lucinda does not immediately align herself with Kate's goal, Kate makes her intended meaning clearer:

Example 22

This is a short extract from a crime novel.[19] *Kate is a detective inspector from Scotland Yard investigating the murder of Lady Lucinda's fiancé. Lady Lucinda has turned up at her late fiancé's flat to retrieve a letter she had written to him:*

Lady Lucinda said: 'May I have my letter?'
Kate replied: 'We should like to keep it for the time being, if we may.'
Lady Lucinda seemed to regard this as a statement rather than a request. She said: 'But it belongs to me. I wrote it.'
'We may only need to keep it for a little time and we don't intend to publish it.'

I do not, of course, suggest that any of these forms of evidence is conclusive (in pragmatics we deal in probabilities rather than certainties) but the cumulative effect of all of them does, I think, give adequate support for the arguments I have put forward.

7.7 Conclusion

I have had some harsh things to say about the unthinking adoption within pragmatics of approaches designed for grammatical description. This should in no way be construed as hostility towards other areas of linguistics! Although my aim in this book has been to show what makes pragmatics distinctive from other areas of linguistics, it would be a mistake to think that a pragmatic analysis can usefully be undertaken in isolation from other levels of linguistic description. On the other hand, pragmaticists should not be apologetic about the difference between pragmatics and other areas of linguistics and, in particular, the fact that ours is a probabilistic rather than a precise science. Within grammar, the linguist is striving to make **rules** which are as comprehensive as possible and which have few/no counter-examples. In pragmatics, we are trying to show how people operate in real-time. In real interactions we are often uncertain about precise meanings/intentions and can tolerate and operate with such uncertainties. What we need, therefore, is a descriptive system which adequately models this indeterminacy and which accords it proper theoretical status.

Finally, I have argued that it is a mistake to adopt an approach to pragmatics which focuses on social factors to the exclusion of cognitive factors, or on cognitive factors to the exclusion of social factors or to adopt an approach which is exclusively speaker-oriented or exclusively hearer-oriented. I have tried to show that in producing an utterance a speaker takes account of the social, psychological and cognitive limitations of the hearer; while the hearer, in interpreting an utterance, necessarily takes account of the social constraints leading a speaker to formulate the utterance in a particular way. The process of making meaning is a joint accomplishment between speaker and hearer, and that is what I mean by 'meaning in interaction'.

Notes

1.   And many other dimensions, of course – cognitive, psycholinguistic, developmental, etc.

2.   Although in 1821 Queen Caroline, consort of George IV, had a good stab at disrupting the coronation of her estranged husband.

3. Bucharest, 22 December 1989.

4. *Hansard*, 22 February 1906, column 555.

5. Desert Island Discs, BBC Radio 4, 30 November 1986.

6. 27 July 1994.

7. BBC Radio 4, 7 August 1994.

8. P. D. James (1994) *Original sin*. Faber and Faber, London, p. 350.

9. *The Sun* is one of the more outrageous of the British tabloids. For many years it had hounded Mr Kinnock, the then leader of the Labour Party.

10. See, for example, Aeginitou (1995), whose PhD thesis was based on just under 80 hours of transcribed classroom data, or Tzanne (1995), who took as her data source the entire body of plays by Tom Stoppard (25 to date).

11. There are obvious practical reasons why writers of all the currently available introductory texts have compromised on the quantity of data used for purposes of illustration. In the first place, they are trying to introduce a very large number of concepts as quickly and as clearly as possible for readers who are new to the discipline — it is not possible to find just one text capable of illustrating adequately a wide range of theoretical issues. Secondly, the text chosen must be readily accessible to readers from a variety of backgrounds. Fairclough's own chosen text (1989: 172–5) shows the difficulty of this: without the extensive exegesis on the part of the author, Mrs Thatcher's speech is unlikely to mean much to anyone born after 1970 or outside the U.K.

12. I owe this example to Celia Bird.

13. BBC Radio 4, May 1985.

14. Colin Dexter (1994) *The daughters of Cain*. Macmillan, London, p. 61. *Old soldiers* is a slang term for *empty bottles* (of alcoholic drink).

15. Grice (1989: 302).

16. Alan Bennett (1994) *Writing home*. Faber and Faber, London, p. 144.

17.   Pepys's diary entry for 22 November, 1663. Robert Latham (ed.) (1985) *The shorter Pepys*. Bell and Hyman, London, p. 325.

18.   Robert Marshall *The haunted major*. Scottish Academic Press.

19.   P. D. James (1994) *Original sin*. Faber and Faber, London, p. 256.

References

Aeginitou V 1995 Facework and politeness in the Greek EFL classroom. Unpublished PhD Thesis, Lancaster University

Alston W P 1980 The bridge between semantics and pragmatics. In Rauch I, Carr G C (eds) *The signifying animal*. Indiana University Press, Bloomington, Indiana, pp 123–34

Apel K O 1991 Is intentionality more basic than linguistic meaning? In Lepore E, Van Gulick R (eds) *John Searle and his critics*. Basil Blackwell, Oxford, pp 31–55

Austin J L 1946 In other minds. *Proceedings of the Aristotelian Society* **XX**: 148–87

Austin J L 1962 *How to do things with words*. Oxford University Press, Oxford

Austin J L 1970 *Philosophical papers*. Oxford Paperbacks, Oxford

Bennett J 1991 How do gestures succeed? In Lepore E, Van Gulick R (eds) *John Searle and his critics*. Basil Blackwell, Oxford, pp 3–15

Benson D, Hughes J A 1983 *The perspective of ethnomethodology*. Longman, London

Blakemore D 1992 *Understanding utterances: an introduction to pragmatics*. Basil Blackwell, Oxford

Blum-Kulka S, House J, Kasper G (eds) 1989 *Cross-cultural pragmatics: requests and apologies*. Ablex, Norwood, New Jersey

Bonikowska M P 1988 The choice of opting out. *Applied Linguistics* **9** (2): 169–81

Brown P, Levinson S C 1987 [1978] *Politeness. Some universals in language usage*. Cambridge University Press, Cambridge

Brown R, Gilman A 1960 The pronouns of power and solidarity. In Sebeok T (ed) *Style in language*. Wiley, New York, pp 253–76

Burt S M 1990 External and internal conflict: conversational code-switching and the theory of politeness. *Sociolinguistics* **19**: 21–35

Burt S M 1992 Code-switching, convergence and compliance: the development of micro-community speech norms. *Journal of Multilingual and Multicultural Development:* **13**: 169–85.

Burt S M 1994 Code choices in intercultural conversation: speech accommodation theory and pragmatics. *Pragmatics* **4** (4): 535–59

Burton-Roberts N 1994 Ambiguity, sentence, and utterance: a representational approach. Unpublished paper presented at Philological Society, March 1994.

Candlin C N, Burton J, Coleman H 1980 *Dentist-patient communication skills.* University of Lancaster Department of Linguistics and Modern English Language/Institute for English Language Education, Lancaster

Carnap R 1948 *Introduction to semantics.* Harvard University Press, Cambridge, Mass.

Coleman L, Kay P 1981 Prototype semantics: the English word 'lie'. *Language* **57**(1): 26–44

Corder S P 1981 *Error analysis and interlanguage.* Oxford University Press, Oxford

Coulthard M 1989 Unpublished paper read at Linguistics Circle (February 1989), Lancaster University

Dascal M 1977 Conversational relevance. *Journal of Pragmatics* **4**: 309–28

Dascal M 1983 *Pragmatics and the philosophy of mind I: Thought in language.* John Benjamins, Amsterdam

Dascal M, Weizman E 1987 Contextual exploitation of interpretation clues in text understanding: an integrated model. In Verschueren J, Papi M B (eds) *The pragmatic perspective: selected papers from the 1985 International Pragmatics Conference.* John Benjamins, Amsterdam, pp 31–45

Davidson D 1967 Truth and meaning. *Synthèse* **17**(3): 304–23

Dillon G L, Coleman L, Fahnestock J, Agar M 1985 Review article. *Language* **61**(2): 446–60

Ervin-Tripp S 1976 Is Sybil there? The structure of some American English directives. *Language in Society* **5**: 25–66

Fairclough N L 1989 *Language and power.* Longman, London

Fann K T (ed) 1969 *Symposium on J L Austin.* Routledge and Kegan Paul, London

Fauconnier G R 1985 *Mental spaces: aspects of meaning construction in natural language.* M.I.T. Press, Cambridge, Mass.

Fotion N 1981 I'll bet you $10 that betting is not a speech act. In Parret H, Sbisà M, Verschueren J (eds) *Possibilities and limitations of pragmatics.* John Benjamins, Amsterdam, pp 211–23

Fraser B 1978 Acquiring social competence in a second language. *RELC Journal* **9**(2): 1–21

Fraser B 1990 Perspectives on politeness. *Journal of Pragmatics* **14** (2): 219–36

Gazdar G 1979 *Pragmatics: implicature, presupposition and logical form.* Academic, New York

Goffman E 1967 *Interaction ritual: essays on face-to-face behavior.* Garden City, New York

Green G M 1989 *Pragmatics and natural language understanding.* Lawrence Erlbaum Associates, Hillsdale, New Jersey

Grice H P 1975 Logic and conversation. In Cole P, Morgan J L (eds) *Syntax and semantics 3: Speech acts.* Academic, New York, pp 41–58

Grice H P 1978 Further notes on logic and conversation. In Cole P (ed) *Syntax and Semantics 9.* Academic, New York, pp 113–27

Grice H P 1979 *Studies in the way of words.* Harvard University Press, Cambridge, Massachusetts

Grice H P 1981 Presupposition and conversational implicature. In Cole P (ed) *Radical pragmatics.* Academic, New York, pp 183–98

Grice H P 1982 Meaning revisited. In Smith N V (ed) *Mutual knowledge.* Academic Press, London and New York, pp 223–43

Gumperz J J 1982 *Discourse strategies.* Cambridge University Press, Cambridge

Habermas J 1991 Comments on John Searle: 'Meaning, communication, and representation'. In Lepore E, Van Gulick R (eds) *John Searle and his critics.* Basil Blackwell, Oxford, pp 17–29

Halliday M A K 1978 *Language as social semiotic.* Edward Arnold, London

Hancher M 1979 The classification of cooperative illocutionary acts. *Language in Society* **8**(1): 1–14

Holmes J 1990 Apologies in New Zealand English. *Language in Society* **19**: 155–99

Holmes J 1992 *An introduction to sociolinguistics.* Longman, London

Hughes J 1984 Group speech acts. *Linguistics and Philosophy* **7**(4): 379–95

Hurford J R, Heasley B 1983 *Semantics: a coursebook.* Cambridge University Press, Cambridge

Hymes D 1962 The ethnography of speaking. In Gladwin T, Sturtevant W C (eds) *Anthropology and human behavior.* Anthropological Society of Washington, Washington, D.C., pp 13–53

Ide S 1989 Formal forms and discernment: two neglected aspects of universals of linguistic politeness. *Multilingua* **8**(2/3): 223–48

Jackson H 1988 *Words and their meaning.* Longman, London

Keenan E O 1976 The universality of conversational postulates. *Language in Society* **5**: 67–80

Knowles G O 1978 The nature of phonological variables in Scouse. In P Trudgill (ed) *Sociolinguistic patterns in British English.* Edward Arnold, London, pp 80–90

Labov, W 1966 *The social stratification of English in New York City.* Center for Applied Linguistics, Washington, D.C.

Labov W, Fanshel D 1977 *Therapeutic discourse.* Academic, New York

Lakoff R T 1973 *The logic of politeness; or, minding your p's and q's.* Chicago Linguistic Society, Chicago

Lakoff R T 1974 What you can do with words: politeness, pragmatics, and performatives. *Berkeley studies in syntax and semantics, vol. 1: XVI.* Institute of Human Learning, University of California, Berkeley, CA, pp 1–55

Lakoff R T 1977 Politeness, pragmatics and performatives. In Rogers A, Wall B, Murphy J (eds) *Proceedings of the Texas Conference on Performatives, Presupposition and Implicatures.* Center for Applied Linguistics, Washington, D.C., pp 79–106

Leech G N 1977 *Language and tact.* Linguistic Agency, University of Trier

Leech G N 1980 *Explorations in semantics and pragmatics.* John Benjamins, Amsterdam

Leech G N 1981 *Semantics* (2nd edition). Penguin, London

Leech G N 1983a *Principles of pragmatics.* Longman, London

Leech G N 1983b Pragmatics, discourse analysis, stylistics and 'The Celebrated Letter'. *Prose Studies* **6**: 142–57

Leech G N, Svartvik J 1994 [1975] *A communicative grammar of English* (2nd edn). Longman, London

Lepore E, Van Gulick R (eds) 1991 *John Searle and his critics*. Basil Blackwell, Oxford

Levinson S C 1979 Activity types and language. *Linguistics* **17**(5/6): 365–99

Levinson S C 1980 Speech act theory: the state of the art. *Language Teaching and Linguistics Abstracts* **13**(1): 5–24

Levinson S C 1981 The essential inadequacies of speech act models of dialogue. In Parret H, Sbisà M, Verschueren J (eds) *Possibilities and limitations of pragmatics*. John Benjamins, Amsterdam, pp 473–89

Levinson S C 1983 *Pragmatics*. Cambridge University Press, Cambridge

Local, J K, Wells, W H G, Sebba, M 1985 Phonology for conversational analysis: phonetic aspects of turn delimitation in London Jamaican. *Journal of Pragmatics* **9**(2): 309–30

LoCastro V B 1990 Intercultural pragmatics: a Japanese– American case study. Unpublished PhD Thesis, Lancaster University

Lyons J 1977 *Semantics* (2 vols). Cambridge University Press, Cambridge

McEnery A M 1995 Computational pragmatics. Unpublished PhD Thesis, Lancaster University

Matsumoto Y 1989 Politeness and conversational universals — observations from Japanese. *Multilingua* **8**(2/3): 207–21

Mey J L 1985 *Whose language? A study in linguistic pragmatics*. John Benjamins, Amsterdam

Mey J L 1993 *Pragmatics: an introduction*. Basil Blackwell, Oxford

Mey J L, Talbot M 1989 Computation and the soul. *Semiotica* **72**: 291–339

Miller G A 1974 Psychology, language and levels of communication. In Silverstein A (ed) *Human communication: theoretical explorations*. Lawrence Erlbaum Associates, Hillsdale, New Jersey, pp 1–17

Milroy J, Milroy L 1990 Language in society: sociolinguistics. In Collinge N E (ed) *An encyclopaedia of language*. Routledge, London, pp 485–517

Milroy L 1980 *Language and social networks*. Basil Blackwell, Oxford

Moore G E 1959 *Philosophical papers*. George Allen and Unwin, London

Nofsinger R E 1975 The demand ticket: a conversational device for getting the floor. *Speech Monographs* **42**: 1–9

Okamura A 1990 Accepting offers: a comparative study of British English and Japanese. Unpublished MA Thesis, Lancaster University

Parret H, Sbisà M, Verschueren J 1981 *Possibilities and limitations of pragmatics.* John Benjamins, Amsterdam

Pyle C 1975 The function of indirectness. Paper read at N-Wave IV, Georgetown University, Washington, D.C.

Rintell E 1979 Getting your speech act together: the pragmatic ability of second language learners. *Working Papers on Bilingualism* **17**: 97–106

Russell B 1905 On denoting. *Mind* **14**: 479–83

Russell B 1919 *An introduction to mathematical philosophy.* Allen and Unwin, London

Russell B 1940 *An inquiry into meaning and truth.* Allen and Unwin, London

Russell B 1956 *Logic and knowledge.* Allen and Unwin, London

Ryle G 1945 *Philosophical arguments.* Clarendon Press, Oxford

Ryle G 1979 Mowgli in Babel. *On thinking.* Basil Blackwell, Oxford

Saville-Troike M 1982 *The ethnography of communication: an introduction.* Basil Blackwell, Oxford

Schegloff E A, Sacks H 1974 Opening up closings. In Turner R (ed) *Ethnomethodology.* Penguin, Harmondsworth, pp 233–64

Scollon R, Scollon S 1981 *Narrative, literacy, and face in interethnic communication.* Ablex, Norwood, New Jersey

Scollon R, Scollon S 1983 Face in interethnic communication. In Richards J C, Schmidt R W (eds) *Language and communication.* Longman, London, pp 156-88

Scotton C M 1983 The negotiation of identities in conversation: a theory of markedness and code choice. *International Journal of the Sociology of Language* **44**: 115–36

Scotton C M 1988 Codeswitching as indexical of social negotiations. In Heller, M (ed) *Codeswitching: anthropological and sociolinguistic perspectives.* Mouton de Gruyter, Berlin, pp 151–86

Searle J R 1969 *Speech acts: an essay in the philosophy of language.* Cambridge University Press, Cambridge

Searle J R 1975a Indirect speech acts. In Cole P, Morgan J (eds) *Syntax and semantics 3: Speech acts.* Academic, New York, pp 59–82

Searle J R 1975b A classification of illocutionary acts. *Language in Society* **5**: 1–23

Searle J R 1979 *Expression and meaning.* Cambridge University Press, Cambridge

Searle J R 1991 Meaning, intentionality, and speech acts. In Lepore E, Van Gulick R (eds) *John Searle and his critics.* Basil Blackwell, Oxford, pp 81–102

Searle J R, Kiefer F, Bierwisch M 1980 *Speech act theory and pragmatics.* Reidel, Dordrecht

Sebba M 1993 *London Jamaican.* Longman, London

Shen Jiaxuan 1994 Bias towards formality: 'you + N' expressions in Mandarin Chinese. Unpublished paper, Institute of Linguistics, Chinese Academy of Social Sciences

Spencer-Oatey H D M 1992 Cross-cultural politeness: British and Chinese conceptions of the tutor–student relationship. Unpublished PhD Thesis, Lancaster University

Sperber D, Wilson D 1986 *Relevance: communication and cognition.* Basil Blackwell, Oxford

Strawson P F 1950 On referring. *Mind* **59**: 320–44

Tanaka N 1993 The pragmatics of uncertainty: its realisation and interpretation in English and Japanese. Unpublished PhD Thesis, Lancaster University

Tarski A 1944 The semantic conception of truth and the foundations of semantics. *Philosophy and Phenomenological Research* **4**: 341–74

Thomas J A 1986 The dynamics of discourse: a pragmatic analysis of confrontational interaction. Unpublished PhD Thesis, Lancaster University

Thomas J A forthcoming *The dynamics of discourse.* Longman, London

Trudgill P 1972 Sex, covert prestige and linguistic change in the urban British English of Norwich. *Language in Society* **1**: 179–95

Trudgill P 1974 *The social differentiation of English in Norwich.* Cambridge University Press, Cambridge

Tzanne A 1995 The dynamics of miscommunication. A pragmatic study of the creation and development of misunderstandings in social interaction. Unpublished PhD Thesis, Lancaster University

Urmson J O 1956 *Philosophical analysis.* Clarendon Press, Oxford

Urmson J O 1969 A symposium on Austin's method. In Fann K T (ed) *Symposium on J. L. Austin.* Routledge and Kegan Paul, London, pp 76–86

Walters J 1979a The perception of politeness in English and Spanish. *On TESOL '79*: 289–96

Walters J 1979b Strategies for requesting in Spanish and English — structural similarities and pragmatic differences. *Language Learning* **9**(2): 277–94

Weizman E 1985 Towards an analysis of opaque utterances: hints as a request strategy. *Theoretical Linguistics* **12**(2/3): 153–63

Weizman E 1989 Requestive hints. In Blum-Kulka S, House J, Kasper G (eds) *Cross-cultural pragmatics: requests and apologies.* Ablex, Norwood, New Jersey, pp 71–95

Wichmann A 1991 Beginnings, middles and ends: a study of initiality and finality in the Spoken English Corpus. Unpublished PhD Thesis, Lancaster University

Wierzbicka A 1987 *English speech act verbs: a semantic dictionary.* Academic, New York

Wierzbicka A 1991 *Cross-cultural pragmatics: the semantics of human interaction.* Mouton de Gruyter, Berlin

Wilson A 1992 The pragmatics of politeness and Pauline Epistolography: a case study of the Letter to Philemon. *Journal for the Study of the New Testament* **48** (December): 107–119

Wilson D, Sperber D 1981 On Grice's theory of conversation. In Werth P (ed) *Conversation and discourse — structure and interpretation.* Croom Helm, London, pp 155–78

Wittgenstein L 1922 *Tractatus logico-philosophicus*, trans C K Ogden, Routledge and Kegan Paul, London

Wittgenstein L 1958 *The blue and brown books.* Basil Blackwell and Mott, Oxford

Wittgenstein L 1958 [1945–49] *Philosophical investigations.* Basil Blackwell, Oxford

Wolfson N 1981 Invitations, compliments and the competence of the native speaker. *International Journal of Psycholinguistics* **24**: 7–22

Index of names

Index of subjects

abstract meaning, *see* 'meaning'
activity type 136, 137, 189–91, 193–4
address forms 154
adjacency pair 138–9
Agreement maxim, *see* 'maxim'
allowable contributions 190
ambivalence 142, 158–9, 195–6, 202
  discoursal ambivalence 202
Approbation maxim, *see* 'maxim'
autonomy, *see* 'optionality'

bald-on-record strategy 169–71, 176

condition
  essential 94–6, 98–100, 103
  felicity 37
  preparatory 95–6, 98, 104
  sincerity 94–5, 98–100, 103
constative 32
context 2, 4–10, 14, 16, 18, 20–23, 46, 50, 57, 58, 82, 88, 89, 105, 106 136, 138, 139, 154–7, 183, 184, 188–90, 193–4, 200–1, 203
conventional implicature, *see* 'implicature'

conversational implicature, *see* 'implicature'
conversational maxim, *see* 'maxim'
Cooperative Principle 56, 61–3, 65, 76, 92, 158–9
co-text 138–9, 207
CP, *see* 'Cooperative Principle'

deference 149–54, 172, 180
deixis 9–10, 133
domain of discourse 3, 4
dynamic nature of pragmatics 22, 183, 185, 203

essential condition, *see* 'condition'
ethnography 188
evidence in pragmatics 40, 57, 75–6, 127, 159, 163, 165, 204
Expressibility, principle of 122
face theory 168–9
face-threatening act 169–76
felicity condition, *see* 'condition'
flouting a maxim, *see* 'maxim'

LIBRARY, UNIVERSITY OF CHESTER